p.100 Pres. firm rule —
"never repeat a clea
If you repeat it, th
always wait for the repetition,"

My Father,
DAVID O. McKAY

Pres & life never quarelled p. 103

My Father,
DAVID O. McKAY

◆ ◆ ◆ ◆ ◆ ◆ ◆ ◆ ◆ ◆ ◆ ◆ ◆ ◆

David Lawrence McKay

Edited by
Lavina Fielding Anderson

Deseret Book Company
Salt Lake City, Utah

Library of Congress Cataloging-in-Publication Data

McKay, David Lawrence.
    My father, David O. McKay / by David Lawrence McKay.
        p.   cm.
    ISBN 0-87579-278-2
    1. McKay, David Oman, 1873–1970.   2. Church of Jesus Christ of
Latter-day Saints — Presidents — Biography.   3. Mormon Church —
Presidents — Biography.   4. McKay, David Lawrence.   I. Title.
BX8695.M27M25   1989
289.3′092 — dc20
[B]   89-38108
                                                                          CIP

Printed in the United States of America

10   9   8   7   6   5   4   3   2

To Mildred
My sweetheart
As Mother was Father's

CONTENTS

· · · · · · · · · · · · ·

PREFACE

◆ ◆ ◆ ◆ ◆ ◆ ◆ ◆ ◆ ◆ ◆ ◆ ◆ ◆ ◆

All of my life, my father has been my ideal, and the loving relationship of my parents has been my ideal of a happy marriage. Writing this book has been an affectionate and respectful attempt to convey some little portion of those ideal qualities of both my parents, but particularly of my father.

I am the oldest of their seven children and was only four years old when my father was called to be an apostle in April 1906. In most important ways, then, I never knew him when he was not a General Authority. But it is not as an apostle, as a counselor in the First Presidency, or as president of the Church that I wish to describe him. He was, simply, a great man. He would have been a great man if he had remained a farmer in his boyhood home of Huntsville or the principal of Weber Academy. He was a man of strong feelings and deep spirituality. He loved the world around him and responded to it sensitively. His most instinctive reaction to other people was affection and helpfulness. The gospel of Jesus Christ was absolutely central in his life, and he allowed no activities or relationships that required compromises of gospel principles.

His feelings for my mother were equally profound. They were in love with each other all their married lives, romantic partners as well as partners in the shared enterprise of rearing a family, managing a household, and fulfilling church and civic responsibilities. At a time when women's roles were private, Father wanted Mother to share his public life as fully as possible and was more pleased by honors and tributes that came to her than by his own.

This volume is not a full biography. It is neither analytical, complete, nor interpretive. What it has to offer are my own memories of treasured experiences with my father and quotations from his heretofore unpublished personal papers.

These papers include his letters to my mother beginning in 1897 and his journals — a mission diary, complete except for a five-month gap, and the diaries he began keeping when he was called to be an apostle, extending from 1906 up into the 1960s. Unfortunately, many of these diaries contain only brief daily entries; often gaps extend for months. The journal of his mission around the world exists in holograph for one two-week period when he was in the South Seas, and in a carbon copy of a typescript for 2 December 1920 through 10 November 1921, with some original typescripts and holograph documents interspersed in the record. After he became a member of the First Presidency in 1934 and had regular secretarial assistance, he began dictating a daily office journal, now in the Historical Department Archives of the Church, which largely replaced his handwritten diary.

As a consequence, this account quotes most extensively from documents produced during only three specific periods: his mission journal; his journal and letters home from his yearlong world tour from 1920 through 1921 and from his service as president of the European Mission from 1921 through 1922; and records of his tour of the European missions in 1952, when I was allowed to accompany him as his secretary. Mother also kept journals of the presidential tours during the 1950s.

All quotations, unless properly cited from published sources, come from documents in my possession.

Father did not often record details of quorum meetings or other administrative details in his journals. Even if he had, a full account of his role as a leading officer of the Church for more than sixty years would have to await the attention of a historian who has full access to his official papers.

The record I have created here includes details and experiences from his diaries, conference notebooks, and letters to supplement my own memories and to let him speak with his own voice; however, the purpose of both the documents and memoirs is the same — to give a measure of this great and greatly loving man.

I have done very minor editing on these documents. I have para-graphed and capitalized in a conventional way for the purposes of stylistic consistency and silently corrected unintentionally doubled words and uncharacteristic misspellings; however, any word that Father may have inadvertently omitted is added in brackets, and all omissions within entries are indicated by ellipses.

My thanks go to many individuals who have contributed to this book, often by sharing their own memories of Father. In addition to those mentioned in the text, I would like particularly to thank Charles Graves, who was a counselor in the New York Mission and who always wanted to hear stories of Father; our children, with their own memories of "Papa Dade" and "Mama Ray"; and Mildred, my partner in this enterprise as in the rest of my adult life.

Chapter 1

A LOVE STORY
· · · · · · · · · · · ·

There is a story in the family that when Father and Mother were living at 1037 East South Temple, a young couple arrived in a car, got out, and then sat down on the front lawn. There, the young man proposed to the young lady. As he later related the story to a member of the family, it was because "I want our married life to be as ideal as that of President and Sister McKay."

I don't know that there was any magic on the front lawn, but there was a kind of magic in my parents' marriage. Father and Mother were an extraordinarily happy couple. Their tenderness toward each other, their loyalty to each other, and their strong commitment to principles of family harmony inspired many husbands and wives to keep romance alive in their marriages.

Father and Mother knew each other long before they developed a serious attachment. Father was graduated from Weber Academy, then taught school for a year in Huntsville. In 1894, he, his brother Thomas E., and their sisters Jeanette and Annie attended the University of Utah in Salt Lake City.

The second year, the two boys rented a cottage on Second West Street from Emma Robbins Riggs, whose daughter, Emma Ray, was then eighteen. One day, as Mother used to tell the story, she and her mother stood together at the window watching the two McKay boys arrive with their mother. Grandmother Riggs commented, "There are two young men who will make some lucky girls good husbands. See

1

how considerate they are of their mother." Ray observed, "I like the dark one." The dark one was David O.

They saw each other from time to time at the cottages where Mother collected the rent, but no serious relationship developed. Father completed his studies in the spring of 1897 and was offered a teaching position in Salt Lake County. He was anxious to begin earning money so that his younger brothers and sisters could also attend school. Then he received a letter from "Box B," the return address of the Church's missionary committee—a call to the British Mission. As Uncle Tommy tells the story, Father was upset with this interruption of his plans; however, Grandfather McKay had accepted a mission calling under even more trying circumstances, and, after his initial disappointment, Father's desire to serve the Lord triumphed over his concern for his family. He accepted this calling, and his first letter to Mother ("Dear Friend Ray") issues a very formal invitation: "A 'Farewell Party' will be given in the Second Ward to-morrow (Fri.) night, at which, if you have no objections, I would be much pleased to have your company. . . ."

He signed it "Your true friend, Dade." His family and friends called him "David O." or "D.O.," but "Dade" was his own version of "David" when he was a toddler and a name he encouraged from no one's lips but hers until the grandchildren began calling him Papa Dade.

Mother arrived with her cousin, Mrs. Bell White, and Father's diary that he labeled "No. 1" has as its first entry on 30 July 1897, "Went to Ogden to meet Mrs. White and Miss Riggs." They participated in the festivities and then "in the evening took a ride over on South hills. Saw purple mts. at sunset. Very beautiful. . . . Went strolling with Ray. Told each other secrets. A memorable night!" Mother, in telling this story later, would add, "Yes, and we held hands all the way home."

Father and Mother corresponded steadily for the first several months, then at longer intervals. His brother Tommy was perhaps his most faithful correspondent next to his parents, and he mentions with deep gratitude letters from his sisters as well.

Father's first letter to Mother, dated 13 August 1897 and mailed from Philadelphia, describes in detail his response to the train ride— his first long journey. It is addressed to "Dear friend Ray" and signed "Your true friend David."

In one paragraph of this letter, Father ventured to be more familiar and to address her by the name he called her in his diary:

"Before leaving the Capitol, I must mention the *Echo* Room as one which interested us very much. Some of the most wonderful echoes in the world may be heard in this hall. Why, Ray (please excuse familiarity) when standing in one part if you say 'how do you do?' the echo will almost say, 'Pretty well, thank you. How are you?' "

He describes the ferry ride from Jersey City to New York by moonlight, the Brooklyn Bridge arching over lines of lighted ships and boats, and the Statue of Liberty looming off to the right. "But I was alone," he wrote, "and don't you know, Miss Riggs, that I cannot enjoy anything like that when I am by myself. I can appreciate it, but cannot enjoy it fully. 'It is not good for man to be alone.' I thought of you when I saw that beautiful sight and wished that you were by my side, showing your appreciation of that scene before you by that most expressive 'mmmm.' Do you know what I mean?"

It was true. Father never enjoyed anything so much as when he was sharing it with Mother.

The next communication with Mother was a letter he received on 7 September 1897 when he was at Lanark. None of Mother's letters has been preserved; but she had apparently expressed concern for the health of her mother, who had died while the letter was on the way.

When Father heard this news in a letter from Uncle Tommy, he wrote tenderly on 5 October 1897:

"In this, your hour of sorrow, Ray, please accept my heartfelt sympathy and condolence. May He who comforts all give you that strength and peace of mind necessary to bear this heavy burden of grief. . . .

"Ray, do not grieve. Remember you have friends who are praying for your comfort. . . . I assure you, Ray, nothing will give your friends more joy than to have the privilege of helping you to take your part cheerfully and well.

"I have often wished that I might be there with you so that I could do something to take your attention from that which grieves you; but of course such a wish is vain. I know that these few lines will fail in the purpose for which they are written; but if you can partake of the same feeling as that with which they are written, I am sure you will know that they come from the heart."

After March 1898, a gap of twelve months in the correspondence follows, possibly prompted by a misunderstanding about their relationship. During that time, Mother left Utah for a while after her mother's death, going to study piano at the Cincinnati School of Music. Prompted by "an indescribable something," Mother reopened the correspondence while she was living in Cincinnati with her father. Six years after their marriage, Father wrote Mother from Harmony, Utah, on 11 June 1907, referring to that period:

"An 'indescribable something' within me is longing for a letter from home. A particular handwriting that used to make my heart beat faster whenever I saw it on an envelope would to-day seem ten times dearer than it did when it first described the 'indescribable something' that sent me letters to Scotland. How well I remember my feelings as I broke the seal, and read your message! I was sure they were those of *Love*. But if I had known Love then as I know it now, I fear the difference in degree between *Love then* and *Love now* would have been so great that I should have thought my heart fluttered just because of warm friendship."

His answer from Scotland, dated 4 March 1899, was warm, playfully alluding to her name:

"As the first spring flowers are refreshed and strengthened by the rays of sunshine immediately following a cold blighting storm, so I was strengthened and encouraged by your cheerful interesting letter. Its warm congenial rays seemed to dissipate the cold dismal clouds of discouragement [about his missionary work], and I basked in the sunlight of Happy Memory! Could you have read my thoughts as I read your letter, you would have changed that opinion quickly, 'That *you* for a long time have held that *I* cared not for further correspondence.' Why you have been entertaining such an idea as that, I know not. . . .

"No, Ray (familiar names bring us closer to each other), you were wrong in your 'opinion.' Your letters, as your company, are appreciated and esteemed more highly than you evidently have thought; and it gives me pleasure to read in your letter that this esteem is mutual."

When Father returned home in August 1899, he had already been offered a teaching position at Weber Stake Academy, later Weber College, in Ogden. He began teaching immediately after his return and, within a few months, became head of the Preparatory Department.

Mother, who was graduated from the University of Utah with a bachelor of arts degree, had accepted a position teaching fifth grade at Madison School in Ogden, just through Lester Park from the academy. When we children teased her about finding a way to teach in Ogden rather than in her hometown of Salt Lake City, she would say with a little laugh, "Well, I believe Ogden paid more."

One of Mother's most cherished experiences that first year made her a firm believer in the principle, "Children respond favorably to praise." She relates:

"The first and only year I taught school, the principal came into my room the first day, which was midyear, and pointing out a child twelve years of age, he said, before the whole roomful of pupils, 'You'll have to watch out for that boy; he is the worst boy in school. He drove Miss B. away by throwing a bottle of ink at her.'

"What a blow for the boy, and for me, too! I thought, 'Now Earl will show me that that record is true by being his worst. I'll try to nip it in the bud.'

"I wrote a little note, saying, 'Earl, I think the principal was mistaken about your being a bad boy. I trust you and know you are going to help me make this room the best in school.' As I walked down the aisle I slipped it to him without anyone's noticing. I saw his face light up, and afterwards his mother told me that he brought the note home and said in an excited tone, 'Read this, Mother, but don't destroy it, for I want to wear it next to my heart.' He was one of my best behaved boys the remainder of the year." ("The Art of Rearing Children Peacefully," address to Brigham Young University Women, 12 Apr. 1952, originally entitled, "Attitudes toward Peace as Fostered in the Home," published by YWMIA as a brochure, *A Message from Emma Rae* [sic] *McKay* [Provo, Utah: BYU Extension Publications, Division of Continuing Education, 1966], p. 11.)

A letter from principal D. H. Adams on 16 June 1900, after school had closed for the summer, testifies to Mother's gifts as a teacher:

"Her discipline was good. Her methods improved throughout the year. She has all the qualifications which go to make a successful teacher. Her pupils without exception loved and honored her. She controlled and taught them by the only true means, namely, a love of the right and a desire for knowledge for its own sake.

"I am sure that Miss Riggs will grow rapidly in power as an educator and my best recommendation for her is that I shall always be glad of her assistance in my School."

Mother went back to Salt Lake City for summer vacation, and two of Father's letters, written within ten days of her departure, have survived. He addresses the second "to my Sweetheart," and it closes:

There are forty miles between us; yet I feel that our thoughts and feelings cover the distance and still keep us in touch with each other. I wonder if, in so short a time, anything more obstructive than distance could ever come between us, so as to sever the happy feeling now existing? I shall dismiss this thought, though, say "goodnight," and ask you to ever remember

Your loving Dade

When a longed-for letter arrived, he answered warmly on 27 June:
"And so you think my reference to the *probability* of that last letter's boring you, 'smacks of the thought that perhaps *I* do not care for a letter so soon from *you!*' Now, Sweetheart, I don't believe you mean that. You know that I never can be bored by a letter from the sweetest girl I know. Then, too, you refer to your letters as being 'long.' Why, Ray, if every word in your letters were a page and every page twice its present size, and two extra pages added as a P.S., I would not think your letter too long. If you sent such an one every day, I would be only too happy. This feeling of lonesomeness would then be partly satisfied, or allayed. Don't ever again mention my being bored by your letters. There is some reason for your being bored with mine."

They were not engaged when Mother left in June, and there is an indication that she planned to look for a school in Salt Lake City, for the cover note accompanying her principal's recommendation regrets "that I cannot be the one to profit by your growing popularity, good characteristics, kindly disposition, and sure success." Apparently she changed her mind, for a later note from William Allison, superintendent of Ogden City Schools, dated 31 August 1900, reads: "I saw Mr. McKay yesterday. We are holding your old place at the Madison school for you. I am glad to know that you have decided to be with us."

Father proposed to Mother in Lester Park early in December 1900. She asked, "Are you sure I'm the right one?" He replied that he was sure. Mother kept the letter Father wrote to her father, Dr. Obadiah H. Riggs, who was still living out of Utah, on 9 December 1900, asking permission to marry her:

"Her sweetness of disposition, her virtue, her intelligence, her unselfish nature, in short, her *perfect* qualities, won my love. When she told me that this affection was reciprocated, my happiness seemed complete. . . .

"I have asked your daughter to be mine in marriage, and now I ask you, Dr. Riggs, her father, if you will give your consent. She has given hers. . . . In return for this I can give her nothing but a true love and a heart and mind whose one desire is to make her happy."

Dr. Riggs's letter to Father has not survived, but he also wrote cordially back to Ray, teasing her: "You are a sly one to be in love for *four* years and not say a word to me about it." He also added some excellent advice about marital harmony that reinforced what Mother must already have known:

"Now my darling daughter, I want to impress upon you the fact that it is not any more difficult to get a man's love than it is to hold it after you have it. There are so many little things that a man appreciates in a woman, that some women never think of. A woman wants to study the likes and dislikes of her husband & try hard to do everything to accord with his likes. Some may say that is not possible. I think it is right & possible. It will pay a wife to do it all along the line. When a true man sees his wife doing every thing she can for his pleasure will he not do likewise for his wife? Surely he will, then there is mutual compensation and mutual happiness. I believe your sweet disposition & true heart will dictate to you to live right along this line. . . . I am very happy to know that you truly love this Bro. David O. McRay [*sic*]. . . . God bless you both."

Mother resigned from her teaching position and went back to Salt Lake City about mid-December to prepare for the wedding while Father stayed in Ogden and looked for a house to rent. Father's letters during that month are tender documents of their affection. One example, dated only "Tuesday evening" but apparently written 11 December 1900, contains noble sentiments:

"Do you know that since I *truly loved*, I can better understand why the gallant knights of old always had a lady love to fight for. The very thought of pleasing her would nerve their arms, steel their swords, and make their courage dauntless. Each one would try to develop the best strength and activity that he could possibly reach that he might be the more worthy of the approbation of his lady. Nobility of character, too, the best would prize, that they might merit the companionship of those who, they thought, possessed the truest and purest of souls."

A second letter has been preserved from a week later:

Tues. Evening, Dec. 18, 1900

My Dearest Sweetheart,

> *I will be happy, I will be true,*
> *When I am married, Sweetheart, to you.*

These words have been in my mind ever since they were repeated to me to-day. It is true they just form the rhyme of a simple love song, yet they express the sentiments of my heart to-night, and in so doing contain a deeper import than the author ever intended. If I am true to you before we are married, it will be much easier after. . . .

It seems a week since I saw you, and it seems about two days since I was last in school. If this feeling continues, it will be eight weeks before I see you again! Every day is a week when I am away from you, every day is but an hour when I am with you! What but *Love* can make Time drag so in the first instance, and make it pass unconsciously in the other?

Yes, it's love—true love, and I feel thankful that I know what pure love is, and that the person whom I love is the truest, sweetest girl that lives.

Sweetheart, is such a love any comfort to you? If it is, try to reciprocate it and give perfect happiness to your loving

Dade

The next letter was written late on Saturday night, 22 December 1900:

Your loving letter written Wednesday night was just received to-day. . . . You say our union will be an eternal one. Eternity alone can satisfy the love I long for, and the love I have to give. . . .

Ray dearest, I have three houses now to choose from. . . . Tonight I got the promise of a six-roomed house and barn for fifteen dollars a month. It is situated two and one-half blocks from the Academy on Twenty-third and Monroe.

...I wish you could be here Monday morning to make the choice. . . . All of these houses are quite modern, two have bath rooms, and one electric lights. All can be attached with little expense.

It is now 12:45 A.M. To-morrow morning — or rather this morning, I must be in Harrisville at 8:30 so I must stop.

I am lonesome without you, Ray, and I long for the time to come when you will always be by my side. Then my contentment will be perfect, if you are happy and perfectly contented. That you may ever be so is the heartfelt wish of

Your loving Dade

It must have been difficult for them to spend Christmas apart. The day after Christmas, Father sent her an affectionate record of how much he had missed her:

Wednesday night
December 26, 1900

My Own True Sweetheart,

No other form of address pleases me more. . . .

Sweetheart, how did you enjoy Xmas? Were you as lonesome as I? Not lonesome, particularly, but — well, were you perfectly happy? I wasn't. Christmas eve was pleasant — the meeting of the folks, the greeting of loved ones in the old home, the decorating of the tree, the children's joy at seeing old Santa Claus come in with their presents, all made us feel truly happy. Tommy's place in the family circle was vacant, however [he was serving a mission in Germany], and his absence made this Xmas eve less happy than last. Then, too, my heart wishes for another's presence. Nor was I the only one, for two or three times I heard the expressions, "I wish Ray were here." "Ray would enjoy this." "Wouldn't it be nice if Ray had come up."

But it was Xmas day that I longed most for your company; and Xmas night, I was lost. Annie, Lizzie, and I went over to the dance about 9:30 but came home again at 11:30. There was no one there, though the hall was crowded. Many of our dear friends were present, but there was no one to satisfy the yearning of my heart. That is satisfied only by the presence of Ray, my treasure. . . .

One week from to-night, Ray! I am anticipating it as the happiest and most important hour of my life. Will it be the happiest? I hope it will be but the beginning of a perfectly happy life for both of us! I'm sure it will be, if your love is like mine, and I believe it is.

Father and Mother were married 2 January 1901, in the Salt Lake Temple, the first couple married in that temple that year. They set up housekeeping on Monroe Avenue, in the first of nine homes they would have over the years. They both wanted a family, believing with all their hearts in the joys of family life, and have told me often with what joy they anticipated my birth and then those of my brothers and sisters. My brother, Llewelyn Riggs, was the second son, followed by Louise Jeanette (Lou Jean), Royle Riggs, Emma Rae, Edward Riggs (Ned), and Robert Riggs (Bob). We were all about two or two and a half years apart, so we usually had both an active toddler and a new baby at the same time in our home for many years.

During those first months of marriage, Father was very busy at the Weber Stake Academy (he was appointed principal the next spring, in April 1902) and serving as an energetic and innovative member of the Weber Stake Sunday School Board.

Mother was not feeling well when she was pregnant with me and, in April, Father prevailed on her to take a week's rest in Huntsville. (All his life he had an unswerving faith in the therapeutic effects of Huntsville.) She had been gone only a day and was only twelve miles away when Father wrote her on 23 April 1901:

My Dear Sweetheart and Wife,

If you and I were separated now for any length of time, what a dissatisfied and unhappy life mine would be! Only one day's separation has made me lonely. . . . When I came home from school to-night, I missed you; as I walked to meeting I wanted you by my side; and since coming home I have longed for you. . . . If the change will improve your health, I feel that I can stand a separation for a week, with an occasional trip or two to see you. . . . I hope to see the roses in your cheeks before many more days have passed. You were dear to me when they were there in courtship, you became *dearer* when you gave them to *our little one*; and you will be even still dearer — if this be possible — when you bring them back.

As children, we accepted our parents' world as the norm. Looking back, we can see more clearly how devoted they were to each other and to the gospel. It was quite clear that their worlds revolved around each other, and it made a happy, peaceful world for us. Father had grown up in a peaceful home where his own mother never raised her voice in speaking to the children or in calling them. Mother noticed these traits and adopted them as her own. Later, in paying tribute to Father's parents and how they reared their family, she said:

"When I was a girl and was visiting the McKay family for the first time, I said, 'Bishop McKay, you have been very successful in rearing a lovely family. Won't you tell me the secret?' He smiled, and said, 'Well, I think one thing has helped tremendously. All married couples have different opinions about various things, but Sister McKay and I make it a point never to disagree before our children. We go to our bedroom and talk things over, and when we come before our kiddies, we are of one mind.' " ("Rearing Children Peacefully," p. 9.)

Father was always attentive to Mother's comfort and treated her with courtesy. Until he was confined to a wheelchair, he always rose when she entered the room, always held her chair, always opened the car door for her, and always bade her goodbye and hello with an affectionate kiss. Once, I remember, he had my brother Bob, a jeweler, make her a necklace—a platinum heart with diamonds encircling it. It was lost for a while, and Mother was so distressed to have lost one of Father's gifts that he had a duplicate made.

We children loved to do things for Mother, not only because she was so unfailingly appreciative and delighted but because Father's joy in these marks of special affection would be so evident.

At the table, he always stopped Mother if she started to get up to fetch something that had been forgotten or to wait on us children. "Now, Ray," he would say and, with a gesture of his finger, he would send one of us children to get the missing item.

Mother, in turn, reciprocated fully. She always wanted to be with Father and to see to his every comfort. Because he disliked eating alone, Mother would serve our meal and sit with us in pleasant conversation while we ate, but keep his dinner hot in the oven while he was at meetings and then join him in a late supper.

Mother made an extraordinarily delicious coconut custard pie—a work of art. The custard itself was tinted pink; and the coconut, delicately toasted, made a beautiful topping. I recall that pie appearing for special occasions to Father's invariable appreciation all the years I was growing up. Then, when my wife and I were having dinner with them at Laguna Beach in California many years later, Mildred noticed coconut custard pie on the menu and called it to Mother's attention.

We were astonished when she remarked simply, "I don't like coconut custard pie."

I exclaimed, "You don't like it! But you've made it all these years!"

Mother smiled at me and said, "It was your father's favorite, and I made it, but I never ate it." And she ordered something else for dessert.

Father used to say, "I like only two kinds of pie—hot and cold." So Mother made pies, splendid pies. For Christmas mincemeat pie, she made her own mincemeat by simmering beef, apples, and spices together. Her apple pies were legendary. Father ate hearty wedges, topped with thick, wrinkled, yellow cream skimmed from the top of our milk pans.

I recall once when we were eating dinner with them, Father poured cream on his own pie and then asked our daughter, Teddy Lyn, "Don't you want cream on your pie?" She answered innocently, "Oh, not on Mama Ray's pies. They're so good."

In 1952, when Mother and Father had been married for fifty-one years, Mother gave an address to the women students at Brigham Young University. Although the topic was the art of rearing children peacefully, she also included a solid section of advice to young wives about how to build a happy marriage. It is likely that her own high commitment to the institution of marriage, combined with her profound love for Father, made her a keen observer of the elements that foster happy unions and produced these principles, which were certainly observed in our home:

"[A husband] wants to see a wife who has made herself as beautiful as she can, a woman who has poise and charm, who greets him lovingly and cheerfully, who studies his every mood, and can tell when he wants to talk and when he would like a complete rest.

"Peace in the home is really a woman's responsibility, and if she wants happiness, she must work for it—yes, and pay for it, too—by being at all times kind, loving, self-sacrificing, ready to help, ready to serve, in fact, loving to do anything the head of the house desires because his desires are also hers. And she must always remember that 'wisdom is made up of two parts: nine-tenths silence and one-tenth brevity.'

" ... There are many qualifications that a woman should have to be a good wife and mother, but the most important is patience — patience with children's and husband's tempers, patience with their misunderstandings, with their desires, with their actions.

"Suppose you ask your husband to carry a mattress downstairs, and instead of carrying it carefully so that not a speck of dirt touches its clean coverage, he throws it through the window upon the lawn below. [Father and I actually did that once with the upstairs mattresses, 'helping' with spring cleaning!] He probably did not think of the grimy dirt from the window frame soiling the cover nor of the possible dirt that might be on the lawn. All he wanted was to save time and energy and get the thing over with in a hurry. Will you rave and rant at him, call him a stupid creature who never does things right, or will you think, 'Oh, what's the use! The thing is done. Better make the best of it'? Always the latter if you can make yourself be calm. Even a slightly sarcastic remark will bring a disagreeable answer, and you'll wish you had not said a word.

" ... A sure way to bring gloom is to show that your feelings are hurt. You cannot live long with any human being and not have something come up at times to irritate you. 'Offense we must expect. The question is what to do with it when it comes. And although we cannot help being hurt, what we can help is showing that we are hurt.'

"I once sat at a table around which were seated several people. The host asked his wife to bring two letters — one written by him, and one by his wife. He read both aloud, and the amused glances the people gave each other as hers was read made her blush deeply. As she was serving at the time, I wondered why, since she felt so keenly about it, she didn't slip her letter, which he had no right to read, out of his hand and thus stop all silent snickerings and wondering thoughts. But she was too polite and patient, and smiled and let it go." ("Rearing Children Peacefully," pp. 1–9.)

Father had observed the same incident and told the same story, but he always pointed out the unkindness and thoughtlessness of the husband. He would summarize this story by emphasizing: "No man should ever tell a joke or make a comment at the expense of his wife.

David O. and
Emma Ray
Riggs McKay at
home on their
golden wedding
anniversary, 2
January 1951

He must be loyal to her above all else, if they are to have a happy and united relationship."

In reading over these principles of human relationships as my mother wrote them, I can honestly say that I never observed either of my parents violate any of them in our home. Theirs was a remarkably loving and appreciative relationship.

And it was romantic. Mother always looked her best for Father. She was petite and Father was tall; but whenever she stood beside him, she unconsciously drew herself up to her full height. Even when they were both in their eighties and nineties, Mother was conscious of her grooming. Whenever she was ill and confined to bed, she urged the nurse to "Hurry!" so that she could greet Father with her hair combed, her lipstick on, and her bed jacket pretty and fresh.

For Christmases, wedding anniversaries, and birthdays, Father wrote Mother little love poems, and she treasured them above any gift that he might buy for her. She had a special box of inlaid wood in which she kept these poems. We still keep them in that box. A few date from the twenties, but she had them for almost every Christmas and birthday during the thirties and forties. One undated but early poem reads:

To

My Sweetheart

Just loving wishes for
a Merry Christmas and many many more!

As my purse is flat, I cannot give
The presents I've had in mind;
And these tokens — mere trifles
Are not what I've tried to find.

So glasses for sherbet, silk stockings and such
As gifts, I'll have to delay —
Later is just as appropriate for your sweetness and love
Make Christmas of every day.

When he gave her some slippers and silver for Christmas in 1940, each came accompanied by its own warm note:

To My Darling Ray:

If my earnest wish were granted,
And your future I could will,
Every step would give you comfort
And make you happier still!

Affectionately,
Your loving husband

To My Sweetheart of Forty Years!

This Silver they claim is Genuine —
And so are you!

This Silver they claim takes Polish —
That's natural to you!
This Silver they claim lasts a life time —
So will my love for you!

Affectionately
Your loving "Dade"

The following chapters present a more chronological view of their life and relationship, beginning with Father's mission and concluding with their declining years. Yet perhaps one more example of their continuing influence on the quality of Latter-day Saint marriages is appropriate. A friend told me that he and his wife were attending a function with James and Elaine Cannon and had driven over to pick them up. James opened the door for his wife and helped her into the car. Smiling up at her husband, Elaine said, "Thank you, Dade." He answered, "You're welcome, Ray," then closed the door. Curious, their friends asked, "What did you mean by that? Those aren't your names."

James and Elaine Cannon, who later confirmed this story to me, explained that they had once, as a young couple, seen Father help Mother into the car and had overheard that little exchange of courtesies. On the spot, "we resolved that we would always do the same thing. And we always have."

Chapter 2

MISSIONARY IN SCOTLAND 1897-1899

◆ ◆ ◆ ◆ ◆ ◆ ◆ ◆ ◆ ◆ ◆ ◆ ◆ ◆

My heart goes out to Father as I read his missionary journal, carefully recorded in lined notebooks. A sensitive, home-loving boy who loved the green hills of Huntsville, he found leaving home difficult:

"Thursday, 5 Aug, 1897. The saddest morning ever spent in Huntsville or anywhere else! At eleven o'clock, bid my home, dear ones, relatives, & friends 'good-bye.' Sobbed. . . ."

Father crossed the continent by train, and then on 11 August sailed for Liverpool aboard the *Belgenland* with some other elders. On their first Sunday out, he had his first experience preaching a sermon, which he called a "poor attempt." When a woman "attacked" his theology, he confessed, "found out I knew nothing about the Bible." As a result, Father launched himself on a serious course of study. In fact, between 16 September and 7 January his journal records twenty-three separate times that he spent a significant number of hours — sometimes a whole morning or afternoon — in study.

Aside from one day's seasickness, Father enjoyed the voyage, playing shuffleboard, meeting the other passengers, and attending performances of a troupe of "Jubilee Singers" on board whose songs he enjoyed very much. He also loved the beauty of the ocean, something completely new to him.

On 25 August, he "looked for the first time at the smoky city of Liverpool" and, upon landing, was appalled at the swarms of "little ragged urchins crying out 'Paper, Paper sir,' 'Matches,' 'Gi'e me ha'e penny!' 'See the Yanks from Philadelphia,' 'Needle Points,' etc."

17

On 27 August, he received his assignment to the "Scottish Mission" and set out for Glasgow. The mission headquarters was two sitting rooms and a bedroom with two beds on Barrack Street: "A gloomy looking place & I was a *gloomy-feeling* boy." Exposure to Glasgow's slums with its open drunkenness repelled him: "Some of the women are bare-headed and bare-footed, ragged and dirty; and such women are rearing children! . . . *Utah* is *dearer* than *ever*."

On Monday, 30 August, he was sent to Lanark to join three other missionaries. The area was hardly receptive to proselyting, for it was closed exactly a month later. Lonesome and homesick, Father records:

"Tuesday, Aug. 31, 1897. Distributed one hundred and fifty tracts, 75 double ones. This was my first 'experience' and although the people treated me courteously, and with a few exceptions, accepted the tracts, yet I never felt so gloomy in my life. I have heaved a *thousand* sighs! . . .

"Sunday, Sept. 5th, 1897. Fast Day. At 12 M. [meridian] went to Newarthill with Bros. Orr & Johnson and held an open-air meeting. The people stood in their doorways to listen. Some stood in the st. one block away. Here, standing in the middle of the st. on both sides of which was a long row of white-washed houses about 6 ft. to the square, I made my first open-air speech. I shall never forget it. The day was cold and cloudy (I had been wishing that it would rain) and the street was dismal and uninviting. Perhaps there were about 30 eager-looking eyes staring wonderingly in mine. My remarks were brief and made in fear & trembling!!! . . .

"Monday, Sept. 6, 1897. . . . Mrs. Wylie told us how the people had expressed themselves about our meeting (Tues. last). 'The preachin' was good,' says one, 'but you should come & hear their singing; it's terrible!' "

As this last entry shows, Father's characteristic interest in people and sense of humor helped him adjust to his mission. For the next four weeks, until early October 1897, Father's typical missionary schedule was to visit members, hold open-air street meetings twice a week or so, and distribute tracts in a given neighborhood. The elders invited people to a nearby meeting or made appointments to call on them in their homes. Their tracting area included all of the outlying villages, so it was not uncommon for Father and the other elders to walk five to ten miles to a particular locale, work all day, often in the rain, and then walk home at night. In one of these villages, he records:

"The people were bitter. One woman tore a tract in pieces as soon as I gave it to her. Another, after finding out what it was shut the door in my face.

"After tracting the town, we had a good dinner at a restaurant and started for Lanark. On our road we distributed more tracts. I met an estimable old lady who, after hearing who I was and what I was doing, became very much interested. We had a long conversation during which she said: 'Weel I've been a long time in my church and I dinna think Christ will forsake me noo.' When I went to leave she extended her hand and with tears in her eyes said, 'God bless ye, for I believe you're doin' a noble work.' She did me a *world* of good."

After Lanark was closed to missionary work, Father and the other elders returned to Glasgow, where Father was assigned to work in the conference headquarters. He kept the mission accounts; tracked down information for emigrants; met arriving members and missionaries; saw off departing ones; received, compiled, and sent out all kinds of reports; handled mission correspondence; addressed and mailed out copies of the *Millennial Star;* supplied the missionaries with copies of the Book of Mormon; and got a thorough education in mission administration that stood him in good stead later.

It was a cold winter with several days running of heavy, smoky fog so dense that the street lamps were lighted by 2:30 P.M., and the branch was plagued by feuds and "enmity." Father uncomplainingly did his duties, even seeing off missionaries, a task that usually made him homesick, with good humor. On November 11, he records a quatrain in his journal that shows he could at least control his loneliness, even if it had not been eliminated:

> As the boat sailed down the Clyde, I thought that,
> Men may come and men may go
> And some from friends ne'er sever.
> But here in Glasgow I must stay.
> My mission goes on forever!

He enjoyed occasional "field trips" to such establishments as a hat-making factory, the Glasgow waterworks, and a coal mine. Father's singing and speaking ability made him a popular figure with the members, and he was deeply involved with branch activities. Choir practice was Tuesday nights, testimony meeting Thursday nights, and most of the branches held four meetings on Sunday. Frequently, Father walked to one of the suburbs of Glasgow to attend these Sunday services with another missionary.

Father's sensitivity to the suffering of others as well as to the kindness of others appears in these journal entries:

"Mon. Oct. 11th. . . . Pres. McM., Bro. Pender, Bro Nielson and I went to Auchinerin to administer to an unfortunate man who has lain in his bed for eight years. He was hurt in a pit. Although he is not a Mormon, still it was at his request that we went there. It is pitiful to see him lying there helpless. After the administration, he seemed to feel easier, and invited us to come again. . . .

"Tues. Oct. 19th. About eleven o'clock while we were preparing our tracts for distribution, Sister Anderson (Catherine) entered carrying a large bundle. After greeting us, she opened it and presented two sheets, one pair of woolen blankets, and a beautiful coverlid saying, 'You Elders have come awa' here to do us good and to call sinners to repent, and I dinna think that we who are in our 'ane beds should let you suffer: so I give you these to keep you warm.' Bro. Pender expressed our feelings by saying, 'Sister A., ye've taken our breaths and we dinna ken what to say to ye.' Her kind act touched the heart of every one. It seemed impossible to express our feelings. She was truly happy for she had done something which filled her benevolent soul with joy. When she was leaving she said, 'I leave my peace and blessing with you.' . . .

"Saturday, Oct. 23. Went with Brothers Anderson and Mitchell to administer to Miss Good. . . . After we administered to her, a dead silence seemed to come over all present. As she lay there, so quietly and peacefully with her pale thin face and steadfast eyes, her long brown hair hanging over the edge of the pillow, we could hear the low *gurgle* in her throat accompanying every short breath. I think her mind just then wandered, for while the stillness yet continued — a stillness only broken by the monotonous ticking of the clock — she began to sing. At first we could scarcely hear her so weak and feeble was her voice; but soon we recognized the hymn she was singing. Her breathing was short and difficult and the words came at intervals but we heard distinctly the words: 'Beautiful home of my Saviour, bright beautiful Home.' That scene I shall never forget. Her white countenance depicting the suffering she had endured; her dark hair streaming in striking contrast to her death-like face, that audible gurgle in her throat; the gloomy surroundings occasioned by the dull day, the dead silence broken only by the seeming knell of the kitchen clock; her feeble plaintive tones as she sang that Heavenly hymn; all made an impression on me that can never be effaced from memory. [Father later preached his first funeral sermon for her.] . . .

"Christmas Day. . . . The plum duff and cake were fine; but I felt homesick.

> I pictured home and all its joys;
> The merry girls and happy boys;
> The private party and social dance
> All seemed my longing to enhance.

"Sat. Jan. 8th. . . . Retired at 1 o'clock A.M. We had scarcely fallen asleep before we were aroused by a knock at the Hall door. I answered it and received the dreadful news from Bro. Cairney that Bro. McDonald was dead. He passed away suddenly about 12 o'clock at his home on Mansion St. Died in his wife's arms. We hurriedly dressed and accompanied them, Bro. C. & little Fletcher, to the stricken sad family. A touching scene followed our entrance into the room. The mother was so sick and heartbroken that she could not control herself. Remained with them until morning."

He also sat up with the family the following evening and then attended the funeral. For several weeks, Father represented the mission president, who was then hospitalized with an unspecified illness.

"Tuesday, Feb. 22nd. . . . In company with Bro. Wood and two returning elders from Scandinavia went to Springburn to attend a meeting previously announced to be held in the Argyle Hall. The Saints of Glasgow were well represented, many of them being there in time to assist in the singing at an open-air meeting held simply to announce the one in the hall. Besides the Elders and local Saints there were present at the regular meeting about twelve or fifteen *unbelievers*. Bros. Mitchell and Montgomery occupied the time. At the close of the services, two or three came to the front and asked about *pre-existence* and *polygamy*. One became very abusive in his language, saying that 'the old prophets who had more wives than one sinned against God, and so do the Mormons.' 'If you believe it to be a true principle you are cowards for discontinuing the practice!' I thought when I heard this of an old saying quoted by father, 'We'll be damned if we do, and we'll be damned if we don't!'

"Sunday, Feb. 27th. At nine o'clock Bro. Edward and I started on foot for Blantyre for the purpose of meeting with the Branch at that place.... After the [evening] meeting was over ... we started on our eight-mile walk. (The trains do not run on Sun., and the last bus had gone.)

"Bro. E. had just recently recovered from an illness, and consequently could not stand much exertion. His shoulders began to ache, his neck would grow quite rigid, so that ever and anon he was compelled to grasp the top of a fence or the limb of a tree and stretch his spinal column! About the time we reached Cambuslang, he was nearly tired out; and I, too, though much stronger than he began to feel 'leg-weary.' We had four miles yet to go! It was raining and the wind blew the *torrents* directly in our faces which were partly shielded by our umbrellas! ...

"We reached '130' at 11:30 P.M., after having walked 20 miles and held two meetings. As we threw ourselves on the bed Bro. Edward remarked, 'I wouldn't do that again for my Grand-mother!'

"Monday, Feb. 28th. When I awoke, I found myself so hoarse, I could hardly speak."

After five months in Glasgow, on 21 March, Father "received an appointment to labor in Stirling with Bro. P. G. Johnston as companion. This means real practical missionary work. I look forward to our coming experience with a feeling of eagerness seasoned with a little dread." At Stirling, he and Elder Johnston, a lifelong friend whom he always visited when he went through Blackfoot, Idaho, found comfortable lodgings, which included a piano, with a family called Sharp on Douglas Street. Father's adjustment to this new area of labor was aided by a beautiful spring that made their frequent walks to neighboring villages a pleasure, although making headway against the prejudice and ignorance that surrounded the name of "Mormon" was an uphill battle:

"Wednesday, April 6th.... Wrote time and place of meeting on about 300 tracts. Distributed one hundred and seventy. The women can hardly understand me when I offer them a 'Gospel tract.' Nearly everyone misunderstands me or asks me what I said. One woman thought I said 'gas bill' and promptly answered, 'No, we don't burn gas'! Today, one old haggard-looking creature took the tract, squeezed it in her hand,

David O.
McKay,
missionary in
Scotland, 1898

and with gnashing teeth, yelled, as she threw the tract at me, 'I'm a lost sinner and I dinna want yer blatherin' Gospel! I hate the name o 't!!' She was a terror! . . .

"Monday, April 11th. [Returned from a meeting out of town.] At Stirling we found everything, so far as we are concerned, all right. Our room was as neat and tidy as the Queen's! It seemed as though I was stepping once more into one of Mama's rooms! It seemed so pleasant and inviting that I couldn't refrain from sitting at the piano, *first thing*, to play 'Home Sweet Home'! . . .

"Thurs., April 15th. Distributed one hundred and fourteen tracts

('second tracting'). Had several interesting conversations. Nearly everyone who took a tract last week seemed pleased to accept this one.
Several asked when we would hold another meeting. This is the most
pleasant 'tracting' day I have experienced."

Then on 9 June 1898, he received a letter appointing him president
of the Scottish Conference (the equivalent of today's district president).
"Realizing to some extent what a responsibility this is," Father wrote
in his journal, "I just seemed to be seized with a feeling of gloom and
fear lest in accepting this I would prove incompetent. I walked to a
secret spot in the wood just below Wallace's Monument and there
dedicated my services to the Lord, imploring Him for His Divine assistance."

That same evening, he responded to President Wells: "Realizing
to some extent the responsibility thus placed upon me, I truly feel weak
and unable to carry it, and if I expressed my own desire, I would say
'Choose another,' yet I feel to say, 'Not my will but thine be done'; and
since God through his servants has seen fit to place this duty upon me,
I shall accept it, depending upon His unerring Spirit for Guidance. And
Bro. Wells, I sincerely ask for your prayers and faith together with those
of your Counsellors. Being young and inexperienced, I feel the necessity
of the hearty support of all my Brethren."

Thus Father left Stirling except for his supervisory visits. He does
not record in his journal the story he later told to thousands of Saints
and investigators in hundreds of audiences. As he and his companion
returned from viewing Stirling Castle, which they did on the second
day they arrived, they passed a building where the stone above the door
had a carved inscription: "Whate'er thou art, act well thy part."

This message struck Father forcefully, and he decided to devote
himself completely and wholeheartedly to his "part," which was the
role of missionary. Father referred to this incident in a letter to Mother
late in his mission, on 25 April 1899:

"As I again read your letter now before me, a warm feeling of
appreciation of your encouraging words comes over me, and your advice,
'Do your work well,' will be remembered, though perhaps not *heeded*
as it should be. It reminds me of a beautiful inscription carved over the
door of one of the cottages in the east part of Stirling: 'Whate'er thou
art, act well thy part.' If one only chooses the good part and does his
work *well*, success and happiness will certainly be his."

An interesting addendum to that story is that in the late 1960s, a missionary in Stirling noticed that the same building was being demolished. Familiar with the story of how it had inspired Father, he asked the demolition crew for the stone, which became the property of the mission. Elder Mark E. Petersen had it brought to Salt Lake City, where it was displayed for several years in the Church Office Building while the Museum of Church History and Art was being constructed. The original is now on display in an exhibit about Father in the museum and a replica is at the Missionary Training Center.

It is hard for me to tell whether Father enjoyed his experience as district president. He had been a missionary for only nine months when he received this responsibility, and he felt it keenly. Certainly there were many joyful and pleasant moments, for the members obviously gave him their hearts and he was thoroughly conscientious; but the responsibilities weighed on him heavily; and for the most part, he was alone in dealing with them. A long-standing feud among some Edinburgh branch families made every meeting potentially explosive.

Many of the members were often ill, and most were poor. Father not infrequently records giving his last sixpence to a hungry family. From early spring until late fall, the elders held open-air meetings several times a week to attract potential investigators. Father had mixed feelings about the value of such activities but cheerfully attended, sang, and preached, frequently expressing gratitude for the support of the branch members. Ships with emigrant parties sailed almost every week, and it was his duty to procure tickets, get the luggage aboard, and organize the sailing party with a priesthood holder in charge.

In addition to these responsibilities, he also supervised the nine branches, so he was sometimes gone three weekends out of four. But these difficult, exhausting months were also months of spiritual growth for him; and his journal records an inspiring portrait of a young man meeting responsibility manfully — sometimes humorously, sometimes discouragedly — and being seasoned by the experience:

"Sunday, June 19th. S.S. at 12 noon. . . . Open-air meeting besides other two. The responsibility is growing heavier. God must manifest his power or I do not know what will become of some of us.

"Tuesday, June 21st. . . . A company of Scandinavians has arrived (by mistake) twelve days before the next boat sails from Glasgow. Mr. Johnson asked me to do what I can to keep them contented. . . . Open-air meeting at Govan Cross. Some disturbance was made by persons in the crowd, but the meeting was nevertheless very good. . . .

"Wednesday, June 22nd. . . . Open-air meeting at Bridgeton Cross. One of the best yet held. The large crowd surrounding us were attentive and interested. At the conclusion tracts were distributed. So eager were they to get them that they literally crowded over each other reaching for them: they saw that the tracts were few and the crowd large. One man expressed himself as 'having been moved' and promised to come to meeting. Another walked toward our lodgings arguing against 'Works.' Others manifested similar interest. . . .

"Monday, July 4th. O how different this *Independence Day* from the one last year! Then I was free as the air. Now I'm tied down with care! letter and M[oney] O[order] from Tommy.

"Sat., July 30th. Visited my cousins, John, Donald, and Bella [in Edinburgh]. Bella is the picture of health and is truly a bonnie Scotch lass. . . . Through the acquaintance of Bella, I met a Mrs. Andrew Mackay and family and learned to my surprise and pleasure that she remembered meeting my father sixteen yrs. ago! We were acquainted immediately."

Most of the month of July 1898 was given over to making preparations for an illustrated lecture Dr. James E. Talmage, a member of the Quorum of the Twelve Apostles, would give about Utah on 2 August. Father had to hire the hall, arrange for an organist to accompany the lecture, arrange for advertisements and tickets, underwrite the financing, persuade someone to introduce the good doctor (the American consul was flatteringly agreeable to the task), and fret about all the things that not only could but did go wrong, including Elder Talmage's missing his train and arriving half an hour late.

"Wednesday, Aug. 17th. . . . At 8 pm. Bro. Edward, Bro. Calder, and I were meeting with some of the Saints at Anderson Cross holding an open-air meeting. Janet Lang and Mary McDonald were there having walked about four miles and a half. I wonder how many of our Utah girls would walk that distance to attend an open-air meeting! . . .

"Saturday, Aug. 20th. . . . Met with the officers & teachers of the S.S. (Bro. X was not there: came to hear "amen" said. He and Bro. Y are not feeling to support the present officers.) A good feeling prevailed and many good suggestions were made. With the exception of the bad feeling awakened by X and Y, all went well. . . . Retired about 11 P.M.

Gloomy! — sad!! homesick!!! discouraged!!!! Angry!!!! Sorry!!!! and what not! . . .

"Mon., Aug. 22. . . . Bro. Calder and I went to Rutherglen to administer again to Sister Faulds. We called to see Sister Taylor whose little baby is very low. Thought best to dedicate it to the Lord and asked Him to call it home if it is His will. . . .

"Tues., Aug. 23. Bro. Taylor came in and reported his baby's death — died this morning at 3 o'clock. Word just received that Sister McDonald has a little girl. As one is called away another is sent in its place. Received an answer from the Editor of the Cummock Express, in which he refuses to publish the article I sent him and denounces the 'New Doctrine' as being as a 'rascally lie', and 'will not defile his paper by discussing it.'

"Thursday, Sept. 8th. Twenty-fifth birthday! Received two kind loving letters from home — from Mama and Nettie [Father's sister Jeanette]. Twenty dollar present from Mama. Their loving words and good wishes brought tears. O if the world would have peace and happiness, let them make every home one where love abounds. The loving confidence expressed today would keep a man from every sin. God bless my parents and loved ones."

In September, Father took the occasion to visit the birthplace of his father in Thurso, an interesting visit that he remembered and told us children about later: "At a 'wee shoppy' kept by a Wm. McKay, I went in to buy sweeties and to see if they remembered anything about my father or Grandparents. The lady remembered hearing about 'The Black Minister' [Father's Grandfather William McKay, so named for his black hair and beard], and directed me down the 'burn' to a wee cottage kept by Angus McKay & wife.

"An old lady answered the knock. As soon as she learned who I am, she said: 'Ye'll com' right in the hoose, and ye'll sit right doon! An' ye're David's son! Weel, I'm right glad t' see ye! An' I mind yer Grandfather weel.' So she continued. I have never enjoyed a visit anywhere as I enjoyed that one. To hear her tell about the time when Grandfather [William] and his family joined the Church was more interesting than a good theatre.

" 'O what times they used to ha'e,' she would say, 'Lots o' folk aboot here were awfu' ill aboot it! awfu' ill aboot it!! O, I canna tell ye what times we used to ha'e. Och-a-ne! Och-a-ne!! 'Deed I'm the one

Birthplace of David O. McKay's father, David McKay, and home of David O.'s grandfather William McKay, in Thurso, Scotland. Inset probably William and Ellen Oman McKay

wishin' to have yer Gran-mother's memory. She could talk like a minister. When she was workin', she wadna' halt all the day!'

"She prepared a nice lunch. When I told her I do not use tea, she exclaimed: 'Do ye no? Well neither did your father. I mind when he was *hame* here aboot sixteen year ago, I was awful put aboot it, I didna' ken what to gi'e him; but ye'll tak' milk.' She remembered this little circumstance 16 yrs! Spent about two hours—two interesting hrs.— with her and then went to another little cottage near by in which my father was born. As I bid her good-bye, she kissed my hand and cried and said, 'I wish ye weel, I wish ye weel!'

"The house to the right is kept by a Mrs. McKiver. She made me welcome, for father stayed with her when he was here on his mission. How I enjoyed the thought of sitting in the same room in which my father first saw the light of day and spent his boyhood hours!! Saw the old chest upon which he sat as he preached to the family and friends who came in to the little room. The kitchen (in which these events happened) is very small with stone floor, boarded roof, and white washed walls. The old fireplace is small and ancient looking. To the right of it is an indentation in the wall containing two shelves upon which the dishes are kept. An old mantle is above it. The furniture consisted of a cupboard, 2 small tables, 5 chairs, the old chest and 1 stool. An old fashioned bed, covered, was also in the room. . . . I enjoyed my visit very very much indeed."

One of Father's most painful experiences involved the death of Elder David M. Muir of Beaver, who had been in the mission for only a month and had earlier served a three-year mission in New Zealand. Soon after his arrival in Dunfermline, he had contracted pneumonia and died 20 October, despite the care of his three companions. In a few months, the family requested that the body be sent home, and Father had the grisly and bureaucratically complicated task of overseeing the exhumation, sealing the coffin, and shipping it home.

In December 1898, Father prepared an article for a local paper refuting some slanderous reports about the Mormons. Addressed to the editor of the *Daily Record*, Father's letter used an impressively mild and reasonable tone for his counterattack, a tactic that he reemployed twenty years later as mission president in refuting exactly the same kind of charge:

"Recently articles appeared in the Glasgow press which misrepresented the object of Mormon missionaries, and which were intended to mislead the public. Knowing that many of your readers do not fully understand why these men travel as they do, and thinking that some, at least, might be interested to know something about these missionaries, I take the opportunity of writing a few lines concerning their work." He then explained that these elders accepted their mission calling and also their particular assignments "cheerfully" as a religious duty, denied that plural marriage had any connection with proselyting but instead affirmed that "the only object that the Elders of the Mormon Church have is to preach the Eternal Plan of Salvation, believing honestly and sincerely that all mankind must accept it before they become members of Christ's church.

"That they are sincere in this is evidenced by their self-denial. Love for home and dear ones is highly developed in their hearts; they feel keenly the scornful look and cynical sneer of those misjudging them; they realise to a certain extent what must be endured as they travel as missionaries; yet, so confident are they that they have the true Gospel, that the ties of affection and friendship cannot hold them, the sneer of the cynic does not daunt them, nor does the prospect of trials and hardship weaken them in their desire and determination to fulfill their calling, which they feel sure is from God. Their earnestness and sincerity is apparent, too, to all who converse with them or who visit their homes. Of course sincerity in a principle does not make it true. Other proofs must be forthcoming."

He then invited everyone to examine these proofs by reading tracts, attending open-air meetings, or participating in Sunday services. He continued:

"They are not aggressive in their manner; and never try to force their ideas upon anyone.

"As to the Mormon's home life in Utah, take the testimony of intelligent, unprejudiced men who have been there, compare their statements with the accusations made by an excommunicate, vainly trying to justify a wrong course of action, and then judge for yourself who tells the truth about the 'peculiar' religious body known as Mormons." He signed the letter "David O. M'Kay, 53 Holmhead Street, Glasgow."

As 1899 began, Father recorded both a personal and a statistical evaluation in his journal that give us a picture of conditions at the time:

"Glasgow, January 2nd, 1899. Sunday. One year ago, I sat in silent meditation wondering where I would be and how I would be feeling one year hence! Well here I am about the same lad as of old. The experiences of the last year have been many and varied, and I hope *profitable*. They have taught me to appreciate the truths of the Gospel, and to feel thankful that I was born of kind, loving parents in the valley of the mountains among a people who in *morals, freedom* of *thought,* and *true* religion lead the world."

As winter settled in hard on Glasgow, Father patiently negotiated jurisdictional disputes between traveling elders and branch presidents ("tired and worried," he confided to his diary) and provided marital counseling for Latter-day Saint couples, many of whom were plagued with drinking problems. He loyally showed up at choir practices, continued to handle most of the massive correspondence within the conference and with mission headquarters himself, organized almost weekly groups of emigrants and saw to their comfort in Glasgow, visited members, spoke at meetings, and blessed the sick.

Toward the last of February, he gave himself a holiday to the birthplace of one of his favorite poets, Robert Burns:

"We were shown the Inn where Tam O'Shanter and Souter Johnny 'sat bousin' at the nappy, and gettin' fou an' unco happy.' A half hour's walk brought us to the birthplace of Burns. The long low old-fashioned house 'stands by the roadside, not far frae the toun, An tho' it is aged an' worn, It's dearer tae some than the mansions in toun—the cottage where Burns was born.'

"By paying twopence each we were admitted to the rooms. The bed in which he was born was pointed to with pride by the old lady who keeps the house, so also was the old chest, and fireplace, and other old relics of the Poet. The roof is just a little over six feet from the floor; and the rooms show that Burns's early life was indeed a humble one." (23 Feb. 1898.)

The holiday probably did Father good since he was quadruply worried. First, Elder Edward had a severe case of bronchitis and Father felt that he should be released, even though Elder Edward begged to be allowed to stay. Father tried all the home remedies he knew and sat up nights nursing his companion, but administrations and fasting seemed to give the only relief to his racking cough and abdominal pain. Second, a five-lecture series on Utah and the Mormons failed to attract the crowds that they had hoped for and left the mission with debts. Third, this financial crisis came at a moment when he was completely out of funds. When the next letter arrived from home, it had been three weeks en route. And fourth, a recent letter from President Lorenzo Snow to all mission presidents had reaffirmed the policy that missionaries did not serve a set length of time and that mission presidents could release or keep elders as they felt inspired. Thus, Father had no idea when he would be returning home.

In Glasgow, in May 1899, a very significant event occurred, involving James L. McMurrin, then a new counselor in the European Mission presidency. He seems to have been a remarkably spiritual man who had taken an interest in Father from their first meeting at a conference in Newcastle, England.

On 29 May, after a day of public meetings, came a meeting of the missionaries and some local priesthood holders. Father's journal account reads:

"As the Elders began to give their reports, it became evident that an excellent spirit of love and unity was amongst us. A peaceful Heavenly influence pervaded the room. Some of the elders were so affected by it that they had to express their feelings in tears. Just as Bro. Young sat down after giving his report, Elder Woolfenden said, 'Brethren, there are angels in this room! I see two there by Bro. Young. One is his guardian angel. The other is a Guardian Angel too; but I don't know whose it is.' Everyone present, impressed with the spirit of the occasion, and sensing the Divine influence could testify to the truth of his (Bro. Woolfenden's) remarks. Although he was the only one who saw them, yet we each felt their presence. Elders wept for joy nor could [they] contain themselves. Sobs came from different parts of the room and they seemed fitting, too, for 'it seemed manly to weep there.' At the conclusion of the reports, all joined with me in a prayer of thanksgiving to the Lord for His blessings and manifestation.

"Pres. McMurrin then addressed the meeting saying among other things that the 'Lord has accepted our labors and at this time we stand pure before Him.' Pres. Naisbitt made a few closing remarks and at 2:30 P.M. the meeting was dismissed by singing and prayer. It was the best meeting I have ever attended."

I think it is significant that Father, with instinctive modesty, did not include in his journal account the portion of President McMurrin's discourse that applied directly to him. On 27 October 1934, responding to a request from the editors of the *Church News* section of the *Deseret News* to share his "innermost thoughts," Father reported the sacred experience he had had thirty-five years earlier. He summarized the events leading up to the prophecy, including Elder Woolfenden's announcement of angelic visitors. Then President McMurrin "turned to me and gave what I thought then was more of a caution than a praise.... 'Let me say to you, Brother David, Satan hath desired you that he may sift you as wheat, but God is mindful of you.' Then he added, 'If you will keep the faith, you will yet sit in the leading counsels [sic] of the Church.' At that moment there flashed into my mind temptations that had beset my path, and I realized even better than President McMurrin, or any other man, how truly he had spoken." (P. 8.)

Immediately after this conference, Father accompanied President McMurrin and several other missionaries and officers to Stirling, one of his favorite cities, and to Bannockburn where Robert the Bruce had won his reputation for valor. "The enthusiasm of Bro. McMurrin and Bro. McFarlane was now at its height and those of our company who were not real scotchmen wished they were," wrote Father on 30 May 1899, "while one or two others by tracing their genealogy back four or five generations satisfied themselves that Scotch blood was in their veins and joined in the enthusiasm."

After seeing off the visiting party, Father and Elder McFarlane visited Aberfoyle — known for the beauties of the Trossachs, the Classic Lakes, and Loch Achray. Father responded ardently not only to the romantic landscape but also to its literary associations as commemorated by Sir Walter Scott. He was eloquent in his description of "lovely Loch Katrine":

"Many poets and writers have tried to depict this beautiful scene; Scott's description of it is grand — but even it as all the others fails to convey to the reader the enchanting beauty of this lake and surroundings! Tranquil beauty, subdued grandeur, enchanting murmurs of a stream or the voice of a warbling songster seem to charm one to the spot! . . . We enjoyed our bread & cheese etc as fully as ever king enjoyed the richest repast spread before him.

"A few minutes walk over a little knoll brought us to the 'Silver Strand,' where 'In listening mood she seemed to stand, The Guardian naiad of the Strand.' "

They inexpertly rowed themselves out to Ellen's Isle and even more inexpertly rowed themselves back after collecting "a few bunches of Scottish Bluebells and leafy ferns as souvenirs of our visit." They got lost the next day and wandered through some beautiful countryside before finding themselves on the shores of Lake Dunkie.

Father commemorated this event in the following comic verse:

> *Auld Scotland, wham ne'er a town surpasses*
> *For beautiful lochs and trackless passes!*
> *Twa exploring youth like a wandering monkey*
> *Got lost ane day on the banks o' Loch Dunkie.*

A few weeks later when President McMurrin was again in Edinburgh, Father enthusiastically conducted his party over the same ground:

"By the time we reached [Loch Achray], Pres. McMurrin was rather quiet. His shoes were too tight for him and the long walk over hard roads had blistered his feet. His pain must have been severe, every step adding to his torture; but he wouldn't give up. . . .

"Before going back to the lodgings secured by the Brig o'Turk, I exchanged shoes with Bro. McMurrin and thus gave him a little comfort.

It was eleven o'clock P.M. when we reached our lodgings, tired, footsore, and sleepy, yet well satisfied with the day's journey. We had walked about 20 miles and had seen some of the most interesting places in Scotland."

The conference and the tour afterwards had refreshed Father and restored his sense of humor. Thus, with equanimity he remarked on 4 June 1899, after returning to Glasgow and plunging into the usual full session of meetings, that "all the time in the Council meeting this morning was consumed by the reading of minutes of two previous priesthood meetings!!"

Father did not mention desires to return home, hopes that he might, or speculations about a possible release date, even when a letter from Grandfather on 24 June informed him that he had been appointed to the Weber Stake Sunday School Board. Instead, he seems to have thrown himself back into his work of supervising the branches and missionaries with zeal and considerable confidence.

In mid-July, Father received permission to go to Wales to attend the famous song festival, the Eisteddfod, and look for relatives of his mother.

"Tuesday, July 18th. . . . The information in my possession as to their whereabouts was very meagre and had I depended upon that alone, subsequent developments proved that I should have left Wales a disappointed boy. But Providentially or otherwise I met an Elder Thomas, who had accidentally met a woman who had been inquiring about a 'McKay in Scotland.' 'She had a letter from Jeanette McKay in Huntsville,' he said, 'and she is expecting you to call on her.' This was just the information wanted; and as I found out afterward, had I not obtained it, I might be vainly looking around Aberdare until now (Aug. 9th) for the persons wanted live in Cefn Coed by Merthyr."

Unfortunately, Father's journal ends in the middle of an entry. We know that he visited his mother's birthplace, even the little room where she was born and where he could hardly stand upright, for he took Mother, my wife, and me back to it when we were visiting the European missions in 1952. Other than that, we have no record of the closing weeks of Father's mission — not even when he learned that he had been released.

He was formally released on 24 August 1899 and sailed for home almost immediately. I wish that I had asked Father more questions about his mission and heard more stories of his experiences there. I know that during my own mission, his letters were tenderly supportive and encouraging, and he seemed to understand my circumstances thoroughly, even though they were quite different from those of his own mission.

How grateful I am that he took the time after long, exhausting days to record what had happened and to give me, almost ninety years later, a glimpse of a boy from Huntsville growing into concerned, responsible manhood. It was this man who returned, married Emma Ray Riggs, and settled down to a career that—he thought—would combine farming and teaching. The apostleship, however, was only seven years away.

Chapter 3

EARLY MARRIAGE, WEBER YEARS, AND APOSTLESHIP 1902-1908

• • • • • • • • • • • • • •

Father became principal of Weber Stake Academy in April 1902, replacing Louis B. Moench, who had asked him to be a member of the faculty while he was still on his mission in Scotland. In addition to his administrative duties, he still taught literature and even headed the music department. He was leading the band one day when Ernest W. Nichols, the father of famous band leader "Red" Nichols, was walking by the school under the open windows. Wincing, Mr. Nichols entered the building, sought out Father, and announced, "You need a band leader." Father hired him on the spot.

It was typical that Father was trying to provide as many opportunities as possible for the students. He sponsored a course of lectures on education, dramatics, and current events that attracted townspeople as well as the student body, oversaw the organization of student government, launched the first track and baseball teams, supported the basketball team, and approved the beginning of the Domestic Arts Department, the Domestic Science Department, and the Conservatory of Music.

Joseph Anderson, a fourteen-year-old student at the academy in 1904, recalled in his oral history that Father, when lecturing on *The Princess* by Tennyson or *The Lady of the Lake* by Scott "just lived it. We all fell in love with him. And he became so absorbed in his subject that he wouldn't even hear the bell ring sometimes." Brother Anderson recalls that later, when he was secretary to the First Presidency, Father

David O. and Emma Ray with their first child, David Lawrence McKay

pounced on occasional grammatical errors with the laughing comment, "Didn't I teach you English?" Brother Anderson also recalled that the force of Father's personality was such that his appearance in a noisy study hall, without saying "a word," brought instant silence. (Oral History, interviewed by John R. Sillito, 23 Feb. 1979, typescript, p. 4, Weber State College Archives, Ogden, Utah.)

My first memory of Weber is of playing with the papers in Father's wastebasket. Father's office was squeezed into the vestibule between the inner and outer doors because the Moench Building, then the only building on campus, was severely overcrowded. Father was determined to do something about these conditions, even though his inquiries to the board of education had produced the answer that it could do nothing more than it already had. Grandfather and the other board members had mortgaged their homes to help finance Weber Academy when it was first begun, and Father was determined to equal their commitment. When the Church agreed to match funds to get the required $120,000, Father felt keenly his responsibility to raise the necessary first $60,000. He later told us how excited he was when Samuel Newhouse of Salt Lake City contributed $5,000.

Many years later, addressing students, faculty, and friends at Weber College Day on 5 March 1952, he recalled for them the experience of having President Joseph F. Smith visit the First Ward, possibly in his capacity as general superintendent of the Sunday School, and then stroll with him in Lester Park. The walls of the new building were standing, but work had been suspended because of the lack of funds:

"President Smith said, 'David, how are you getting along with the building?'

"I said, 'Not very well. At first we had large contributions as you know ranging from $5,000 down to $25, etc., but now the contributions are small and slow. It reminds me of an experience when I was a boy in Huntsville. Mother had molasses in some cans in the cellar. When I inverted a can, molasses would come out in a great glob, but no matter how long I held that can inverted, I could not get out the last drop.'

"He smiled and said, 'Shall I tell you how to get out that last drop?'

"I said, 'Yes.'

" 'Warm the can.'

"We followed that advice and were pleased to dedicate that building which is now west of the Moench Building."

I was present with Mother and Llewelyn when the last pillar for the portico of the new building was swung into place. By then, Father had been an apostle for two years but was allowed to continue serving as principal to complete this project.

On 8 April 1906 Father was called and sustained to the Quorum of the Twelve. As he told us children the story later, he and Mother had gone to Salt Lake City at conference time, taking Llewelyn and me to visit Mother's cousin Bell White and her husband, Parley, for lunch. During the meal, a telephone call came, asking Father to come immediately to the office of Francis M. Lyman, president of the Quorum of the Twelve Apostles.

Father had a premonition of a calling—but to a different position. He was then assistant to Thomas B. Evans, superintendent of Weber Stake Sunday School, and had been involved in innovative efforts to train members of the stake board to select an "aim," arrange the subject in a logical way, gather interesting enrichment materials, and make practical applications to the lives of the students. At monthly "union" (stake preparation) meetings, the board members taught the same principles to ward teachers and outlined lessons for the coming month. In weekly ward faculty meetings, the ward Sunday School superintendencies worked with individual teachers on their lessons.

President Joseph F. Smith, then president of the Church and general superintendent of the Sunday School, may have been impressed by the new quality of teaching in Weber Stake. Father had been invited to prepare an article on these principles, which was published in the April 1905 issue of the *Juvenile Instructor* under the title of "The Lesson Aim: How to Select It, How to Develop It, How to Apply It."

Thus, when he received that urgent telephone message between morning and afternoon conference sessions, he felt that perhaps he might be asked to become a member of the Church Board of Education. Elder George Albert Smith, then an apostle, met him at Temple Square and escorted him to the office of President Lyman.

As Father told us the story later, Elder Lyman opened the conversation: "So, you're David O. McKay."

"Yes, sir."

"Well, David O. McKay, the Lord wants you to be a member of the Quorum of Twelve Apostles."

Father was speechless.

"Well," continued Elder Lyman, "haven't you anything to say?"

Father finally was able to respond, "I am neither worthy nor able to receive such a call."

"Not worthy! Not worthy!" exclaimed Elder Lyman. "What have you been doing?"

Father explained, "I have never done anything in my life of which I am ashamed."

"Well, then," pursued a calmer Elder Lyman, "don't you have faith the Lord can make you able?"

"Yes sir," responded Father humbly. "I have that faith."

"Very well, then," said Elder Lyman briskly. "Don't say anything about this until your name is presented in conference this afternoon."

Father, somewhat dazed, returned to the Whites' apartment. On his way, he encountered his father, who asked if he had been called to the Board of Education. "I've been asked not to say anything about this until it's announced," Father explained, and Grandfather replied, "Then don't say anything."

Father didn't. It must have been very hard for him to say nothing to Mother—and equally difficult for her not to ask. They left Llewelyn and me with our cousins and went to the afternoon session. It was in the last few minutes of the closing session that President Smith presented the names of the General Authorities for sustaining, including the new apostles in the list, without commentary. When Mother heard, " ... George F. Richards, Orson F. Whitney, and David O. McKay," she burst into tears. She heard someone behind them say, "There's the wife of one of them. See, she's crying."

Among the flood of congratulations and good wishes that accompanied this call came a letter from Grandfather Riggs radiating sincere pride in Father's calling. Mother cherished this letter.

> Kansas City, MO, April 9th 1906

My Dear Son:

I was called from the breakfast table to the 'phone this morning.... It was Prest. F. M. Smith at the other end of the phone, who called my attention to an item on page 7th [in the newspaper], in which it states that D. O. McKay of Ogden, G. F. Richards of Tooele, and Orson F. Whitney of Salt Lake City, were unanimously elected apostles.... This struck me like a thunderbolt. The first one named above is my own boy and I write now to learn if it is really and truly and unmistakably true, that my son David has been made an apostle in the Utah Church....

I suppose that position would take you away from home more from wife & babies than the school work, still your dear little wife will feel so proud of her apostle husband that she will be willing to make the sacrifice no doubt.

... An old Patriarchal blessing on me stated that I would be an associate with apostles. It may be as that prediction has not been fulfilled in me, that satisfaction may come out in another member of the family....

> Pater Familias
> O. H. Riggs

I'm sure that this calling made certain differences in our lives. Father now had conference assignments out of town virtually every weekend and meetings in Salt Lake City at least once and sometimes three or four times a week, but certainly, staying in Ogden while Father continued his responsibilities with Weber Academy minimized the visible changes to our lives. And never, by a word or look, could we children surmise whether Mother wished Father's schedule different in any way.

One clue about Father's absences lies in an often-told story that occurred when Lou Jean was about four years old. Father had been away on an assignment, and Mother had made Father's welcome-home dinner something special by way of celebration. Father complimented Mother on it—which was not unusual. Lou Jean, however, recognizing the compliment as something visitors frequently said, responded with perfect courtesy, "Come again some time."

I also recall that we grew up knowing that we had to "set an example." What that meant, as I interpreted it in my youthful days, was that we couldn't play baseball on Sunday. All of us children felt a real obligation to do the right thing. I'm sure we didn't understand the importance of doing the right thing for the Lord's sake at first—but doing the right thing to please Mother and Father was certainly no unworthy substitute.

Father's ability to catch the train from Ogden to Salt Lake City on the fly became something of a local legend. He became expert at sprinting down the street and swinging aboard the moving train with his grip in his hand. Once a woman in an automobile saw him rushing down the street and gave him a lift. Even more colorfully, he was hurrying down 24th Street from Weber Academy, desperately late, hailed a boy on horseback, and hitched a ride to the station. A student saw them; and the *Acorn*, the school's literary paper, carried a cartoon of Principal McKay riding the horse, the boy clinging behind grinning broadly. This pattern, incidentally, did not alter. I remember often riding on the handlebars of our bicycle while Father pedalled urgently toward the station, then riding it back at leisure after he had leaped aboard the train.

Weber students seem to have been proud of their principal, but I gather that their pride grew out of personal liking for him and his teaching, not because he had an important ecclesiastical position. The unpaginated but carefully printed and illustrated *Acorn* souvenir issue for the spring of 1906 after his calling has several tributes to him, but they all center on his character, not his calling.

Father had begun a journal on 7 April 1906, the day after his calling. It is perhaps indicative of the rest of his life that he was interrupted while telling the story of how he was called and was never able to finish it, even though he left two pages blank for it. Between 19 April when he made his next entry and 15 July, he attended stake conferences every weekend but one—and on that one exceptional weekend, he was attending the Weber County Sunday School conference.

Two weeks later—and just two months after his calling—he went to the St. George Stake conference. He sent Mother a hurried postcard from Modena, Utah, which was the railroad terminal:

Modena, June 15, 1906—Noon

Dear Ray:

We are now 300 miles from Ogden, and 60 miles from St. George. We now start on a 60 mile buggy ride.

Love and kisses to you and the boys.

Lovingly, Dade

Stake conference assignments were demanding. In addition to the difficulties of travel, a grueling schedule awaited General Authorities on the other end. This particular conference had Saturday sessions at 10 A.M. and 2 P.M. and a priesthood meeting at 4:15 P.M. On Sunday were a regular Sunday School session at 10 A.M., a general session at 2 P.M., a "special" Sunday School session at 4:30 P.M., plus another session at 8:30 P.M. (Often there were Saturday night sessions as well.) At this conference, Father gave four addresses, administered to two people, and got to bed at 11:35 P.M. He was awakened Monday morning at 3:45 to return home. The party stopped for breakfast at 8:30 A.M. at the home of a good sister, whose menu was so astonishing that Father recorded it all: *"For three persons.* 3 dishes of mush, 9 fried eggs, 6 boiled eggs, 3 plates of potatoes, 2 dishes of radishes, 3 dishes of lettuce, 6 slices of ham, 3 pieces of cake, 3 pieces of pie, 6 dishes of fresh and preserved fruit." He traveled all day Monday and all Monday night, finally reaching Salt Lake City at 6:30 Tuesday morning.

Four days later, he was at Parowan Stake conference with nine meetings on Saturday and Sunday, at eight of which he spoke. Around most of these meetings, he squeezed in ordinations and blessings of the sick.

There are no letters dated during the winter of 1906–07, and his journal has a gap between July and December. Probably Father was given more local assignments during the winter because of his heavy administrative responsibilities at the academy. One touching entry on

9 December at the Brigham City conference records his pleasure at a Sunday School conference especially for the children: "It was a beautiful morning; and as the rays of sunlight came through the window and shone on the smiling faces of the children, it seemed that Heaven was approving the spirit that prompted the great gathering of children that morning. . . . I then spoke to the children, telling the story of 'The Other Wise Man.' "

He frequently directed one of his talks to children in stake conferences. A favorite topic was weeds, explaining how weeds are plants growing in the wrong place at the wrong time to be useful.

On the weekend of 9 December 1906, he attended a stake conference, stayed over Sunday night, caught the early train Monday morning and "went directly from depot to school. A large attendance of students, enrollment 315. Went home to Ray & the babes at 12 M[meridian]. At 1:15 P.M. went to Salt Lake taking the boys with me." That means Mother saw him for an hour and fifteen minutes between Friday evening and Tuesday evening.

It also gives a glimpse of some of the problems the principal of Weber Academy had. The next morning, Tuesday, 11 December, he wrote briefly but humorously: "6:00 A.M. 'Rustled' coal for school, by hiring job wagon to take coal from home." He was still fund-raising for the new school building, writing outlines for Sunday School lessons, serving on the Ogden Civic Improvement League (Betterment League), which tried unsuccessfully to rid Ogden of saloons and houses of prostitution, and teaching a parents' class in Sunday School that took an assertive stand toward community problems.

Father seldom kept a detailed account of his daily activities. Thus, I was interested in his account of one week in January 1907. Monday morning he attended to academy duties, taught a parents' class in the afternoon, and took Mother to a production of *Monte Cristo*. He then sat up late working on a report for a Quorum of the Twelve committee:

"Tuesday, Jan. 27th 1907. 7:30 A.M. Advanced Rhetoric class. 'autocrat' [by] Holmes. 8:45. Devotional Exercises—academy. 9:25. Theology class. 10:30. Eng. Literature class—Hamlet. 11 to 12 Finished [report] . . . 12:30 Dinner. 1:15 P.M. At depot intending to take train to Salt Lake but was disappointed by not meeting messenger with [typed report]. . . . 3:10 P.M. Went to Salt Lake City. 4:30 P.M. Meeting of Sub committee. . . . 6 P.M. Informal meeting with Bro. Pyper arranging for

evening meeting. 7 P.M. At meeting of S. S. General Board. Several
important topics considered. 11:45 P.M. Boarded train for Ogden. 1:30
A.M. Wed. retired.

"Wed., Jan 30. 1907. 7:30: Faculty meeting the principal business
being a consideration of How Best to Entertain Wm. J. Bryan who comes
to Ogden Sat., Feb. 2. under the auspices of the Academy. 9 A.M. Took
train to Salt Lake City. 10 A.M. Special meeting of the Quorum of the
Twelve. . . . It closed at 12:55. 1 P.M. Meeting of Sub-committee . . . 2
P.M. Meeting of Gen. Committee. . . . Dismissed at 5:45 P.M. 6:15. Dinner. 7. Special session Gen. S. S. U. Board. Considered 'outlines' until
11:40 P.M. Tired out, so instead of going home secured a bed in a hotel
and retired at 12:15."

He then spent all day Thursday in the Quorum's regular council
meeting in the temple, Friday at school ("busy all day — regular work
and new building matters,") and Saturday making arrangements for
William Jennings Bryan's evening lecture. This event was not without
its comic moments:

"Sent Prof. McKendrick to Salt Lake to meet Mr. & Mrs. Bryan.
At 6:50 P.M. the teachers, a committee of prominent citizens, and Ni-
chol's band were at the depot. The visitors' failure to come on the R.
G. W., as we thought they would, disconcerted us somewhat. The band
thought he had arrived, and after playing their welcome, as they thought,
started up to the hotel to meet Mr. Bryan there. Knowing that our
guest had not come in, and learning a few min. after the band's departure
that they had gone, I started up 25th St. on a run through the slush
and rain, to stop them. Caught them near Lincoln and ordered them to
return to welcome Bryan. In the meantime Bryan came in, the band
getting back just in time to give their welcome selection which was
followed by three cheers by the large crowed gathered in the station.
Lecture on 'The Old World and Its Ways' at 8:30 P.M. Opera house well
filled. Bryan is a refined orator, Mrs. Bryan, a refined, intelligent woman.
The lecture was the most clever advertisement of Bryan that I have
ever listened to."

Sunday, February 3, he was most uncharacteristically at home in
the morning — but the reason is tenderly apparent in the next line: "Fast
meeting in the 4th Ward, at 2 P.M. at which I blessed our little baby
girl, giving her the name of Louise Jennette. May she ever be as pure
and sweet as she was that hour! We were all present — Ray, Lawrence,

Llewelyn, Baby and I." An hour later, he caught the 3:10 train to Salt Lake City for another meeting.

I was five, old enough to remember the birth of this little sister. We knew the baby was coming, of course; and when I heard Mother crying, I thought it was the baby and came scampering downstairs to ask, "Is it a boy or a girl?" Father, obviously upset and worried, sent me back upstairs to my room and told me to keep very quiet. A few minutes later, he burst into our room upstairs, beaming from ear to ear, and announcing, "It's a girl!" I was confused but relieved at the sudden change in mood.

While Mother was recuperating from the birth, Father's sister Ann McKay Farr, who lived just four blocks away on Adams Avenue, took care of Llewelyn and me at her home. When Aunt Annie reprimanded us for some misdemeanor, I took five-year-old umbrage, seized my brother by the hand, and said, "Let's go home." She headed us off at the corner and persuaded us to come back.

Father's journal contains a wistful little note the week after Lou Jean's blessing. He spent Monday at school, Tuesday going straight from school to meetings in Salt Lake, and Wednesday going straight from the morning train to classes: "Met my family at noon. I feel that I am away from them too often." He then adds some details about some pressing financial worries incurred through his own generosity:

"The knitting factory has gone into the hands of a receiver. This means that we lose all our stock in it amounting to one thousand dollars. Besides this I may have to pay $1500 of a $3000 note on which I am security; and I might have to pay as a director for some subscribed stock another thousand. Thus we lose at one sweep $3500.00! Pretty hard blow just after building and our house not paid for!

"Ray hasn't uttered a complaining word. She has nothing but encouragement for me. I sometimes feel pretty 'blue' over the loss; and no doubt she does, but she doesn't show it. She is a brave little woman and a true devoted wife. How I love her!" (6 Feb. 1907.)

An entry very important to me appears on Friday, 22 March 1907, when Father was assigned to attend the Hyrum Stake conference in Cache Valley: "Took Lawrence, my little boy, with me. This was his initial trip. I hope to take him as often as I can." Because the railroads offered half-price tickets to children under the age of eight, Father made a point of taking one of us children with him on his conference assignments when it was practical, especially since Mother was seldom able to accompany him until we were older.

That spring he made an effort to have someone else appointed president of the academy. In fact, Horace S. Cummings, who occupied the position that would later be commissioner of Church Schools, suggested that perhaps Uncle Tommy would be a suitable candidate; but the unfinished building was a great concern and a change of leadership did not seem advisable. Father, at the request of the First Presidency, remained in charge for another year.

The new building was used for the first time at the end of May for graduation. Father was obviously pleased with how things had gone — particularly the benefit concert for which he had arranged notable performers including his brother apostle, Heber J. Grant:

"Mon. night. Junior reception to the graduating class in new hall. A success! Tues. night. Commencement exercises in the new hall — a grand success! The hall was crowded. My dream of two yrs. ago was this night realized. The building was not yet finished but it is near enough completed to serve our purposes for commencement week. It was truly a pleasing sight to see the graduates and their many friends in the new hall. Wednesday May 29, 1907. Class night. The exercises were successful — probably [scored out] undoubtedly the best we have held.

"Thursday, May 30, 1907. . . . At night was held in the new hall the benefit concert. The artists were Miss Edith Grant soprano, Elder Heber J. Grant (Perhaps he would not desire to be classed with artistic singers but he was one of the leading attractions), Miss Phylis Thatcher, and Bro. Ballard of Logan; Fred Tout, the Tabernacle choir, and a male double quartette under the direction of Prof. Squire Coop, from Ogden."

That summer, he was sent again to southern Utah. He left Salt Lake City by train June 5, a Wednesday, and returned almost two weeks later on Tuesday, June 18. He traveled by stage and buggy where the train ended, holding as many as three meetings per town in ten towns. Three loving letters home have been preserved. One, dated 8 June 1907, from St. George, tells about capturing the Gila monster exhibited for years in Weber's laboratories:

My dearest Ray:

We arrived at Modena Thurs. morning at 11:25 and were driven from there, in a stage, to Enterprise, twenty miles toward St. George. Reaching Enterprise at 4:25 P.M., we commenced meeting at 4:30. The people were already assembled. Out of a membership of 210, there were present 158.

This is a good attendance when we know that the ward covers an area of nearly a thousand sq. miles. Everybody in the town was present. After the meeting, we shook hands with all. Just as we reached the Bishop's home, it commenced to rain, and continued nearly all night. We were comfortably housed, and had a good night's rest.

Next morning, Fri., we started at 7:30, drove six miles, changed teams, and continued our journey, Bp. Holt, driver. The day was chilly, exceptionally so, for this time of the year; but we managed to keep fairly comfortable. In the afternoon, as we were coming along the "trail" just this side of the burned-out crater nearest St. George, we overtook a young man driving a team. As we neared his wagon, he said, "Did you see that alligator?" "An alligator?" we shouted. "Yes, it's just back there." "Let's go back," said I, and jumped out of the buggy. Our teamster turned around, and we were all soon in the sage brush looking for something. Soon the young fellow shouted, "Here it is!" and there, sure enough was *something* — not an alligator, and not a lizard, but the missing link between the two — a lizard-like reptile about 14 inches long, known as the "Gila monster." Its bite is deadly poisonous. I took a satchel strap, made a noose, and by Bro. Lyman's and Bp. Holt's skillful maneuvering, got the animal's head in it. Bro. Lyman pulled the strap and was the first to hold the "monster" in captivity. Bp. Holt emptied his clothes out of his telescope [collapsible suitcase] and let us use it as a prison for the captured animal. This morning, we chloroformed it, bottled it in alcohol, and prepared to carry it home to the Academy.

On 11 June, he wrote longingly from Harmony: "Until this afternoon we have been busy every moment — driving, eating, preaching, or sleeping; and I have not had much time to *center* my thoughts for a continued length of time on home. You are always in my mind, but in the midst of duty, you have to pop up between thoughts, like a beautiful flower I saw today blooming in a bed of "prickly pears"; but today we arrived here several hours before the time of meeting and I have wished every moment of waiting that I could spend the hours with my loved ones. To do this being impossible, I've longed for a letter. I am glad I feel this way. Love is the greatest and the purest power in life, and I am thankful that it rules our home and reigns supreme in our hearts. I strolled alone up the hillside here this afternoon, and spent just two hours of lonely happiness (if you know what that is) thinking of you and the babes. I have never loved you more dearly in my life."

Father's journal fills in some details on 12 June: "Left Kanarra at 1:47 P.M. arrived in Cedar at 4 P.M. . . . After a shave, wash, and general brushing made so necessary by the dusty, windy drive, I called at Pres. Jones' for letters. I was not disappointed. There was one from my sweetheart Ray, the dearest, truest wife on earth, and the letter is the sweetest I have ever received. The last word in it is

> *My Dearest, I'm lonely without you,*
> *My heart yearns ever for thee;*
> *And with fondest hopes I am thinking*
> *When your bright, cheerful face I shall see.*
> *I miss you so much at the fireside,*
> *When the shadows of evening appear;*
> *And without you my life is so gloomy*
> *I were wishing the end to draw near.*

" 'With best wishes that you may have a good time, I am, as always,

" 'Your loving Ray' "

He answered Mother's letter and sent her the following lines:

> *There are those who live for Pleasure,*
> *There are those who yearn for Wealth,*
> *There are those who seek Position,*
> *There are those who pine for Health,*
> *There are men who delve in Science,*
> *Mighty truths of life to find;*
> *And they strive to find the Author*
> *Of Life, the Soul or Mind.*
> *All these things should be commended,*
> *If the end in view be pure;*
> *And great truths we all should strive for,*
> *Every blessing made secure.*
> *But for me life's one great object —*

> *And it leads to God above —*
> *Is to long, to search, to live for*
> *The Divine eternal* love.
> *I have found that Love in you, Dear,*
> *It contents my soul each day;*
> *And I thank my Heavenly Father*
> *For my darling Emma Ray.*

The letter that he sent with this poem, written immediately after he read Mother's letter, expresses the devoted love they shared:

My darling *Wife:*

You have never written a *sweeter* letter in your life, and I have never appreciated one more than the *love* letter you wrote on the 6th, and which I received just an hour ago. . . . True love is like all truth; *the more one gives the more one has.* Six years ago, as I told you yesterday, I thought my love for you was all my heart could hold; but it seems so little now compared with what is in my heart to-day that I wonder that I thought it full. To-day I think my soul is filled, and it is; and yet forty-four years hence, it must be stronger and purer still. This simply means, as our experience proves, that Love feeds and grows on Love, and while it grows, it increases the capacity of the soul for loving. So our love was perfect when I kissed you at the altar; it is perfect to-day; it will be perfect when the century strikes "half past"; it will be perfect eternally!

Feeling as he did about marriage, it was with tender feelings that he officiated at the wedding of his sister Jeanette and Dr. Joseph Morrell on 19 June 1907, in the Logan Temple. Festivities continued the next day in Huntsville where Aunt Lizzie had prepared a wedding dinner. "It was delightful to meet all together once again in the dear old home of our youth," Father records in his diary. His mother had died 5 January 1905, and he wrote wistfully, "I missed her kiss at the doorway, her smile in the parlor, her laugh at the table by Papa's side, and the evening talk before going to bed."

On 29 June 1907, he was off to stake conference in La Grande, Oregon, the earliest trip I can remember taking with him. My only recollection of that experience is being awestruck by the plank sidewalks — huge one-by-twelve-inch slabs of the region's lumber, laid together end to end, but warping and curving in a way to make walking on them a most interesting experience.

On Independence Day, 1907, his diary contains the uncommon report: "A day of rest. There is nothing I have to do, there is nowhere I have to go. A day of relaxation. Drove to Huntsville with Ray and the Babes. Enjoyed a family reunion at the old home. Drove back to Ogden at night."

I developed "rather a severe attack" of whooping cough on 13 July, and had the honors mostly to myself until Lou Jean also came down with the sickness just when Father left for his next conference to San Louis and San Juan stakes in Colorado and New Mexico.

At that time, the Western States Mission was a pioneer in the service of sister missionaries, and on 19 July 1907 Father observed approvingly, "Young boys and young girls together, and under conditions, too, where love sparks, no doubt, strike fire in the youthful hearts; and yet very very few, if any, of these young people forget themselves in regard to the strictest of propriety between the sexes."

He wrote with feeling on 22 July: "Received a letter from Ray. . . . She said she and babes are pretty well, but I know from interruptions she had while writing that the babes are unwell." He answered promptly, datelining his letter from "Fruitland, alias Kirtland, alias Burnham, Nearly-off-the earth" on 27 July 1907:

My dear Ray:

This has been a long trip, a hard trip, and one full of worry. At Durango night before last, I went to the telegraph office to send you a telegram asking how you all are; but the line was out of order, and the operator told me I could not get an answer before I had to leave. There is no office here, but last evening tried to telephone to one, but was unsuccessful. I will try again this morning.

Physically, I am over a thousand miles away from you, but there is not an hour passes without my seeing everyone of you in our lovely home. My soul is with you. When in imagination I hear those little ones coughing, and see your worry, my whole being is wrung in sympathy. . . .

With truest love, and daily prayers for your health and happiness, I am your own Dade

XXX to the babes and xxx Mama.

On 8 September 1907, his thirty-fourth birthday, he wrote intro-spectively: "Thirty-four years ago today I was nestled to my mother's bosom! What would I not give to hear her greeting and receive a loving kiss from her this morning! Half my life is spent. Where shall I be thirty-four yrs. from to-day? How shall the intervening time be spent?" He spent that particular day at the Sanpete Stake conference and, by strenuous efforts, reached home at 5 A.M., just in time to put in a full day at Weber Academy.

Although Llewelyn had escaped and I was slowly recovering, little Lou Jean was still very ill. On 20 October 1907, Weber Stake held its conference and Mother, sleepless from a night spent nursing Lou Jean and without any hired help, made a "good dinner" for "Bro. and Sister Grant, Bro. & Sister Whitney, Bro. and Sister Shurtliff, and several others. . . . Lizzie [Father's sister] was kind enough to come over and help. She is one of the most unselfish girls in the world. She possesses true beauty—beautiful without, noble within."

By another week, Lou Jean's fever had developed into pneumonia. Friday, Father was scheduled to go to another stake conference in Woodruff, Wyoming. He telegraphed home on Saturday and, after four hours, received the chilling message, "Lou Jean is worse. You had better come home at once." When he saw his own father waiting at the station as the train pulled in Sunday morning, he braced himself to hear that Lou Jean was dead. Instead, Grandfather assured him that she was still alive, though worse than when he had left.

"Dr. Morrell had been at the house all night—the nurse had been constant in her attentions, but not so much so as Ray and our folks who loved her. Bell and Nell were both untiring in their attentions.

"The Lord blessed Lou Jean; and it was through His blessing and the skillful attention and direction of Dr. Morrell that her life was spared. Our friends were exceptionally kind, and prayed earnestly for the res-toration to health of our little girl.

"All day Mon., Mon. night, Tues., and Tues. night, her life lay in the balance, but Tues. night the crisis was reached; and, although but little change was noticeable for the next few days, she began to im-prove." (27–29 Oct. 1907.)

At some point during Lou Jean's illness, an experience occurred to confirm in my six-year-old mind the power of prayer. Father and Mother were both extremely worried and, when Sunday came, stayed at her bedside while Llewelyn and I went to Sunday School. Father asked me, before I left, "Will you please ask the superintendent to have the Sunday School pray for Lou Jean?" I transmitted the request and noticed that the prayer was given at about 11 o'clock.

When I returned home, Father told me that Lou Jean had reached a crisis at that time and then had relaxed and fallen into a refreshing sleep. I recall being grateful but not astonished; I took it for granted that the Lord would intervene on our behalf in response to the prayers of the faithful.

Father spent the rest of November and December raising money for the Weber Academy, administering to the sick, attending scattered stake conferences throughout Utah every weekend until the Sunday after Christmas, and continuing his Sunday School work.

The day after New Year's, he recorded:

"Thurs., Jan. 2, 1908. Seven years ago today Ray and I were married. We have had seven years of life and happiness, and are blessed with three beautiful children. We are happy and contented in each other's love. Ray has been a true devoted wife and an ideal mother! May our next seven years and seven times seven be as successful!"

In February 1908, Mother accompanied Father east to Chicago, Kansas City, and Independence. Mother, in the first stages of pregnancy, was ill for much of the trip; but being together was worth a great deal of discomfort to them both.

Although William McKendrick had taken over much of the internal administration of Weber Academy, Father had retained the responsibility for raising the rest of the money for the new building and was still teaching four classes during the spring of 1908. Finding contributors, getting pledges, and then collecting was very difficult; and many refused to contribute further. Father was extremely worried, for the dedication had been scheduled for 27 May 1908. Exhausted by his schedule that spring, he confessed sorrowfully on 1 May 1908: "There is yet due on the new Building $5500.00 or more, and the funds for current expenses are not sufficient to meet the bills due, and to pay salaries. My being away so much makes my labors here in school a burden. They used to be a pleasure. Thirty more days and, I hope, I shall be relieved."

When graduation rolled around, the necessary funds had still not been found. On class day, 25 May 1908, the graduating class "presented me with a beautiful set of Dickens' Works. The thought that this was my last week in school had made me somewhat sad during the evening, so when this expression of good-bye came, it quite unnerved me. Tears mingled freely with our mutual expressions of appreciation."

It is obvious that Father made the next day's entry with a full heart and tender feelings:

"Tuesday, May 26. I received a telephone message from Bro. Geo. D. Pyper [assistant to the general superintendent of the Sunday School] requesting me to come to Salt Lake without fail on the 10:40 A.M. train. In the midst of all my school work, I was loath to do it but consented. The teachers didn't seem to mind my going.

"Attended to S. S. Union Board work from 1 P.M. to 6 P.M. Came back to Ogden at 7:20 P.M. and prepared to attend the reception to the Board and faculty. . . . When Sister McKay and I arrived at the Academy, we were met by Bro. McKendrick who chided us for being late. We went upstairs together. I felt that something unusual was going on, but was not prepared for the magnificent scene that I found myself in the midst of when the lights were turned on in the old study hall. There sat 300 students, all the faculty, members of the Board, and their wives, President Smith, Sup't. Horace Cummings and others — all extending from their countenances a welcome such as I have never before experienced. As soon as the lights were turned on, the assembly applauded and the Academy band struck up the Weber Academy March.

"I was surprised!

"The brilliancy dazed me; I experienced every kind of feeling of embarrassment known to man. It was a glorious gathering, skillfully planned, and successfully carried out. Bro. McKendrick had me called to Salt Lake so that teachers and students could prepare. The principal feature of the evening was the presentation of the following letters by the chairman, Bro. McKendrick.

#1

Ogden, Utah — May 26, 1918

Dear Bro. McKay:

The enclosed check of $1050.00 is handed to you with the best wishes of the Faculty and student-body of the Weber Academy. It represents the combined efforts of both, and will help some to liquidate the indebtedness of the new building, before its dedication; a hope that has nestled close to your heart, and for the realization of which you have earnestly prayed and worked.

Permit us now to relieve you of $1050.00 worth of anxiety and responsibility.

> Very truly your friends,
> Faculty and Student-body

#2

> Ogden, Utah, May 26, 1908

Dear Brother McKay:

Enclosed please find check for $2000.00 which we have the great pleasure of contributing for the purpose of liquidating the balance due on your beautiful building.

> The Church of Jesus Christ of
> Latter-day Saints
> By the First Presidency

#3

> Ogden, Utah, May 26, 1908

Dear Brother McKay:

Enclosed please find check for $1500.00, which we have the pleasure of handing you in the midst of your festivities and just before the dedication. It represents in a small degree, the high regard we have for your past labors relative to the Academy and the young people in our several wards. Verily is this true: If ever a man lost himself for the good of others, you are that man.

> Your friends and brothers,
> The Bishops of Weber Stake

"I tried to respond but made a poor failure of it.

"The toasts were excellent, and contained a great deal more than I merited. Bro. Middleton's was exceptionally good, and so was Bro. Ridges', a copy of which he handed me, and which to preserve, I insert here:

Toast: "Who is this man McKay?"

That is what Saul said to Abner. "Whose son is this youth?"

To *us*, he is David, the son of David, the Huntsvillite.

He has put to flight the army of doubt, and has slain the giant "I can't"; and tonight, as in days of old, we sing and feast in his honor, and can say as did the woman of old, "David hath gathered his tens of thousands."

To *me*, he is the man whose handshake I cannot forget.

The man who will undertake to do two days work in three hours and eighteen minutes, and expects the rest of us to do the same.

The man who never forgets a kindness, who appreciates thoughtfulness, and delights in making others happy.

The man who thinks this might be his last day on earth. If you do not agree with me, walk down town with him and endeavor to talk at the same time.

The man who is as kind and gentle to his horse as to his children.

The man who never takes more than four minutes and nine seconds to catch a train.

The man whom we love, we admire, and respect.

The man who has become as a little child.

The man who will ask, "Is it right?" and says, "Then we will do it."

Father always cherished the memory of his years at Weber Academy and kept a warm place in his heart for his many friends made there.

In August 1908, Father was sent on a three-week conference assignment to Taylor Stake and Alberta Stake in Canada with the third conference in Big Horn Stake, Wyoming. Mother, four months pregnant and feeling well, was able to accompany him. Unfortunately, she caught cold either just before they left or in the first days of the trip. It turned into a severe, racking cough; and though she carried on cheerfully, Father's journal chronicles a growing worry that counterpoints their sightseeing, meetings, and visits.

They had scheduled three days of camping at Waterton Lakes with a party of local leaders, but Mother's cough kept her from sleeping. During the ride to Cardston, "Ray was seized with an intense pain in her shoulder, and suffered agony for several hours. By hot applications, the pain was reduced, and she slept again towards morning." The depth of Father's worry—he was actually afraid for her life—appears in his entry for August 22:

"Ray still unwell, and suffering from pain in her shoulder. Her cough is not much better. She makes little mention of it, and always seems cheerful; but her looks show that she is a pretty sick girl. I feel encouraged to-day, however; for I have an assurance that the Lord wants her to live to rear her children. It's our duty now to take care of her, and not let disease overpower her."

He attended to his duties at Alberta Stake conference, 22–23 August 1908; but during the Sunday School convention held in Byron, Wyoming, on Monday, 31 August, Mother began to miscarry:

"She suffered intense pains during the meeting, and also during the ride to Cowley. . . . Putting the four-months-old foetus in a little box, we boarded the train for Toluca Junction. Our fears and apprehensions can only be imagined. When Ray felt sure that she had lost a little unborn infant, she felt sad and downhearted. She found some relief in tears, and then became fearful lest some complication should arise, and she far away from medical aid. However, she endured the ride wonderfully well. . . . Bro. McMurrin and I administered to Ray. Soon after the administration, she went to sleep, and had a good night's rest."

There were no further complications; but a few days after Mother and Father returned, Father celebrated his birthday and wrote, somewhat pessimistically:

"Tues. Sept. 8, 1908. One half my life is now past. Thirty-five years old to-day. [He lived to be ninety-six!] As I look back, the thirty-five pages are not half so well written as they should be—only a few good deeds recorded."

He had been an apostle for two and a half years, lacking one month. Although he was at last able to lay down some of his responsibilities at Weber after five and a half years as its principal, in the next twelve years, he and Mother would add four children to the family and Father would take on even heavier responsibilities.

Chapter 4

FATHER AT HUNTSVILLE

◆ ◆ ◆ ◆ ◆ ◆ ◆ ◆ ◆ ◆ ◆ ◆ ◆ ◆

Huntsville had a special place in Father's heart all his life, even when there were many, many competing demands. Often, even as president of the Church, Father would get up at 5 A.M. or earlier and go to the farm in Huntsville; but he would still be at his desk by 8 A.M. and put in a full day's work. For him, even an hour on the farm was worth the trouble of the drive, and contact with his land and his animals — even Huntsville's air, he said — was deeply refreshing to him.

These visits were prompted not only by Father's great love of the land but also, I think, by his desire for us to grow up learning the lessons of hard work and responsibility that he himself had learned on the farm. Every summer, Llewelyn and I milked nine to twelve cows, night and morning. Some of my memories of those animals are exasperating, and some are affectionate. I always milked Nellie first. She was a beautiful purebred Holstein, almost pure white, who gave nearly two pailfuls at every milking — six gallons at a time. She insisted on being milked first and followed me around the corral while I was getting things ready, anxious to be relieved.

Another cow with personality was Bossie — sometimes just Boss, for short. She had no horns, but she made up for that loss in dominance, and she ran the herd. In the winter, we took her with us to Ogden where I continued to milk her to provide the family's supply night and morning. A beautiful brown Jersey, she also was a prolific producer.

Every fall, we loaded her in the wagon and transported her down

David O. McKay's birthplace in Huntsville, Utah, as it appeared in 1955

to Ogden. After a few years, she walked into the truck by herself, knowing that she could look forward to a comfortable barn all winter. But in the spring, she would get restless. One year, I left her untied while I went into the house for something and returned to find that she had disappeared. I ran quickly back to the house to tell Father, who was actually amused. He surmised that she would go up Ogden Canyon, so we set out that way. We found her at the mouth of the canyon, about six blocks east of our house, tied to a telephone pole by a helpful passerby.

"Let's see whether she'll go the rest of the way," Father suggested. He wrapped the rope around her neck and put a note on her halter: "Please let me pass; I'm going to grass." Then we turned her loose. (Canyon traffic was not then what it is now.) She set off determinedly up the canyon and, we found out later, arrived in good time on the farm. Powell Evans, who was taking care of the herd at that time, didn't recognize her sleek summer coat and tried to chase her away. She had no intention of leaving but instead butted her way into the herd to remind them who she was. Then he recognized her and let her stay. After that, we simply turned her loose every spring to go home.

Milk production then was a hand chore. We poured the milk into two ten-gallon cans, put the lids on them, and then carried the cans into the stream in Dry Hollow to get the milk cold enough to be freighted to Salt Lake City. When we heard the streetcar at the mouth of the canyon, we loaded the two cans on the back of a buggy, hitched up Mike, and drove down to the village general store a mile and a half away.

During one summer, we bought a cream separator, put up a tent in the meadow, and made our own butter, churning it with a crank-handle churn. We sold the butter to the store in Huntsville. Jerry, our bull, didn't care for the tent. He hooked it with his horns and tore it down, nearly demolishing the separator in the process.

Jerry was one of our more interesting animals. A young Jersey with a protective streak, he accepted Llewelyn's and my coming to milk the cows but pawed the ground when strangers arrived. Father was a stranger. Once when Father came with us, he ordered Jerry sternly, "Don't do that to me." The bull, to our astonishment, put down his head and charged. Father sprinted for the fence, but Jerry hit him in the middle of his back. Father's hat went flying, and, distracted, Jerry hesitated long enough for our hired man and me to chase him away.

Father, shaken, jumped on a horse, roped Jerry, and dragged him bellowing to the chute where our local expert dehorned him. The operation made Jerry safer but did not improve his disposition. After that he had to be kept in a pen ten feet high made of two-by-six boards. He recognized the sound of Father's motor and always bellowed at him when he heard the car drive up. He was the only animal on the farm that did not learn to love Father.

An example of Father's kindness to animals occurred one summer when a swallow built her nest in the saddle house next to the barn in Dry Hollow. Father left the window open on purpose so she could get in and out to tend her nestlings. One afternoon, Aunt Lizzie saw that the window was open and closed it. She mentioned the event in our casual family conversation, and Father promptly traversed the mile between the house and Dry Hollow to reopen the window for the frantic little mother.

Father loved the birds so much that he wouldn't have cats in Huntsville, preferring to keep the mice under control with bait, even if it did mean losing a little grain. But our dogs accompanied us from Ogden to Huntsville and back again. Billy was a beautiful purebred collie, a gift from C. C. Richards, the father of Franklin D. Richards, who was later a member of the First Quorum of the Seventy. One year he won a gold medal in the collie category at the state fair. Winnie, another purebred collie, joined the family later. They both learned to ride on the running board of the car, Winnie on the right and Billy on the left, the twelve miles from Ogden to Huntsville. Once in a while, they'd lose their balance at a sudden jolt or an emergency swerve, but they were amazingly stable and learned to crouch at the corners. When they could see that the family was getting ready to go, they would dance and prance in the driveway, barking anxiously, but neither of them would touch the car until Father would nod and say, "All right." Then they would both leap aboard.

On one occasion, Billy was riding with Father and me when we came to a flock of sheep being driven from one place to another. Father and I noted with amazement and pride how Billy, who had never seen sheep before, instantly jumped down and began rounding up stragglers and steering the leaders, acting on instinct alone.

Billy was an amazingly patient dog. When I was little, Father had a harness made for him, and we hitched him to our sled. At Christmastime, Father would ask me to deliver packages to relatives and friends. I put them on the sled, and Billy pulled it.

Billy always waited at the corner near our Ogden home where the streetcar stopped in the evenings, greeted Father with dignified delight and, with great pride, carried Father's newspaper home, dropped it in the dining room, and went to lie down in his assigned place in the hall.

Later, Father was without a dog, and word got around that he wanted one. Members of a priesthood quorum in Delta, Utah, got together, identified a suitable sheepdog for presentation, and then told Father about it. He was delighted and told us all that he was going down to get the puppy. Back he came with a full-grown sheep dog, Spike. We all burst out laughing at the misunderstanding, and Father explained, "He won my heart when he put his paw on my arm while we were driving back."

Spike was very well trained and a much-loved dog. Just once—and I'm sure for good reason—he forgot his manners, nipped at a man delivering something, and tore his trousers. Father told the man to go have a new pair of trousers made by the Deseret Gym tailor. When the tailor explained that he could reweave the tear so that it would be invisible, the man thought Father had spoken to him privately about it to avoid paying for the suit. He complained to the police, and we were given the choice of killing the dog or getting rid of him.

His previous owner was glad to have Spike back and, with a heavy heart, Father returned him. "You'd better shut him up," he warned the man when he was ready to leave. "Oh, no," said the man. "He'll stay here." But Spike jumped into the car, proudly wagging his tail, hoping to go back home with Father.

Father exercised a magical influence even over other people's dogs. Peanuts belonged to Morgan, his younger brother. I recall one day when we were driving from Huntsville to Ogden in the buggy with Peanuts following us. We encountered Morgan driving up to Huntsville and stopped to visit. When we started up again, Peanuts followed us, then ran toward Morgan, then back toward us, and then sat in the middle of the road and howled from pure frustration. Morgan resolved the dilemma by calling him.

Among our other memorable livestock were pigs. We had a large black boar named Caesar, and it was my duty to keep him supplied with water, which I had to carry in a bucket from the pump. One day just after Father had left for a conference, in a hurry as usual, he began to worry that Caesar might be forgotten and fired off a telegram: "Don't forget Caesar. He may be thirsty."

Telegrams had to be phoned from Ogden to Huntsville; and anything passing through the Huntsville telephone exchange was in the public domain. The next time I went to the store, a half-dozen people asked, "Lawrence, who is Caesar? Why should he be thirsty?" I got the same question the next day and the next. I'll never forget Caesar.

Another memorable pig was Peter, the only survivor of a litter of nine, the mother of which had also died. We nursed him with a bottle, and he considered himself a full member of the family. When he grew up, he learned how to open the barnyard gate and come across the road to the back porch, where he would push Billy, the collie, off the doormat with his snout. Billy, who regularly drove cattle and hogs with aplomb, was always so astonished at Peter's impertinence that he would retire from the field in bewilderment. Then Peter would snooze on the door-mat, one ear cocked for the sound of anything that might be food. I remember once (only once!) when he trotted briskly into the kitchen. Mother took the broom and swept him right back out again, exclaiming, "I will not have a pig in my kitchen."

In retrospect, I think that living on the farm must have been difficult for Mother. That is my guess, for she never uttered a syllable against the moves to Huntsville every summer and even took the children to Huntsville in the summer of 1921 when Father was on his world tour. With no indoor plumbing and a lack of other modern conveniences (we had to pump our water at the well outside, for instance, and heat it on the stove), preparing meals and keeping busy children clean must have been a monumental task. But for her, Father's joy in the farm out-weighed her inconvenience.

Father's love of horses is legendary. He kept horses until his death and rode until he was in his eighties. In his late eighties, he had to be helped to mount, and at one point we asked anxiously, "Are you sure you should be riding?" Father reassured us, "Sonny Boy takes care of me."

Stories about Father and his horses are legion. One of the most influential experiences I had involved Daisy Mae, a Wyoming horse I bought from Deseret Livestock for our own daughters to ride. She had been raised on a ranch and apparently mistreated, for she was afraid of men. She liked girls and would let our daughters approach her, but she'd shy away when I tried to catch her. One afternoon, I was trying to catch her to put a halter on her when Father saw me.

He stopped me at once and said, "You mustn't chase her. She'll just learn to run away from you." That's when I first heard the famous dictum that he and Mother had lived by in rearing their own family: "Lawrence, don't ever give a command to an animal or to a child that you don't see is obeyed." I think it actually hurt him to think that an animal might try to avoid him. He dropped all of his plans for the afternoon and spent the next four hours training Daisy Mae. He put a rope on Daisy Mae's halter, called her, and—when she came—patted her, praised her, and gave her oats. If she tried to run away, he brought her up short with the rope and tingled her leg with a whip. By the end of the afternoon, she came to him willingly and quickly and also learned to come to the rest of us when we called.

Mike, half of Father's matched team, didn't like to be tied up and would gnaw at the knot until he got loose—but then he would simply stand quietly. I guess it offended his dignity not to be free. I enjoyed reading this notation from Father's diary on 24 May 1912: "Mike drove the distance [from Ogden to Huntsville] and returned in 2 hours and

45 minutes. 15 minutes at the old home made the entire trip 3 hours—and the little horse did it easily. He is the best driver I have ever owned. A good horse is a pleasant companion."

Another of Father's favorite horses was Dandy, a beautiful and well-trained animal who loved Father so much that he would, if Father put him before an object he feared, go up to it. But Dandy was also a foolish young horse. He would nibble and nudge his tie ropes until they came loose. In the pasture, he would move along the fence until he found a stretch of smooth wire and then would paw it down carefully until it was low enough that he could step over. He even learned to open the door to his stall and the gate to the corral. Once he wandered out on the highway and was hit by a car. The machine was demolished, he was injured, and the driver was slightly hurt. Father redoubled his efforts to keep Dandy under control—even wiring the gate shut—but Dandy had not learned his lesson.

One day, he found the gate unwired, unlatched it, and wandered out with another horse, his pasture mate. They explored a neighbor's field, and Dandy pushed open the door to an old house that was being used to store tools and grain. They promptly set to work on the oats—poisoned bait for gophers. Within a couple of hours, they both were dead. Father felt Dandy's loss keenly and often told his story to make the point that young people who never learn where the limits are frequently meet Dandy's disastrous end.

Some of my favorite hours with Father were spent riding the range on the hills above Huntsville, checking to see that the cattle were where they belonged, and doing the spring branding. Father's preferred costume for such activities was a khaki shirt and trousers, gloves, and high-laced boots. His fine beaded gauntlets, a gift in later years, are on exhibit in the Museum of Church History and Art.

Father's horses recognized the sound of his car and would be waiting at the barnyard gate by the time he came up the lane. He often gave them sugar. Father's favorite horse for riding was Sonny Boy, a sorrel gelding with a white blaze and a white stocking on his off forefoot. He was not only beautiful but sure-footed and fast. An entry from Father's 1956 office journal that has been copied into his Huntsville scrapbook tells how well-trained Sonny Boy was. Father had just celebrated his eighty-first birthday two days earlier:

"I drove up to Huntsville—road is now paved right up to the gate of my farm. Upon arrival, I got out of the car, and walked over to the gate where I called my horse Sonny Boy who was out in the pasture with his head turned away from me. When I called, he picked up his head, turned around, and started toward me, with all the other horses in the field following him. I had several lumps of sugar in my pocket and the horses came up to me. I gave each a lump of sugar. Then Sonny Boy came over and stood patiently waiting for me to put the halter and bridle on him. I led him to the car and put my "gift" bridle [a birthday present] on him, then took a thirty-minute ride. Even on the highway with cars whizzing by, Sonny Boy was in perfect form and did everything I wanted him to. I think he is now perfectly trained, and I am delighted with him!"

Uncle Tommy has told us a revealing story of Father's fondness for his horses. While Father was traveling around the world, visiting the far-flung missions of the Church, Uncle Tommy suggested that he might sell some of the "surplus" horses. Father demurred but finally wrote authorizing Uncle Tommy to sell Star, an older horse that he had not used for range work or farm work for some time. After Father returned home, he saw Star in the new owner's pasture and thought she looked "a little homesick." So Star became one of Father's horses again.

In June 1954, someone broke into the saddle house and stole four saddles. In August, President Rulon P. Peterson of Lake View Stake made an appointment to meet with Father at the Huntsville house to discuss "some stake problems." To Father's astonishment, eleven of the Ogden stake presidents or their representatives came to the meeting. He laughed and, according to President Peterson's account, observed: "It has been said that if one of the General Authorities goes to visit a stake, it is just ordinary business. When two of them go, it's usually a division of a Stake; but when several of them go, they say 'Hell's a poppin'.' "

The group then proffered, not a problem, but a custom-built saddle created by J. G. Read & Bros., Co., of Ogden with a quilted seat, a foam rubber fill, and Father's name inscribed in gold on the back of the cantle. Accompanying this gift were a matching bridle and a Navajo saddle blanket. With tears in his eyes, Father said, "I have never been more surprised in my life. I am overwhelmed, not because of the gift . . . but because you, my friends of Ogden, have remembered me."

Upon request,
David O. McKay
and Sonny Boy
model the
surprise gift of a
custom-built
saddle,
Huntsville,
21 August 1954

It was raining slightly and Father was wearing his business suit, but he insisted on trying out the saddle immediately. The entire group moved over to Dry Hollow where he called Sonny Boy to him and cinched up the saddle himself. It fit perfectly. Even the stirrup lengths were just right. He recorded in his diary on 21 August, "No gift could have pleased me more — but aside from its value, the thoughtfulness, the planning, and the true brotherhood of these noble men thrilled my soul. I was deeply touched by this event, and shall ever hold their visit this morning as one of the precious events of my life." (Huntsville scrapbook, n.p.)

Father was not a hiker or hunter. He liked fishing, but I recall that his chief pleasure came in preparing the tackle, an act that got him in a "vacation" mood. The only "camping" trip I recall was one July when the General Authorities had their vacation, and Mother, for some reason, needed to be in Ogden. He took Llewelyn and me, then in high school, on what he called a picnic. He put hay and quilts for bedding in the wagon and drove us to Dry Hollow. We worked all that day, slept at night in the wagon, and worked the next day, bringing a ditch from the spring down to the farm.

When we were digging potatoes with him, he sang the beautiful Samoan farewell song, "Tofa My Felini" (Good-bye, My Friend), one of the cherished souvenirs he brought with him from his tour around the world.

We also played hard on the farm. It was traditional to make hay on the Fourth and the Twenty-fourth of July. We would begin early in the morning, work hard, eat a gigantic dinner at midday and, later in the afternoon, play an all-family baseball game with everyone—even little children—participating. Teddy Lyn, our second daughter, remembers Father's enthusiastic encouragement when she was little and afraid to take her turn at batting.

Cutting the season's growth of grass on that large lawn on the south side of the house was as much a haying tradition as filling the barn itself. Our farm was not large by today's standards—about a hundred acres all told, some of it in pasture, with summer range for the cattle in the mountains above town. Our primary crops with Huntsville's short growing season were hay, oats, potatoes, and peas. Father's Huntsville scrapbook contains a red ribbon he won for his Cobbler Potatoes at the Third Annual Utah Intermountain Seed Show in January 1928.

Being in Huntsville is indelibly associated in my mind with being part of the extended family. Grandmother died in January 1905 when I was three, and I have only one memory of her. I was upstairs in the big Huntsville house and saw a dead bee on the window sill of the south bedroom. I picked it up and discovered that it wasn't dead after all. I let out a yelp and Grandmother, downstairs with Aunt Lizzie, who later told me about it, instantly said, "It's Lawrence. He's been stung by a bee. That's a special cry." She came upstairs, took me outside, and put soothing mud on my finger. I'll always be grateful to that bee for my sole memory of Grandmother.

Writing in the *Improvement Era* in a Mother's Day tribute, May 1958 (p. 303), Father paid Grandmother a heartfelt tribute:

"I cannot think of a womanly virtue that my mother did not possess.

Undoubtedly, many a youth, in affectionate appreciation of his mother's love and unselfish devotion can pay his mother the same tribute; but I say this in the maturity of manhood when calm judgment should weigh facts dispassionately. To her children, and all others who knew her well, she was beautiful and dignified. Though high-spirited she was even-tempered and self-possessed. Her dark brown eyes immediately expressed any rising emotion which, however, she always held under perfect control.

"In the management of her household she was frugal yet surprisingly generous, as was father also, in providing for the welfare and education of their children. . . .

"Her soul, to quote the words of the poet, was 'As pure as lines of green that streak the first white of the snowdrop's inner leaves.' In tenderness, watchful care, loving patience, loyalty to home and to right, she seemed to me in boyhood, and she seems to me now after these years, to have been supreme.

" . . . I have often wished that I had told her in my young manhood that my love for her and the realization of her love and of her confidence gave me power more than once during fiery youth to keep my name untarnished and my soul from clay."

In one of our last trips with Father to Huntsville, he stood in the smaller upstairs bedroom in the original part of the house that he had shared with Uncle Tommy. With light streaming in from the east windows, he repeated to us his experience about hearing a noise downstairs while his father was on his mission. There were no interior stairs; the two little boys had to climb up a stair on the outside of the house to get into their second-story bedroom. Father knew that Indians had threatened his mother once; and terribly frightened that something would happen to her, he crept out of bed to kneel on the icy floor and pray that his mother and the family would be safe. As he prayed, "a voice answered me, just as if someone were standing there: 'Don't be afraid. Nothing will hurt you.' " I think all of us children knew on the basis of Father's experience, until we had our own, that our prayers would be heard and answered.

He also showed us the place downstairs where he had been playing marbles next to the south porch that leads off the dining room when the stake patriarch called him in, gave him a blessing, and afterwards told him that he had "something better to do than play marbles." I remember his telling us that his mother was very busy preparing dinner, but she could see he was upset. She set the preparations aside and took him in her arms to ask what was troubling him. Defiantly, he replied, "I don't care what he says. I'm not going to stop playing marbles!" Lovingly, Grandmother explained that the blessing was for the future and that he could play marbles as long as he wanted. His burden lifted, the future apostle returned to his game and she returned to her stove.

In the dining room stands the old pump organ that Father used to play and in the living room is the beautiful Chickering grand piano of Mother's that was one of the first three to come across the plains, brought by her grandfather. We spent summers close to our cousins, aunts, and uncles, listening to the old family stories, playing baseball, croquet, and Rook, reading, swimming, and helping on the farm.

As children we loved playing in the huge barn with its big loft full of sweet hay. It was very solid, like everything Grandfather built, with a sandstone foundation and beams up to a foot thick. In 1986, snow broke a tree, which fell on the barn and broke the main beam. We were all sad when the barn came down.

Grandfather was a great gardener—so particular about the soil that he wouldn't walk on the ground between the rows when he was planting. He carefully laid out one-by-twelve planks that we all had to stay on when we came into his garden. I'd lose myself on purpose in his big raspberry patch. He also had a special red rhubarb that he'd brought over from Scotland.

I remember seeing him wheel a wheelbarrow, full to toppling with some kind of materials, and saying something about the size of the load. He stopped, laughed, and said, "That's a lazy man's burden." I stared. He explained, "A man who would rather wheel a load like this than make two trips has to be a lazy man."

Another favorite memory is his long prayers. He was famous for giving the Lord complete reports on the well-being of the family, the community, the Church, and the nation. He also offered petitions up with the same detail. We children would take heart, however, when we heard him say, " . . . for thou hast said that we are the salt of the earth, and we know that if the salt loseth its savor . . ." That phrase always came close to the end.

He made a beautiful croquet ground behind the house. We children thought it was for us, but the adults played there, too—playing croquet and eating gooseberries.

Grandfather was very lonely after Grandmother died but, to my knowledge, never considered remarriage. He felt that a bishop should be married, so he resigned as bishop of Huntsville Ward after her death, serving on the high council, as stake patriarch (Father, as an apostle, set him apart to that position), and as one of Weber Academy's most loyal board members. He survived Grandmother by twelve years, dying in November 1917.

Every Memorial Day, the extended family gathered—it still does—to decorate the graves. While the cousins played games in the afternoon, the David and Jennette McKay (also spelled Jenette) sons and daughters would have a business meeting. No in-laws were invited, and neither were the grandchildren. They made an exception for me, the oldest grandson, after I was practicing law so that I could advise them on legal matters. Aunt Lizzie kept meticulous minutes as the secretary. Father was the president.

They were all very close, and family feeling ran deep. Father's secretary had standing orders, even when he was president of the Church, to admit his sisters and brothers at any time. Father and Uncle Tommy looked a great deal alike, but I hadn't realized how much until I met both of them at the station in Ogden when they were returning from Salt Lake City. An acquaintance came up, saw them together, did a double-take, and then explained, "Now I understand why David O. McKay sometimes greets me affably and sometimes ignores me. This [pointing to Father] is the David O. McKay who always speaks to me and this [pointing to Uncle Tommy] is the David O. McKay who ignores me."

On 9 May 1950, Father wrote to his friend Preston Nibley, explaining an accident at the farm that had caused a limp Brother Nibley noticed. Father was seventy-seven and still using a team of horses!

"My son Llewelyn and I were having a jolly day on the farm two weeks ago last Saturday. I was enjoying driving a team that cooperated with us perfectly in pulling some large dead trees that we heretofore couldn't move. The largest at first seemed to be too much for us. However, I turned the team a little to the left and they moved it, but the log hit my heels and down I went with both legs pinned helplessly and painfully. The log was too heavy for Llewelyn to lift, so he swung the team to the right and pulled it off. Luckily no bones were broken, but I have had a very badly bruised right leg; the other one somehow escaped with little injury.

"By the way, after resting awhile, and being quite sure that no bones were fractured, I said to Llewelyn: 'Now we have started, let's finish the job!' And we did. After returning home Saturday night, getting a little necessary medical care, I continued to fill appointments from Sunday to Wednesday following.

"And that is why, eventually, I had to go to the hospital." (Huntsville scrapbook, n.p.) Although Father made light of this injury, he had actually crushed veins and muscles quite seriously and had to receive extensive treatment.

Father was in his seventies right after World War II when the creation of Pineview Reservoir backed up the water into our little valley, leaving Huntsville on the new shoreline. Later, the size of the reservoir was increased and Dry Hollow was flooded. I can still feel Father's sadness at the change. "I remember helping my Daddy clear rocks and sagebrush off so we could have a farm here," he told me. His office journal for 12 October 1957, when he was eighty-four, records his feelings: "It is sad for me to see the change at Dry Hollow since the government took over the land for the dam — the barn, hayshed, granary, and the farm itself look dilapidated." (Huntsville scrapbook, n.p.)

He loved land passionately and could not be without it. After the reservoir was put in, he bought an additional twenty-two acres on the east bench above the rising water and retained the title to his own land all his life.

His Christmas parties for the grandchildren were lots of fun. Into his eighties, every Christmas vacation he took the children on a bobsleigh ride, bells a-jingle, Father driving in his long thick raccoon coat and big gloves, beaming from ear to ear.

Our daughter Joyce remembers that the littlest grandchildren rode in the sleigh and the others whizzed along behind on their own sleds, each one attached to the bobsleigh with a rope of a particular length so they wouldn't run into each other. Preparations, as you can imagine, became quite elaborate. Planning the course was one of Father's chief activities, especially after the city started scraping the snow off its main streets.

The children gave no thought to the preparations, however; they

David O. McKay driving the horses for family members to enjoy a sleigh ride at the Huntsville farm

just enjoyed the snow, what seemed like the incredible speeds, the jingle of the bells, the snorts of the horses, and the shrieks of laughter if they fell off and had to race after their sleds to jump back on.

These sleigh-riding sessions sometimes ended with caroling around the piano, and they blend in my mind with our Christmas Eve parties where each grandchild performed on a family program. In the caroling that followed, Father would slip away and come back with the bells which he would shake merrily while we all sang a rousing chorus of "Jingle Bells." These evenings ended with "Love at Home."

Although we had full-time help in running the farm as far back as I can remember, there were still matters that required our attention through the winter months. I clearly remember that the snow got deep enough that I could walk over the picket fence on its crust without particularly noticing a rise. The fireplaces in the front bedroom and living room and the stoves in the dining room and kitchen kept the downstairs warm, but upstairs, we hurried to get under the covers.

In his seventies, Father decided to build the Cottage across the road from the old home. Our good friend Edward O. Anderson, then

David O. McKay
and Sonny Boy
preparing for a
bobsleigh ride as
Edward looks on

Church architect, built it for them as a private commission. Next door
was a generous pasture for Sonny Boy.

Mother and Father loved the Cottage. It had electrical heat, fully
modern appliances, and the main living areas on one floor, making it
much more practical for weekends than the old home across the road.
It also gave them a place for many favorite pieces of furniture when
they moved out of their South Temple house to their Hotel Utah apartment in 1960.

We took advantage of their absence in California for a weekend to
move the furniture into the Cottage. We put their favorite chairs — the
two overstuffed wing chairs upholstered in powder blue — in front of
the cozy fireplace. As we took them through the house, there were
many exclamations of delight and appreciation; but the real reward for
our work came at the end when they went to those chairs, settled down,

reached out to hold hands and smiled at each other, beautiful contentment on their faces.

Many's the day during those years that I got a call from Father at
the office inquiring, "Lawrence, what are you doing this afternoon?" I
always answered promptly, "Driving you to Huntsville!" (That was the
correct answer.) How he and Mother enjoyed going up for a weekend,
or even for an afternoon and evening at the Cottage!

I recall one snowy day in the heart of winter when we found the
Cottage wrapped in deep drifts. I shoveled a one-person path to the
doorway; but given Father's unsteadiness and the slippery footing, I
should have made it wide enough for two. As it was, I was walking
behind Father, trying to steady him from that awkward position, when
he slipped and collided against me. We both toppled over into the snow.
Mildred, coming along behind us, was instantly alarmed but hurried up
to find us both "laughing our heads off," as she put it, and rolling in
the snow. Father was like a boy in his ability to enjoy such things.

Two significant experiences of Father's in Huntsville occurred
when he was a young boy, and I would know nothing of them if his
lifelong friend, John C. Peterson, had not written to Father from his
home in Cardston, recalling these incidents. The letters are preserved
in Father's Huntsville scrapbook:

Dec. 19th, 1955

Do you recall when we were Deacons[?] Sister Eliza R. Snow was
at a conference at Huntsville[,] we Deacons sang a song and Sister Snow
in her address to us said ["]I can see in that group of boys Bishops of
wards, Presidents of stakes, Apostles, and some of you will live to see
[the] Saviour["] and I often wondered. But now that you have been
Ordained President that question has been answered.

Oct. 1st 1958

How proud I have always been to think back of the days in Huntsville
when we used to go on the East hill of Huntsville to sleigh ride and I
remember one time when a fog came up and we could not tell which
way to go and I started to cry and you said don't cry John let us Pray
and you offered a Pray[er] and the clouds Passed.

Chapter 5

GROWING UP
WITH AN APOSTLE
1908-1920

◆ ◆ ◆ ◆ ◆ ◆ ◆ ◆ ◆ ◆ ◆ ◆ ◆

I was an adult, driving Father through Ogden Canyon, when Father explained the rule by which he governed his life: "I never make a decision without asking myself, 'How will I explain this to the Savior when I meet him?'" I do not know when he formulated this standard for himself, but I see it running like a thread through his long life of love and service.

Much of the background for Father's activities during the early decades of the new century comes from two national movements: prohibition and the Progressive Movement. Father actively campaigned for prohibition in several forms throughout this time and strongly opposed repeal, which occurred in 1933. The Progressive Movement focused on social betterment — working against the evils of poverty, crime, juvenile delinquency, and preventable ill health. Father's involvement in the Ogden Civic Betterment League and the enormous popularity of his parents' classes in Sunday School reflected a personal commitment to these political and social ideals. Later, during World War I, he was actively involved in Red Cross work for Ogden. He does not comment on these movements in any great detail, but his journal records a number of speeches that he gave and his resource notebooks contain frequent statistics, anecdotes, and quotations on the subject.

An undated partial draft of a letter in pencil to an unidentified correspondent gives something of how he must have approached critics of his position in favor of prohibition:

"On this question of prohibition, we differ, and no doubt shall continue to do so until the experience of the future proves the wisdom of one side or the other.

"I will admit frankly that there are two phases of that question which have given me serious concern, viz., (1) the antagonism and, in at least one instance, the ill will, that has been engendered in the minds of some of the men who have been friends to our family for years; and (2) the depreciation in the value of the property owned by the brewers. As to the first, I have come to the conclusion that a man is not justified in sacrificing what he considered a true principle merely to gain or to hold the good opinion of his friends. He who is afraid to make an enemy seldom merits a friend. In the second, I find the most potent argument of my friends who oppose prohibition. Personally, I should be willing for the state to compensate in some measure for this loss, if it could be estimated fairly. On all other questions — such as restriction of 'personal liberty,' 'injury to business,' 'Prohibition does not prohibit,' 'the evils of blind tigers [illegal drinking establishments selling home brew],' 'the drug store menace,' etc. etc. — I have satisfied myself absolutely, and feel sincerely that I am working for the best interests of our State and Nation when I devote all the energy I have towards the state-wide and eventually the nation-wide prohibition of the manufacture and sale of all intoxicants.

"I think none the less however of you and others of my friends who disagree with me in these views. Let each one work conscientiously and fairly for what he thinks is best, and whatever may be the outcome, let us abide by it, and still work together for a bigger, brighter, and more prosperous Utah."

Father's journal during the fall of 1908 records some of his prohibition activities:

"Saturday, Oct. 10, 1908. In the afternoon, Prest. Thos B. Evans and I went to Huntsville, and held a special meeting with the Priesthood of that ward, in regard to the Temperance movement. I spoke for one hour and fifteen minutes, after which the following resolution was unanimously adopted: 'Resolved that we the priesthood of the Huntsville Ward do all in our power to create a sentiment against the saloons in our town, and to use our influence to close them entirely. This influence to be exerted individually, upon those with whom we have influence, upon the city council and upon the legislators to pass prohibitory laws against the liquor traffic.' . . .

"Sunday, Oct. 18, 1908. . . . At 7 P.M. in a blinding snow storm, through darkness and mud, we drove to Garland where at 8:15 pm. I addressed the young people at that place . . . [on] Temperance."

During the fall, Father gave a course of eight lectures on Church leadership in Ogden so popular that leaders attended from other stakes as well. He records, on the evening of his last lecture:

"Tues., Dec. 15. . . . At 7:30 P.M. I went to the Academy, Ogden, and met the quorums and auxiliary organizations of the Ogden Stake, and visitors from other stakes. Spoke for one hour and twenty-five minutes on Fast Day Exercises. I was blessed by the Good Spirit, and so were those present. Just when I thought we were ready to dismiss, Bro. Samuel G. Dye in behalf of the High Council stepped to the platform, and in a most appropriate, I might say eloquent speech, moved that the officers of the stake express their appreciation of the talks given during the past nine weeks. This was seconded by the following, each speaking very kindly and appreciatively of what has been said: Bro. Sanderson, in behalf of the S.S. Stake Board; Sister Barrows in behalf of the Primary; Elder H. H. Goddard, in behalf of the Religion Class. Sister Taylor, then, came forward and presented me, in behalf of all present, thirteen volumes of Emerson's Works. . . . I was very much impressed with the spirit of the occasion, and tried to express my appreciation of people's kindness. They were free indeed in their remarks about the talks."

In 1909, the third year of Father's apostleship, he was extremely busy preparing outlines of course work for the priesthood quorums— the first year there had been quorum curricula. It was a project dear to Father's heart, and he was also very pleased when the General Authorities decided that the seventies, who had always met separately, should meet at the same time as the rest of the priesthood holders in their wards. "Thus was my most earnest wish for the last twelve months granted," he wrote in his journal on 4 January 1909. "It's the best thing that could be done."

In March, one of Father's conference assignments took him to Omaha, Nebraska, through Denver and Kansas City. Mother saved two of his letters from that assignment:

On the train
Near Rawlings,
March 12, 1909

My dear Sweetheart:

I am wishing we had money—a pile of it!—and I have wished so continuously nearly all day. Lonesomeness has produced the wish—a longing lonesomeness that only one can dispel, and she my sweetheart Ray. I have been thinking that if we had a large income, you and the babes and a girl to take care of them in hotels could all go with me on these trips. Then I could attend to my duties and be at home also; for home is anywhere if loved ones be there.

Well, we haven't money, so we can go together only occasionally. Such trips then become oases, and trips like this to-day, sandy deserts. . . .

Yes, I wish for money, but not because I don't feel rich. With you and the boys and "papa's Tomboy"—"Papa's dirl," and our happy home surroundings, with papa still with us, and all the folks one, with the bright prospects in life, and our membership in the Church—with all this wealth, and more, I feel the richest man in the world! But I wish you were with me just the same.

Good night, and happy dreams. Mine will be sweet because like my thoughts to-day, my dreams will be of you.

Lovingly,

Your own Dade

x x x Kisses to Lawrence, Llewelyn, and Lou Jean.

Union Pacific Railroad
March 20, 1909

My Dear Sweetheart:

Yesterday we had an excellent time in Omaha, holding meetings from 10:30 A.M. until 10 P.M. Intermission from 5:30 to 8 P.M. I had one of the hardest struggles that I have ever had to keep up. About 1 P.M. when I arose to speak to the Elders in Priesthood meeting, I turned suddenly sick. I had been suffering from my old complaint all morning, but this attack was an all-over sickness. I struggled for a few minutes, but finally had to give it up. Beads of perspiration stood all over me,

David Lawrence,
Llewelyn, and
Lou Jean McKay

and then I felt a chill coming on. I went out of the hall, and walked a
mile or two just as rapidly as I could. At two o'clock I was back at the
hall, and joined in the opening exercises of the meeting. About two-
thirty I started to speak, but in less than ten minutes I had to give it
up again. I went out, put my finger to my throat, and struggled for a
little relief. Returning to the room, I took a little nap while Brother
Herrick was speaking. At 3:15 P.M. I tried it again, and this time succeeded. I told the people that this was the first time I had given a
sermon in sections.

"After the afternoon meeting, we continued the Priesthood meeting, which [had been] discontinued at 1:30. This lasted until 5:30 P.M. After hearing their reports, I succeeded in finishing my instructions to them.

"I then went to the hotel, and rested until 7:45. My head was aching and I felt faint, not having been able to eat anything since morning.

"At 8 P.M. the hall was crowded. I prayed for strength, and after Pres. Redd had spoken a few minutes, I arose to make a short talk. Bro. Herrick and I thought it best for me to speak first, so if I had to give up, he could take up the theme as he had done in the morning; then if I felt better I could close the meeting.

"I was remarkably blessed. I have never before felt more freedom in talking, and have never spoken better in my life. I was surprised when I took my seat to know that it was just ten o'clock. I had spoken one hour and a half! It had been a wrestle all day, but the spirit of the Lord conquered. . . .

"There are a good many I's in this letter, but it is written to the one girl in the world who is most interested in me, so I have given personal details. . . ."

His journal entry for 20 March 1909, the return leg of his trip, reads: "Arrived in Denver. . . . At the mission house, I received a letter from the sweetest and truest wife in the world. She said all well at home. I was happy." Mother was two months pregnant, and Father was concerned about her health; but Royle Riggs McKay was born safely on 21 October 1909.

Neither Father's journal nor a conference notebook for the remainder of 1909 have survived, but a few letters from his many conference assignments give the flavor of his experiences. On 20 May 1909, he wrote from St. Johns, Arizona:

My dear Sweetheart:

Just before leaving Snowflake, I received your letter; and you don't know how good it seems to get a few lines from Loved Ones, even though I've been away less than a week. When everything is alright at home, and you and the little children are well, I'm happy, no matter where I am. How is that annoying cough? Have you overcome it yet? Dear Ray, please take good care of yourself. Take plenty of rest, break up that cold, and don't let anything make you tired, weak, or nervous.

I am just so contented and happy in my home life that sometimes I find myself fearing that our peace and happiness might be marred. One thing is sure, if we can just train our children to keep true, and we set them the example, our union is an eternal one no matter what comes here. But I believe in living now, and to love is to live. O if I could only step in the dear old dining room to-night—just long enough to carry my boys on my "sodjers," kiss them and Lou Jean good night, and then sit down with my sweetheart on my knee and her soft arm around my neck, and talk over our blessings, our duties, or visits, or even our debts, how happy I should be! . . .

We are hundreds of miles apart, but I feel that our hearts meet in a sweet goodnight!

God bless and keep you always!

> Your loving
> Dade

Early that fall, just before my eighth birthday, I went with Father on another of his stake conference assignments to Panguitch. We took the Denver and Rio Grande Railroad from Salt Lake City to Marysvale. I was thrilled to spend the night in a Pullman, drawing the curtains and joggling along in the upper berth with Father in the lower. Charles S. Hart, one of the Seven Presidents of the Seventy, was also assigned to this conference from one of the general boards. At Marysvale, which was the end of the line, James Houston, Jr., president of Panguitch Stake, met us with his son about my age, Crawford Houston. They drove us to Circleville where we arrived at 1:45 A.M.

We stayed what was left of the night there, then set off early for Panguitch, thirty-two miles away, and arrived in time for the Sunday School conference at 10 A.M. It had begun to rain; and by nightfall, the storm was intense. An evening meeting had been scheduled, but virtually no one came because of the storm. Then next morning, we started out in two buggies for Cannonville where Father was to choose and ordain a bishop.

I remember watching the red mud come up on the spokes and drop off, come up on the spokes and drop off, as mile after mile passed. That was virtually all I could see. We had a leather cover snapped from the top of the buggy to the floor, covering us and sheltering us from the rain with two isinglass windows for the driver and two slots for the reins. We drove all day in the unrelenting downpour and reached the village of Tropic about 5 P.M. The main road to Cannonville had been washed out, and we had to take a side road. There were no bridges on this road, and we had to ford the river several times. I remember that Father was very calm and cheerful; otherwise, the swirling water and the tense moments when the horses had to brace their feet and lean into their collars to drag the carriages up a steep incline in the thick red mud would have alarmed me.

It was nearly dark when we reached a house beside the road, almost the only dwelling we had passed on that deserted way. The men debated whether to ask for shelter or continue on. They decided to continue on, and we forded the river again. By this time, the water came right up to the horses' bellies. A little farther on, our way was blocked by a torrent dashing from the mountain on our left across the road and into the river. One of the men volunteered to take his horse and buggy through, but President Houston refused. "You'd be dashed to pieces," he said.

We turned around to seek shelter at the house we had passed, but the river had risen so much in just a few minutes that the horses and carriages would have been swept downstream. We were stranded in the triangle edged by the river, the mountain, and the torrent.

I was terrified. I thought it was the end of the world and started to cry. Father took me on his lap and held me in his arms all night. I must have slept soundly, for I do not recall waking up or having nightmares. During the night, the rain stopped and the torrent subsided markedly. In the morning, even though we had had nothing to eat or drink, we were much more cheerful. Men on horseback rode out from Cannonville to find us. By leaving the buggies there, we were able to complete the trip, and Father held his meetings.

In October 1910, Father went to a California conference, taking six-year-old Llewelyn. Father wrote from San Francisco on 24 October:

"The first place we visited was the post office. We were not disappointed; for there awaiting us was your sweet letter. . . . I was at once favorably impressed with San Francisco. (Now that I've written that sentence, I see there might be two meanings to it.) I do *not* mean that after reading your letter, I wanted to stay in San Francisco; but that your letter made me so happy that even San Francisco seemed to extend a welcome, or at least be a desirable place for a few days. Love, you know, changes the aspect of the whole world!

"I am sorry that our darling baby boy [Royle] still has that cold. I hope he will soon throw it off. You needn't worry about his heart: There is nothing the matter with it, I am sure.

"Llewelyn is standing his trip heroically. He gets lonesome, though, for Mama. I read your letter to him, and watched his face when I was reading about the baby in the book case. I knew that part especially would take him right home. He said, 'My, we've been away so long, I guess baby "bover" is a big boy. Maybe we won't know him. Maybe he's walking' and many more little surmises that told me too plainly how his little heart was longing for just one glimpse of baby and a loving caress from Mama. As we were going out of the room, he said, 'When you were reading Mama's letter, I pitty near cried.' I asked why, and he answered, 'I guess it was because I wanted to see Mama.' This morning, he was counting the days when we should start for home."

When Llewelyn wrote a letter home in careful printing, Father added a postscript begging Mother not to tell anyone when he expected to be home: "I should like about two days home without interruption of telephone calls and appointments," he wrote wistfully. "Just two days of *peace* away from the hurry, worry, and buzz of the world."

On 14 July 1911, Father was mounting his horse Trixy when "the saddle turned, Trixy started to run, and I jumped to the ground with such force as to break my right leg." Father was so seldom ill and inactivity was so foreign to him that this record of his convalescence is rare indeed:

"Saturday, 15 July 1911. How quickly a man can get undone! Both bones broken just near the ankle. Suffered considerable pain from the mass of blisters that came on the ankle. Bp. Olsen stayed until midnight last night. He is an excellent Bishop, and a true friend. Friends very considerate. Uneasy all night—considerable pain. Ray attended me constantly, changing bandages every two hours, night and day. Many friends have called to-day, among them my dear friend Elder Orson F. Whitney. He and Pres. Shurtleff administered to me.

"Monday, 17 July. Easier today. Serenaded at night by . . . boys from Sixth Ward. . . . Their singing of the dear old hymns quite overcame me, for they sang from their hearts to do me good. . . .

"Friday, 21 July 1911. One week gone—in bed a week! The time has not dragged wearily either, for with the presence of many friends and 'Lorna Doone,' which I have finished, the days have passed rapidly and pleasantly. So our lives will pass — and before we are aware, we shall sight the journey's end before we have accomplished anything worthy of mention. . . .

"Tuesday, 25 July 1911. Almost entirely free from pain. In the evening, Mssrs. Griffin, Pickett, Purdy, and Klomp came in and gave me an hour of song. Their singing was excellent, but the spirit in which they expressed their solicitude was beautiful. Such manifestations of friendship are handsful of sunshine thrown into the gloom of this world. . . .

"Thursday, 27 July 1911. Walked with crutches. . . . I have never before considered it a blessing to get on the porch."

In the fall, Mother was able to take another trip with Father, this time to Mesa, Arizona, to a Sunday School convention with a week added in California after the conference. He noted on 8 November 1911:

"Kissed babies goodnight at 8:40 and went to Salt Lake. Annie offered to stay with the children. Her kindness is appreciated more than we can tell; for the pleasure of Ray's trip depends upon a contented mind. Annie's care of the children gives her this."

They spent a day in the orange groves near Phoenix, visited an ostrich farm near Pasadena, California, saw three plays in the evening, took their first swim in the ocean ("delightful"), and were taken to a dance hall by some misguided friends. "Saw some of the most vulgar actions . . . that one can imagine," wrote Father in disgust. "What degradation women can reach!" (18 Nov. 1911.)

They both caught colds on this trip, and Mother's, a week later, had turned into a case of "rheumatism" so excruciating that she was unable to join the McKay clan's celebration of Thanksgiving. Father mentioned that she was still not fully recovered when he made his last entry for the year on 20 December.

When spring arrived in 1912, Father branched out into the cattle business, purchasing one hundred calves at $19.50 each. He was not completely satisfied — called the price "exorbitant" — but had high hopes for the venture. (8 Mar. 1912.) Mother was pregnant and, as usual, very ill during the first trimester. Father noted on 5 March 1912: "Ray is not feeling very well, but she is always sweet and uncomplaining."

Simultaneously with Mother's pregnancy, Royle, then two and a half, became ill. Father's conference notebook for 23 February 1912 indicates that, as Father left for a stake conference in Wells, Nevada, Royle developed a fever of 105°. Then in early April 1912 come these heartrending entries:

"Wed., 2 April 1912. . . . Upon returning home, we found our darling baby peevish and ill. He complained of pain in his right knee. He suffered nearly all night. It seems to be an attack of rheumatism.

"Thurs., April 4, 1912. . . . Baby's leg is no better. He is feverish today.

"Fri., April 5, 1912. . . . Learning by telephone that baby is worse, I returned [after second session of general conference] at 4:45. Poor little Royle! He is suffering from an infected knee, probably caused by a fall. The doctors do not know what is the matter; but Dr. Morrell thinks the infection has been in his system since his recent illness.

"Sat., April 6, 1912. Baby seems a little better, but his fever is still around 104 degrees. . . . At noon, I learned by telephone that Royle will probably have to be taken to the hospital. Felt that I ought to miss the afternoon meeting and go home to my wife and baby boy, but finally concluded to remain until 4 P.M. Followed Bro. Orson F. Whitney in addressing the Conference. Up all night with our sick boy. Fever has been 106 degrees.

"Sun., 7 April 1912. . . . At 3:30 this morning, Royle had a convulsion, and another two hours later. The Doctors have concluded that his only hope is in having an operation and this is extremely hazardous because of the congenital weakness of his heart. The operation was performed . . . Dr. Morrell supervising. Everything was successful. The diagnosis had been just right. At 10:25 A.M. all was over, and we felt encouraged. He soon recovered from the effects of the anesthetic, and was less feverish and entirely conscious all day, but towards night his breathing became short, and his fever began to rise. He was evidently in great pain from some other cause besides his little afflicted leg.

"Mon., 8 April 1912. O what a night of suffering for our darling boy! Every breath he drew seemed agony to him! The doctors examined him this morning, and discovered that his pain was due to pleurisy on both sides. At this we almost lost hope; but later when Dr. Morrell told us that by an examination he knew what germ had caused the infection and that he had the anti-toxin, we again took courage.

"But Royle was too weak and the complications of diseases too many. He battled bravely all day, taking the little stimulant given him at intervals as willingly as a grown person would. At 9:30 P.M. Papa, Thomas E. and I again administered to him. Ray felt very hopeful, and lay down on the cot beside him for a little rest. Soon his little pulse weakened, and we knew that our baby would soon leave us. 'Mama' was the last word on his precious lips. Just before the end came, he stretched out his little hands, and as I stooped to caress him, he encircled my neck, and gave me the last of many of the most loving caresses ever a father received from a darling child. It seemed he realized that he was going, and wanted to say, 'Goodbye, Papa,' but his little voice was already stilled by weakness and pain. I am sure he recognized his Mama a moment later. She had rested only a few minutes; and noticing that the nurses were somewhat agitated, she was bending over her darling baby in a second and did not leave him until we gently led her from the room from which Death had taken our baby boy.

"The end came at 1:50 A.M., without even a twitch of a muscle. 'He is not dead but sleepeth' was never more applicable to any soul, for he truly went to sleep. He did not die.

"Dr. Morrell, three nurses, Ray and I were with him when his little spirit went home to his Grandmama. In the midst of a deep sorrow, one learns of the value of true friends. While they cannot lessen the grief following the death of a loved one, they do give a comfort that is second only to the peace that comes from God. May God bless our many friends, as they in hearts and by their many kind words and deeds have blessed us today!"

I was ten and Llewelyn was eight when Royle died. I remember reprimanding Llewelyn for sobbing out loud in public as we stood beside the casket in our parlor. Father said gently, "Let him cry."

A month later, on 31 May 1912, in writing to his good friend and colleague, Professor Wilford M. McKendrick in Boise, Idaho, Father related Royle's death, calling it "our first sorrow in parenthood." He added: "His suffering and plaintive little cries pained us even more than his death; but oh, we do miss him so much! Our home seems vacant and lonely. I can stand it, for my life is filled with varied scenes and duties with which Baby was not associated; but poor Ray is home all the time seeing little things that call up all fond associations and loving caresses of her baby boy. She is brave, but she suffers. Just the night before I left home (Wed.), she sobbed nearly all night. She says she knows she will meet him again, but this knowledge does not take away the yearning for the sound of little pattering feet now silent, and the sweet little voice now stilled."

Father had earlier recorded finding "Ray in inconsolable grief. She had attempted to sing Rowland [Aunt Nettie's son] to sleep, but the memory of little Royle emphasized keenly her loss, and she could only weep and sob for comfort — and poor comfort too. O this yearning of the heart for our baby boy!" (28 April 1912.) I remember that Royle's favorite song had been a little gramophone record about Santa Claus's workshop which he would listen to over and over again. Mother put it away. She just couldn't bear to hear Royle's music again.

In 1949, after Father and Mother had moved to Salt Lake City, they bought a family plot in the Salt Lake City Cemetery, exhumed Royle's little coffin, and brought it down for reburial, with Father rededicating the grave. By then, Royle's death was almost forty years in the past; but Mother stood by my wife as they lowered the little coffin into the new grave and whispered, "Oh, Mildred, I hope you never know such grief."

Another sorrow came when Mother's pregnancy ended in a miscarriage in August when she was about six months pregnant:

"Tues., Aug. 20, 1912. Today's Ray's sickness [labor] was very severe her condition necessitating the Doctor's use of instruments. The climax was reached about 6 P.M. This is the third miscarriage she has suffered. A little baby would have been such a comfort to her now since losing our little boy Royle. But we are again deprived of this blessing. . . .

"Fri., Oct. 25, 1912. Ray and I bade goodbye to the children, and started for Denver to attend conference of Western States missionaries. Ray hesitated to go because of expense, but when I insisted, she consented. These trips together, though few and far between, are like wedding trips."

Since they attended meetings from 10 A.M. until 10 P.M. during the entire time they were in Denver, essentially their only time together was the two days spent on the train. Father's entries give some measure of how starved they must have been for this companionship and what balm it must have been after the trauma of the last few months.

The sadness of Royle's death is one of the few sorrowful times I remember in our family life. Our much-loved home on 21st Street in Ogden was a warm, welcome, and interesting place. It is inseparable in my memory from my Mother and Father. In fact, one of my earliest memories — possibly my earliest — is watching the workmen build the house in 1903 or 1904 and later, walking with "Papa" through the park from the old home to the new one. I was "helping" him push a wheelbarrow full of things to put in the new home.

Quite frequently we shared our home with other people. When Mother and Father were first married, his sisters lived with them and attended Weber Stake Academy. Another long-term guest was Aaron Tracy, a brilliant student at Weber who came to Father and said he would have to drop out because he couldn't afford to go on with his education. Father immediately invited him to live with us. In 1922, he became principal of Weber, fully vindicating Father's faith in him. I was enthusiastic about having him in our home because he repaired Llewelyn's rocking horse.

I found among Father's papers a letter from Aaron Tracy written 2 February 1913 in a beautiful hand:

Dear Bro. McKay: —

Every time I read something very good I always see you in it. I am reading Sir Launfal and when I got to those lines where it says,

> *The Holy supper is kept indeed*
> *In whatso we share in another's need;*
> *Not what we give, but what we share,*
> *For the gift without the giver is bare;*
> *Who gives himself with his alms feeds three,*
> *Himself, his hungering neighbor, and me.*

I thought of what you shared with me, you and your kind wife, just seven years ago about now. I am very thankful for what you did and am becoming more so every day. I hope you will never think me ungrateful because I don't seem to show my gratitude; but many times in my prayers I have thanked my Heavenly Father for your kindness to me.

Seven years ago now I was going to leave the dear Old Academy and go out to work for a wage of $20 per month, but you would not permit me. You took me in the library and made me accept the opportunity of my life by sharing your home with me. At this time you did not even know me, yet you served me an unending blessing. I could mention many, many things to prove this but would rather tell you of them sometimes. I often look back upon those days and count the blessings which have come to me through you and the training I received at the Academy.

. . . If there is ever anything you want me to do for you I would leave everything and do it. There is one thing I know I can do to show my appreciation for your goodness to me, and that is to live and do right.

Music was an important part of life in our home. Father and Mother both played the piano. Father had played for priesthood meeting and dances in Huntsville, held on the second floor above the village mercantile store. Sometimes he'd sit down and play hymns at home, but he did not have time to maintain his proficiency with the instrument in a serious way. Mother, however, kept up her music. She could transpose and play by ear; but as soon as Lou Jean began to play, Mother quietly turned aside invitations to accompany our singing or performances by saying, "I'd rather hear Lou Jean play." We knew she loved music, but only later did we realize that she did this to encourage Lou Jean.

Father was anxious for all of us children to have music. By the time Lou Jean played the piano, Llewelyn the clarinet, and I the violin, we were able to produce passable trio music. Father's favorite was "Believe Me, If All Those Endearing Young Charms." I suspect that it was a bit of a special love song between Father and Mother, although she would always make a mock-wry face when we got to the line about the "dear ruin." We played selections from the operas, popular songs, and trio arrangements from the classics. The high point of our joint career was being invited to perform over KSL radio for one program.

I'd have to attribute whatever proficiency we gained to Mother's persistence. Her method was the direct approach: "Lawrence, have you practiced yet?" I don't recall her nagging, however, or following up on that question, and certainly there were no bribes or threats. She simply assumed that we would know what was right and would do it.

For many years, our piano was an old Chickering that Mother's grandfather had brought across the plains by wagon. Father, to surprise Mother, bought a new upright Chickering and had it delivered when she was at a Relief Society meeting. He installed it in the library the day before Christmas. I went in to look at it; but Father hustled right in after me and ushered me out again, explaining that if Mother saw the light on and came in to see what I was doing, the surprise would be spoiled. I can't remember now what subterfuge he used to send her into the library on Christmas morning, but I can still remember her cry of delight.

Mother and Father also enjoyed singing together and with us. We sometimes spent hours singing hymns and popular songs such as "After the Ball."

Once, years later, when Mildred and I were driving Mother and Father to Huntsville, the topic turned to music and the songs they enjoyed. They were both in their eighties, but they started singing the songs from their youth—"Just Tell Them That You Saw Me," "A Bicycle Built for Two," ballads, and other love songs. The duet lasted for the entire trip—Father singing melody and Mother the harmony. How I longed for a tape recorder!

Reading was always important to our family. Lou Jean remembers sitting on Father's lap while he read us *The Lady of the Lake*, *Ivanhoe*, and Maeterlink's *The Bluebird*. His diary for 24 February 1914 records: "With David Lawrence, Llewelyn and Lou Jean, I . . . went to the Theatre to see "The Blue Bird," a most beautiful drama by Maeterlink. Children enjoy the scenery and the children actors; the grown people, the philosophy." *The Lady of the Lake* was a family favorite, sometimes continued over several tellings. We loved the poetry and the Scots dialect in which Father told the story. It's hard for me to separate his telling it from the books that we later discovered on our own. I recall reading Walter Scott's *Marmion* but without much enthusiasm because Father had never told us that story.

Always anxious to spare Mother's strength, Father wrote insistently from Mesa on 9 March 1913:

"Just before I left, Ray, I suggested that you try to secure some good help, and you protested, as usual, that you didn't need it. Now, I want to *insist* that you get a girl to do *all* your housework. Our trip to California proved to me that you have been using more reserved energy than is good for you; and I still regret that we did not remain another two weeks. But we didn't. Now the right thing to do is to take rest, exercise and fresh air at home. . . . It is *economy* to keep strong. I say economy, because I think the main objection you have to a girl is the expense. . . . Discontinue that housework drudgery. Remember what house cleaning has cost you in the past. Perhaps five or ten dollars to a woman would have avoided much pain and sorrow. Now, sweetheart, no *house cleaning* for you this spring. For *once* I want my way."

Mother was pregnant with my sister Emma Rae, and Father's conference report notebook for 1913 records on 3 November: "Ordained my son David Lawrence to the office of Deacon. . . . Started for Bear River Stake Conference, but turned back at Brigham City on account of worry over Ray's condition." Emma Rae was born 12 December 1913, and Father blessed her on 1 March 1914, recording her name as Emma Ray, the same spelling as Mother's. It was later changed to the more usual feminine spelling, Rae.

Father's next letter to Mother that has been preserved came from Great Falls, Montana, on 30 April 1914:

My Dear Sweetheart:

When I opened my satchel last evening, and found those oranges snugly crowded in, I thought, Just one of the thousand thoughtful things Ray is always doing to make my life a heaven! Those dainty little considerations, which always bring sunshine in our pathway, spring more spontaneously from you than from me, but I appreciate them just the same, though I may not often say so. . . .

What a dark old life this would be without you, Dearest, so please guard carefully your health. As a wife, you have made our home the dearest place on earth; as a mother, you are rearing in that home the dearest children in the world. You and they grow dearer to me every day. Indeed, if I keep falling more deeply in love, my soul will absolutely rebel against filling some of these long appointments. The trouble now is that even when I do get home, there is so much to do on the farm that we have very little time in each other's company.

Three weeks later, he wrote from Cardston, on 8 May 1914:

My dear Sweetheart:

When I learned by telephone last night that your letter was in town, there was no sleep for me until I had it, though to the postmaster's house and return is a walk of nearly two miles. When I am away from home, Ray, I like a letter every day. . . . I was almost sorry when I received your sweet letter that I had ever said anything to you about your "epistles." It was altogether too short. It is your letters to *others* that should be shortened; those to me, lengthened.

In about 1911, Father began keeping both a journal and a separate notebook for the stake conferences he attended. In these conference notebooks are summaries of the meetings, statistics, speakers, changes in officers, observations on the spirit of the people and the officers, and, infrequently, personal information. In 1910, the Church had sixty stakes, each with four conferences a year. If 1914 were typical, Father visited thirty-five stakes a year on assignment, not counting Sunday School conventions. That means he would have seen each stake every other year and, after six years, would have developed a considerable amount of personal information about the stake and the people in it. Under such circumstances, for someone with an outgoing, loving personality like Father's, it is easy to see how each year created more strands in the network of friends, acquaintances, and colleagues that ultimately encompassed three generations of Church members. For interest's sake, I tried to reconstruct what Father was doing on the nineteen Sundays in 1914 when he did not note a stake conference assignment. General conference and general Sunday School/MIA conferences accounted for four, a national Sunday School convention in Chicago accounted for another two, and he organized a Scandinavian ward in Salt Lake City on another weekend. That left twelve Sundays, an average of one per month, including Christmas Sunday, when he presumably was home with us. In fact, on most of these other Sundays, he spoke in a local ward, and he usually spoke in our home ward on Christmas Sunday.

Father had long wanted an automobile, admiring their speed and efficiency in whittling down the long hours spent on the road for conference assignments. Ford produced the first Model T in 1908, and my recollection is that Father and Uncle Tommy jointly bought one soon after these cars reached Utah. Within a few months, it was obvious that each family needed one, so Father bought one for us.

While the twentieth century was in its teens, Father was in his late thirties and early forties, a period when most people are settling down to consolidate the gains made during their previous decade. I was entering my teens with the other four children following. Emma Rae was our baby, and the death of Royle was behind us, though still present. I do not know what ecclesiastical assignments Father had during this period other than his numerous conference assignments, his work with the Sunday School General Board, his calling as general superintendent of the Sunday Schools on 2 January 1919, and his appointment as Church Commissioner of Education only four months later. He had been able to turn most lesson-writing assignments over to other qualified people and was no longer teaching or administering affairs at Weber, but he still served on its board of education and spearheaded the drive to raise funds for a new gymnasium beginning in 1918.

A highlight from September 1915 was Father's appointment by the First Presidency to lay the cornerstone of the temple in Cardston, Alberta, Canada. This was the first temple outside the boundaries of the United States and the first temple authorized since the completion of the Salt Lake Temple in 1893. President Joseph F. Smith had presided at its groundbreaking ceremonies in 1913 and in June, three months earlier, had gone to Hawaii to break ground for the temple there. Father was alone on this trip with no member of the First Presidency and no other General Authorities present for the ceremony. I cannot help wondering if Father's experience here sensitized him to the possibilities of international temples, which would be such a feature of his presidency. His conference notebook records briefly: "This principal corner stone of the first Temple to be built in this dispensation beyond the borders of the U.S. by the Church of Jesus Christ of L.D.S. is now duly and properly laid in honor of God our Eternal Father and may it remain unmoved during the completion of the entire structure and until all the divine purposes for which the Temple is erected are consummated." He notes among those present, "Major Hugh B. Brown," his future counselor in the First Presidency.

When he returned, Emma Rae's tonsils were removed. The timing was most unfortunate. Emma Rae was very ill for three days afterwards, general conference began the day after the operation, and Mother gave birth to Edward Riggs McKay (Ned) the third day, October 5.

Among my most important memories is a traumatic but spiritual event that occurred the next spring, when I was fourteen. In March 1916 the Ogden River swept the old iron bridge at the mouth of Ogden Canyon off its moorings. Uncle Tommy had come down the canyon from Huntsville by car, parked east of the bridge, and then made his way cautiously across the loose structure on foot. He spent the night with us and, at breakfast next morning, asked me to drive him back to the bridge in Father's Model T.

Father said, "I'll take you, Tommy. Go ahead and get ready for school, Lawrence."

They left as soon as they'd finished breakfast. We children were almost ready to leave when Uncle Tommy drove hastily back to the house and helped Father inside. Father's face was a mass of blood, and I watched in shock as he stood over the sink, spitting out pieces of bone and teeth. Even more frightening to me was his disorientation. "What was I doing?" he asked repeatedly. "Where was I driving Tommy?"

At first, he refused to go to the hospital; but Mother and Uncle Tommy prevailed and took him while we children obediently went to school. Later we learned the story. A rope to show that the bridge was closed had been stretched across the highway, but it was almost invisible in the early morning fog. Uncle Tommy spotted it and shouted, "There's a rope! Look out!" and ducked. The rope struck the radiator of the Ford, bounced to the windshield, which opened from the bottom, pushed it back on its hinges, and hit Father squarely in the mouth, breaking his jaw and knocking him unconscious. Uncle Tommy grabbed the wheel, stopped the car, moved Father over, turned the car around, and drove back home.

Father tells of regaining consciousness to hear one of the nurses say, "Isn't that too bad. Well, at least he can wear a beard." Our bishop, Edward A. Olsen, heard of the accident and hurried to the hospital where he blessed Father that he would have no pain. The blessing was literally fulfilled on the instant. Dr. Morrell and Dr. R. S. Joyce operated on his broken jaw and torn cheek. President Heber J. Grant came up from Salt Lake City and blessed Father that he would not be scarred. The first time Father was able to attend a quorum meeting, President Grant looked down the table at him and said, "David, from here I can't see any scar."

Father responded, "Because there is none, President Grant."

Dr. Morrell used to say, "President Grant gets all the credit for that operation."

Father later told us that he had had a prompting of danger ahead, "but I disregarded it." I suspect that he seldom disregarded such warnings again.

He may have saved a life by his sensitivity to the Spirit on another occasion. I was hauling a load of beet pulp from west of Ogden over the viaduct when Father, who was having a rare moment's leisure to read at home, suddenly closed the book and stood up.

"Where are you going?" Mother called as he hurried down the hall.

"To save Lawrence's life," he called back over his shoulder.

He got into his automobile and met me at the top of the viaduct, just as I was about to start the descent. He reminded me that I was driving a team of four horses abreast (I didn't need a reminder of that!), that they were pulling four tons of beet pulp, and that the wagon had no brakes. While I held the reins, he got out of the car to block a wheel by chaining a spoke to the body of the wagon. Unfortunately, we were holding up traffic, and a car honked behind me. I moved the team to get out of the way, but we had started the descent. The team could not stop. By the time we reached the bottom, the horses were racing out of control on the left side of the road. We hit a car that emerged from behind the candy factory, smashing the motor but sparing the driver. One of the horses slipped and fell down. I seized the momentary check to leap down and sit on his head, keeping him from getting up. We were saved.

If Father had not stopped us and if that car had not come out at that moment, we would have careened onto busy Washington Avenue, Ogden's main street, and probably knocked over pedestrians. My feelings of gratitude can only be imagined.

A sad but not tragic event occurred the fall after Father's accident when Grandfather died peacefully after an operation 9 November 1917, conscious to the last moment.

American troops entered World War I in 1917, and many boys Father knew were involved, including his own younger brother, Morgan. A letter from Morgan dated 11 February 1918 describes a visit from Father "in camp" somewhere in Virginia:

"It was pretty hard to say good bye, and see you get on the boat, just as bad if not worse than leaving home, but it wasn't very long after, that the thoughts of our delightful visit together replaced those of our parting, and since then I have been living over and over again those two memorable days. They were surely red letter days for me. I did

David O. McKay
in his early years
as an apostle

appreciate your visit D.O. and can never tell you the amount of good
it has done me. . . .

"All of the fellows here whom you talked to have told me several
times how much they enjoyed your visit and were all disappointed that
you couldn't stay longer. I wish you could have stayed two or three
days and met every one of them. They are all mighty fine fellows and
send best wishes to you. I can tell you I was mighty proud to have them
meet you. I surely am proud of our family and surely hope you will
always have cause to be proud of me."

To another local fellow serving in the navy, Father wrote: "I appreciate very much, too, your excellent letter. It breathes the spirit of

the true missionary. Indeed, I look upon your position now as one of as great importance as any you ever had in the Mission Field. Opportunities for preaching the Gospel are many, I am sure. It is not that so much that will influence your companions, but your manly character, your noble ideals, and your clean righteous life. These will speak louder than words. . . . God bless you." (Letter to Byron G. Miller, 24 Oct. 1918.)

The influenza epidemic that slew so many in 1918 lingered for several weeks in our household but eventually passed over. A letter from Father to a mission president on 24 October 1918 apologizes for a delay in answering his letter and explains:

"Everything during the last week has had to take second place to the demands of Influenza. You will be able to judge how serious this malady is here in your own town, when I tell you that for the last five days I have attended from one to three funerals each day, and one of these a double funeral. Three of our little ones have not escaped, but I am very thankful to be able to tell you that they are all far along the road to recovery."

President Joseph F. Smith, age eighty, became seriously ill with the flu and died in November 1918. Thus, Heber J. Grant became president of the Church, and Anthon H. Lund and Charles W. Penrose became his counselors. In fact, President Grant was sustained to his position on 23 November 1918 and, both to avoid the epidemic and also to seek needed repose, went to California less than a week later. He invited Father and Mother to accompany him, and Father's conference notebook for 1918 contains an interesting record. They went by train to Los Angeles, and then by car to "Deseret," a Church-owned residence in Santa Monica:

"Sunday, Dec. 1. . . . Pres. Grant is evidently under high nervous tension, able to sleep only two and three hours at night. Have concluded not to tell him of President Lund's sudden illness. . . .

"Monday, Dec. 2. Pres. Grant received an honorary membership in the Brentwood Golf Club, and I the courtesy and privileges of the golf course for the month of December. Used Bishop Nibley's clubs. Played my first game of golf, and concluded that it is the game of all games. [We children knew nothing of golf. When Father wrote us his and President Grant's scores — his own being considerably higher — we congratulated him on winning.] Drove to Los Angeles & back. Spent

Emma Rae and
Edward McKay,
July 1919

the remainder of the week playing Golf and driving in auto. President
Grant, Bishop Nibley, Nephi W. Clayton, E. Wesley, Rae *[sic]* and Mae
were companions. Pres. Grant has improved very much."

President Grant was a prolific and warm letter writer, so it is not
surprising that Father's private papers include letters from President
Grant; but they seem to be unusually personal and candid. Within five
months of President Grant's sustaining, Father was appointed general
superintendent of the Sunday Schools and Church Commissioner of
Education in 1919. The next year, President Grant selected Father for
an unprecedented year-long tour of missions around the world.

Entries from Father's diary for 1919 give these pictures of our family life:

"Thurs., 9 Jan. 1919. Traveling back and forth between Ogden and Salt Lake is becoming irksomely grinding.

"Sun., 12 Jan. 1919. On account of the increased number of influenza cases, the First Presidency and Council of Twelve have advised that all Latter-day Saint assemblies be discontinued until further notice. . . .

"Tues., 14 Jan. 1919. Drove Rae [sic] around the ward as she distributed her workers literature, cards, and buttons for those who contribute to the 'Armenian and Syrian Relief Fund.' Rae as Relief Society President has charge of the 4th Ward. [As matters turned out, Father was on hand in Syria in 1921 when Joseph Willard Booth, representative of the First Presidency, distributed those collected funds to the suffering Armenian members of the Church.]

"Friday, 18 April 1919. Very busy preparing to go to Beaver. Drove to Huntsville, gave a few directions to Carl [the hired man], and returned to Ogden. Left for SLC at 2 P.M., left S.L.C. at 4:45 P.M. Barely caught last car of Los Angeles Limited. Met Pres. Grant on train; and talked over Church School Superintendency matters. . . .

"Sat., 3 May 1919. . . . Rae and I started by auto for Manti, 160 miles where we arrived at 10:45 P.M.

"Sun., 4 May 1919. . . . At 5:30 Rae and I left Manti by auto, and in 5 hrs and 30 min. reached S. L. City—2 hrs later were in Ogden. Tired, very tired—Rae especially.

"Mon., 5 May 1919. Assisted in house cleaning. . . .

"Sunday, 11 May 1919. . . . Thomas E. McKay set apart Pres. Ogden Stake. . . .

"Sun., 22 June 1919. . . . At N. Sanpete Stake Conf. . . . We traveled 318 miles by auto, and held 4 meetings—a 23 hr. day.

"23 June 1919. Mama Ray's 42nd birthday. She is as sweet and true as when we married Jan. 2, 1901. . . .

"Mon., 30 June 1919. Last day of saloons in America! Thank heaven!"

I know very little of his activities for the rest of 1919, and only a sketchy conference notebook has survived for 1920. By then, I was a young man, ready to go on my mission. Llewelyn and Lou Jean were teenagers, Emma Rae was in grade school, Ned was getting ready to start kindergarten in the fall of 1920, and Mother was pregnant with her last baby, Robert Riggs McKay. We were growing up.

an out-of-the-w   en's nest. The eggs were hardly fresh, but Llewelyn
didn't know that   in a very businesslike way, collected them and
trotted off to the   grocery store about two houses up from our
street's intersectio   Madison Avenue where he exchanged them
for candy. As I reca   proprietor generously concluded the trans-
action and then pho   other. Later that evening when Father got
home, he and Llewely   nt back to the store to exchange fresh eggs
for the ones Llewelyn   d t n in. Again, there were no scoldings.

Another incident I r c   urred when Llewelyn was a little older,
possibly eight or nine. H   esponsible for feeding his rabbits and,
in an effort to simplify t   helped himself to alfalfa from a farm
lot on Madison Avenue.   razed" quite an area when the owner
noticed it and brought it   s attention. Without scolding, Father
explained carefully that   't the thing to do and, as I recall, went
with him to apologize.

I can recall only   casion where he even sounded impatient,
and he certainly had pr   cation. He was playing baseball with Llewelyn
and me in the backy;   at our Ogden house. I was pitcher, Llewelyn
was batting, and Fath   was catching and coaching simultaneously. We
were just youngster;   and when Llewelyn smacked the ball, he was so
excited that he flun   the bat behind him, hitting Father in the head.
"Don't ever throw ;   at!" Father exclaimed. "If you can't play baseball
better than that . .   ' And words failed him. He went into the house
to tend his goose   g, and Llewelyn and I contemplated, wide-eyed,
the close call we   inflicted on Father.

As a result of   gentle, loving discipline, we children were never
afraid of our par(or afraid of getting into trouble for trying new
things. An incid(that to me most beautifully epitomizes this relationship occurre   hen we went to California for the first time, in
February 1910   was eight, as I recall. I'm sure it involved some
church busines   ather, because the president of the California
Mission met u;   ailroad depot in Los Angeles and drove us out
to the house v   enting on Hill Street in Ocean Park. We drove
out on Wilshi   rd, then just a wild country road.

On our v   my first glimpse of the ocean, and a very disappointed bo   . The tide was out, and the ocean just looked
like a lake, f   ing, though big. We settled into our duplex on
Hill Street ;   bed.

I woke up very early next morning and set off with innocent enthusiasm to inspect the ocean close up, an expedition that involved crossing the speedway. The ocean was much more exciting this time. The tide was coming in, and the waves were thundering on the beach. I was totally engrossed in the spectacle when I realized, after some time, that someone was beside me. It was Father. He smiled at me and said, "It's beautiful, isn't it?" Then, hand in hand, we went back and had breakfast.

In retrospect, particularly as a father myself, I can imagine how alarmed Mother and Father were when they awoke to find me gone and with what concern Father set out to look for me. But finding me safe, he chose not to communicate any part of that alarm to me. Instead, he simply shared the beauty of the ocean with me and made it an unforgettable memory for me.

Another illustration of Father's great restraint as a parent occurred when I was a returned missionary studying for a year at the Sorbonne. Father and Mother, then presiding over the European Mission, had come through Paris to leave the three youngest children with Lou Jean and me while he and Mother toured the mission. They had returned to pick them up just when a friend of mine, returning from his mission in Germany, was at the apartment. He had wanted to see the show at the Folies Bergère, much known for its gaiety, color, and dashing music but quite tame by today's standards, I would say. As we bade Mother and Father goodbye, Father asked, "Where are you going?"

"To the Folies Bergère," I answered.

"Have a good time," he smiled.

Down in the street, my companion let out a long breath. "Imagine being able to tell your father that you were going to the Folies Bergère!" he exclaimed.

I gazed at him in wonder. It had never occurred to me to conceal anything from Father.

Father was a firm believer in free agency. I don't know that there was any proscription against face cards, but we just never had any in our home. Llewelyn got a streak of independence when we were in high school and bought a volume of Hoyle's rules and a deck of cards that he kept in his top drawer. I recall that Father once came in to look for something and found the deck of cards.

"Whose are these?" he asked.

"Mine," answered Llewelyn.

Father looked at him, put them back in the top drawer, and walked out. He never referred to them or mentioned them again to Llewelyn; but as I recall, they didn't stay in the top drawer very long.

I never heard my parents disagree, let alone quarrel. The incident that comes closest to a disagreement came when I was in my early teens and saw an advertisement for a combined subscription to the *Literary Digest* and the *Youth's Companion.* I asked Mother whether we could take advantage of this offer.

"I think we can," she answered, "but ask your father."

When I asked Father, he said, "No."

I knew we were on a very strict budget and thought no more about it, but Mother gave me a look that I couldn't interpret. A few days later, Father said, "You were asking about a subscription to the *Literary Digest* and the *Youth's Companion.* That will be all right." I'll never know what went on behind the scenes.

As a result of the closeness of our parents and their consistent affection for us, I recall life with my brothers and sisters as usually pleasant and happy. I was very close to Llewelyn, naturally, and we formed a duo in most of our pleasures and mischiefs. We were certainly not perfect children, and among my memories are a few incidents of which I know Mother and Father would not have approved. I recall once in their absence mischievously teasing Lou Jean and a friend who were playing tea party. My sister chased us down the street with a broom.

On another occasion, Llewelyn and I were playing "sword fight," I with my violin bow and Llewelyn with a butcher knife. I got quite a bad cut on my hand and felt lucky that it wasn't worse.

Obviously Father was gone a great deal too much to wait for him to resolve problems or judge cases. Mother made the decisions in his absence, often mentioning, "Your father would want . . ." Father always supported Mother's decisions.

Mother was wise and thoughtful in her parenting and seldom had to change a rule because she never made them impulsively. I recall her saying, "Lawrence, if you always do what I say, you won't get into trouble." She considered motherhood her career, and she gave it the kind of intelligent consideration and planning that made her a wonderful success at it.

When she spoke to Brigham Young University women students in

1951, she had been a mother for fifty years and shared many wise precepts about that important role:

"Nearly every woman can be a mother, but not the right kind of mother. The successful mother must plan, and arise early to carry that plan out. If she does not, the meals are late, the dishes drag, the husband is cross, and the woman is flustered. If she does not plan a week ahead, the meals are of a sameness and unappetizing. If she doesn't plan three months ahead, the sewing is not done in time for school. There is discontent and perhaps whining. If she does not plan a year ahead, the gardening, the house-cleaning, and the education of the children are neglected. . . .

"If the mother doesn't have obedience when the child is very young, two or three years of age, she is going to have much trouble as the child gets older. . . .

"It is so much fun in the early walking stage to pull all the pans from the cupboard a dozen times a day, to climb to the sink and play in the water, to sprinkle mother's clothes on the floor, to pull open parcels, to be doing something every minute. This is the time when mother must have no nerves, when she must pick up after baby—or, better, to help him pick them up—when she must be gentle, never scolding but helping him to learn pleasantly the many hundreds of new things, to him, in the world.

"If she says, 'Don't do that,' every other minute, he will pay absolutely no attention to her. It is useless to tell children not to do things unless at the same time you give them a suggestion of something they *can* do. Instead of saying, 'Stop playing that drum; it is driving me crazy,' try saying, 'How would you like to make a tower with these blocks?' If he says, 'No,' try something else that you know he likes. Keep him doing.

"But if there is something that he must not touch or play with, and you tell him that he must not, and gently lead him away, be sure that you do not permit him to handle the article the next minute, or your desires will mean nothing to the child.

". . . A mother should make promises rarely, but when she does, she should keep them religiously.

"The time baby starts to notice things is the time to start making him polite by thanking him for everything he gives you, by saying,

'Please' to him when you want something; by excusing yourself if you walk in front of him, or if you accidentally knock over his blocks. . . .

"Treat all your children with equal affection. Sometimes parents do not realize how much more their eyes shine when they look at a special child. How they praise him, how they favor him with special gifts because he has been an outstanding child in looks, in his studies, in music, in everything that makes a beautiful character, while another not quite so wonderful in the parents' eyes secretly observes these things and is hurt and jealous because of the contrast in treatment. Parents should be most careful to see no difference in children or, rather, never to show it so that all hearts may rest. Never deceive a child . . .

"I remember as a child how I loved and respected my mother because she did not discuss my failings with the neighbors. She certainly did not approve of the way some of the neighbors aired their children's weaknesses before us. I can see now the children's bowed heads and disappointed facial expressions when their mothers pointed out the fact that they were poor students at school, that there was no music in their souls, that they were disobedient, bad children. Oh, for more wisdom for mothers!" ("The Art of Rearing Children Peacefully," pp. 6–10.)

Mother followed these principles scrupulously. Correct grammar was very important to her, and she always corrected us children instantly if we made a mistake — unless a friend was present. She would never think of embarrassing us by correcting us in front of a friend.

Her emphasis on correct grammar reminds me that when I went to school for the first time, she was greatly concerned that I might be exposed to coarse or profane speech. I remember her asking, when I came home the first day, "Did you hear any bad language?"

Cute

"Yes," I answered honestly.

"What was it?" she asked, concerned.

"Someone said *is* for *are*," I innocently answered.

She and Father were scrupulously honest with us. I remember that Mother never tried to slip out of the house, leaving the younger children to be tended in the hopes that they wouldn't notice she was gone. Even if her leaving upset them for a few minutes, she always explained where she was going and when she would be back.

As another example, she would not allow even April Fool "fibs," but she bent the rules enough to allow misrepresentation by implication. I remember that Winnie, our collie, was expecting puppies any day. We children were very eager for them to come. On April Fool's, Mother greeted us in the morning, "Look what's in the kennel." We rushed out and found only Winnie. When we came back, Mother smiled and said, "April Fool's."

I remember once teasing Lou Jean on April Fool's, "You spilled gravy on your dress." Mother corrected me, "You can't say that, but you could say something like, 'Oh, look at your dress.'"

I should also mention how supportive my parents were in what we did. Emma Rae remembers that the first year she taught high school in McCammon, Idaho, she also directed the students in a play. How thrilled she was to peer through the curtains on opening night and to see Father, Mother, and Bobbie enter the auditorium. When Emma Rae later taught school in the Granite School District in Salt Lake City, Mother and Father always made a point of seeing the plays she directed.

Llewelyn and I once performed a comedy routine of Box and Cox that was popular at the time. My parents were there. My wife recalls that once, after we were married, she was performing at a Mutual event and said, "I don't want any of the family there. It would make me so nervous to see Lawrence in the audience." As she tells the story, my mother instantly exclaimed, "Oh, Mildred, that's wrong! We want to go, to give our loving support and prayers." That was our family's perspective.

As another example, when Llewelyn was student-body president at Weber and Father was president of the board, the student officers had planned to hike up Mount Ogden and raise the Weber flag. Not many students had signed up to go, and Llewelyn was quite worried. "How would it be to announce that I'm going up with you?" suggested Father. Needless to say, practically the whole student-body turned out to accompany Father and Llewelyn up the mountain.

Mother and Father both enjoyed games. We played Rook, Pit, and Croquinole for hours when winter weather kept us indoors. Mother was never one to sit and fill the time with idle chatter. If our work was done, she would sit down with us and propose, "Let's play a game!" We enjoyed playing with her and, when we could, with Father. One of our favorites was "McKay Pirate Rook," a combination of bridge and Five Hundred played with Rook cards. Father just loved it and would bid up a hand with utter recklessness. His brother-in-law, George R. Hill, had devised the game after the feeling developed among Church leaders that members might be spending too much time playing bridge. Favorite outdoor games were croquet and baseball.

A sweet expression of Mother's feelings about motherhood is an undated poem that she wrote, which was printed in *The Relief Society Magazine*, June 1967. A framed copy of this poem now hangs in the old Huntsville home:

Mother Love

When you were a girl in the long, long ago,
With no cares except lessons, or maybe a beau,
Were you asked by a neighbor, a very dear
    friend,
To be with her babe and your services lend?
With your arms about baby in tender embrace,
Examining each line of its dear little face,
As it dropped off to sleep under your rhythmic
    line,
Did you ever say lightly, "I wish it were mine"?

And when you were married to that handsome
    beau,
Who courted you gallantly years, years ago,
And God blessed you with babies with eyes
    brown and blue,
With features of yours and your dear husband's
    too,
Did your soul burst with happiness, satisfaction,
    and joy,
As you gazed with fond love on the face of your
    boy?
As you sang to it, crooned to it, thought it divine,
Did your heart throb the murmur, "I'm thankful
    it's mine"?

And then as the years hurried happily on,
And the mates of the children in time came
    along,
When you held your first grandchild pressed close
    to your heart,

*Did you wish for one like them — to make a new
    start?*
*No! woman's life is divided in three in life's
    test —*
*Maidenhood, motherhood, then — self culture and
    rest.*
*As you look on the forms of the grandchildren
    nine*
*You're content to say glowingly, "I love them as
    mine."*

Chapter 7

A MISSION
AROUND THE WORLD
1920-1921

◆ ◆ ◆ ◆ ◆ ◆ ◆ ◆ ◆ ◆ ◆ ◆ ◆

The fall of 1920 was a busy one for us. Father had sold our home on Twenty-first Street, probably in preparation for moving to Salt Lake City, and we were living in Grandfather's home on Madison Avenue.

Mother organized the move during the last stages of pregnancy with her seventh child, Robert. Father's conference notebook reports that he missed the Saturday meetings in Cache Stake on 4 September because "a message from 'Baby Land' required my presence at home."

I turned nineteen at the end of the month and was getting ready to leave for my mission in Switzerland. When Father and I drove away from Dry Hollow for the last time, I stopped for one last, long look; and Father recognized what I was feeling. "You're feeling it already," he said, "the loneliness." With the same sensitivity, he sat down and dictated a letter to me the day after I left:

Oct. 22, 1920

My Dear Son, David L.:

We have been wondering, almost every waking minute since you left, how you fared as a traveler. . . .

Emma Ray was the first in the family to write you a letter. You will find it enclosed herewith. The love she expresses comes from her dear little heart; and that is the love, my dear boy, that we all have for you. We are proud of your manliness, and grateful for your high ideals and keen sense of honor. Our confidence in you is absolute, and we feel sure that you will do your best to prove worthy of the Priesthood and to magnify every Calling you may receive as a true servant of the Lord.

May Heaven's choicest blessings be yours during your entire mission!

Statements like those were typical of Father, who always expected the best. No one ever wanted to disappoint him.

Needless to say, letters from home were very important to me. Father wrote a second letter on 29 October 1920, responding to my first letter and giving me a piece of excellent advice along with the family news:

"One reference in your letter emphasizes the fact that you are just at a very impressionable age. I mention the fact simply to remind you that a young man's affections are very much like a young colt that is just being trained—he's alright so long as the trainer has a firm hold on the lines, and can keep him in the road. He wabbles around a good deal, but as long as he keeps going straight ahead, there's no need for worry. More than one pretty girl will make your heart go pit-a-pat; but keep your mind's eye on your missionary Road.

" . . . When I reminded Llewelyn that he would soon have the entire responsibility, he gently suggested that we rent the farm. I think, however, that he can manage it—the responsibility will do him good. . . . You have some sweet brothers and sisters, and an ideal Mama, and they are all proud of their missionary brother and son. Such a family, I think makes life worth living. The success of parenthood may be rightly measured by the nobility of its sons and daughters!"

While this letter was following me across the ocean, my parents were suddenly involved in an amazing adventure of their own. It is obvious from Father's letter on 29 October that he had no intimation of what was to occur; but within a very few days, President Heber J. Grant asked Father to travel around the world, visiting the remoter missions, holding conferences to strengthen and motivate members of the Church, examining the operation of Church schools in the Pacific, and, if he felt so inspired, dedicating the land of China for the preaching of the gospel. His companion was Hugh J. Cannon, a son of George Q. Cannon, and a stake president in the Salt Lake area.

Father and Brother Cannon were set apart for this calling in the temple on 2 December 1920, President Grant voicing the blessing upon Father and stating among other things:

"We bless you with every gift and grace and every qualification necessary for you to possess to fully magnify this calling. We say unto you: Go forth in peace, in pleasure and happiness, and return in safety to your loved ones and to the body of the Church. We bless you with power over disease, not only in your own person but with power so that when you lay your hands upon the sick and the afflicted . . . that many shall rejoice in the blessings of the Lord that shall come to them through your administrations. . . . We bless you with great wisdom, with a retentive memory, with capacity and ability to comprehend and understand the needs of the various missions that you shall visit. . . . You shall be warned of dangers seen and unseen and be given wisdom and inspiration from God to avoid all the snares and pitfalls that may be laid for your feet by wicked and designing men. We bless you that you may have the spirit of love and fellowship and goodwill."

Then, on 4 December, Father and Brother Cannon bade farewell to their families. Father's journal reports his tender feelings:

"Every little household duty when performed seemed to say, This is the last time for awhile; even the fire in the furnace looked gloomy when I threw in the last shovelful of coal. . . .

"[Ray] reminded me of one of the pretty little geysers in Yellowstone—it would remain placid and peaceful for awhile, but soon the forces, hidden and turbulent, would stir the surface of the water until it swelled, bubbled, and boiled over at the rim. . . . I hope the tears that bedimmed Ray's eyes so frequently during the day proved a relief to the rising emotion she so heroically tried to subdue. . . .

"I kept my feelings pretty well under control until I began to say goodbye to the children. . . . [Neddie] couldn't realize why his daddie was sobbing. . . . The parting moment with my Sweetheart and true devoted wife, my life's companion and Joy, I cannot describe. Such sacred scenes, anyhow, are not for expression in words—they find expression only in the depths of a loving soul. . . . Parting from [the three oldest children] at the station stirred my feelings wholly beyond control."

Father and Brother Cannon were off on a journey that took them more than sixty-one thousand miles, into fifteen missions, to meet with more than three hundred missionaries. They embarked in Vancouver,

David O. McKay, center, and associates aboard the *Empress of Japan,* 22 December 1920

British Columbia, for Yokohama, Japan, on 7 December. Father was both terribly seasick (less so as the months passed) and terribly home-sick (more so as the months passed).

Once aboard the *R.M.S. Empress of Japan,* a Canadian liner, Father penned two quick letters, the first to me and the second to Mother:

Dec. 7, 1920

My beloved Son:

My last message before leaving American shores is to be to you who so recently experienced the loneliness that overwhelms me as one sees the outlines of one's native land receding gradually but surely from view! . . .

The kind friends at home were exceedingly lavish in their good wishes and expressions of love. I was really overwhelmed by their kindness and assurances of confidence notwithstanding it all—indeed partly because of this—the parting from home last Saturday was a pretty sad one for me. Your Mama,—bless her dear, sweet, soul, was all broken up. She couldn't go to the station—neither did little Ned. The others did. I leave you to picture the scene for you saw it but a short time ago. . . .

Well, my dear boy, the gang plank is dropped, and we are off. I am comforted in the thought that we go in the interest of the greatest *Cause* known to humanity — the Gospel of Jesus Christ. I glory in the fact that you too are devoting your talents and loving personality to the preaching and the teaching of everlasting truth. God bless and guide you always!

Remember, my boy, that your darling little mother has the hardest part of this missionary work; so write to her often and regularly. Your letters do her so much good. . . .

> Affectionately,
> Your loving father,
> David O. McKay

Here is his tender farewell to Mother:

> Dec. 7, 1920 9:30 P.M.

My Own Sweetheart:

We have been sailing along the Coast for about five hours. Another hour or so, and the chance to send you a message on this side of the ocean will have passed; and I want you, the dearest and sweetest of sweethearts, to have the last letter to go ashore to-night. . . .

Ray, though thousands of miles of ocean separate us, we shall be closer together than ever before in our lives; for never were you dearer to me than you are now. The beauty of true and competent Motherhood has crowned the beauty and sweetness of your girlhood, the charm of which has only increased with the glory of true motherhood. My most fervent prayer to our Heavenly Father is that He will keep you and our beloved children in perfect health until we meet again. To be reunited as a loving family, each one healthy, virtuous, and true, is the only great blessing I pray to enjoy! . . .

Good night and pleasant dreams! Remember, I'm with you always!

> Affectionately,
> Your loving
> Dade

The first of Mother's letters to me in my possession is dated 14 December 1920. In retrospect, I marvel at how cheerfully she writes about a cold kitchen, a five-year-old with tonsillitis, and a three-month-old baby with colic!

My Dear Boy, Lawrence:

. . . I am glad in a way that you have been homesick for it shows us that you love your home, but I am sorry if it has made you miserable. Papa says he felt the same way the first few weeks away from home. We surely are miserable without you, dear one. Home is very different without you & Daddy. It seems as though our family is very small indeed. I cannot get used to it.

But I am very proud of you, Lawrence.

. . . Our furnace acts fine, all but the kitchen. That flue does not act at all. . . . Ned has had tonsillitis for over two weeks now and he is a peaked little boy, but thoroughly angelic. He follows me around from morning until night wanting me to read to him. Reminds me of his oldest brother. . . .

Your little Silas [baby Robert] is still growing beautifully. Tonight for the first time he wanted to play with the paper. His eyes grew so big, and his fingers twitched and he looked a darling. Wish you could see the little dear. He has considerable colic yet. Suppose it is six months' colic. . . .

Everybody sends best love. Especially your

Mama

As a new missionary, I realized that although I had accepted and believed in the crucial principle of the Atonement all my life, I was far from understanding it. I had asked Father to explain his understanding of it, and he kept his promise on 20 December 1920, thirteen days out of Vancouver:

My dear son David:

. . . In one of your letters you asked for my views on the Atonement, and I think that this is an opportunity for me to attempt to give them to you. In the first place, I have been impressed with the fact that the Doctrine and Covenants says so little about the necessity of the shedding of blood for the atonement of sin. The explanation in the Book of Mormon, too (Alma 34:14–16) is a very good one, although it leaves unanswered your query as to the necessity of it. I think the passage given above gives the best reason thus far revealed.

But back of the orthodox Christian view of the Atonement, I see ever working toward the salvation of the human family, the sacrifice spirit as exemplified in the life and by the death of the Redeemer.

In the beginning whenever that was, man found himself shut out from God's eternal Presence. He remembered little, and in time would have remembered nothing of his associations with eternal beings. "In his humiliation his judgment was taken from him." Earth and earthly things were everything to him.

When he became hungry, it was earth that satisfied him;

When he became thirsty, it was an earthly element that quenched his thirst;

When he became cold, it was the skins of animals that protected him and kept him warm, or it was the great moving luminary in the sky that shed his genial rays on man's chilly limbs.

When he sought comfort in repose, it was . . . the trees or skins or vegetation of the earth that gave him a downy bed.

In short, the earth became not only man's "foster mother," she was to him the source of his very existence.

Self-preservation became not only the first law but, I can imagine, *the only law he knew*. As the race increased and the struggle for existence became more acute, selfishness and strife would manifest themselves. Man would struggle with man for supremacy, as for the best things Nature could offer for the prolongation or the comforts of life—Thus would man become "carnal, sensual, and devilish by nature" (Alma 42:6–13).

Now what was there in man to lead him up to a Godlike life? The divinity within him, I grant you, would be ever urging him to rise above himself. But his searchings for the Infinite could express itself only in a worship of the manifestations of Divine power—the *sun*, the *moon*, the *thunder*, the *lightning*, the cataract, the volcano etc etc.

How significant is that passage, then, which says "By grace are ye saved through faith; and that not of yourselves; it is the gift of God."

The Lord revealed to man the Gospel and one of the very first commandments given superseded in essence the *self-preservation* law. *It was the law of sacrifice*. The effect of this was that the best the earth procured[,] the best specimen in the flock or herd should not be used for self, but for God. It was God not the *earth* which man should worship. How this simple test of sacrifice affected the divine nature as well as the carnal in man the story of Cain and Abel graphically and appropriately illustrates. For one, the best the "firstling of the flock" was all too poor as a means of expressing his love and appreciation of the Relation of Life that God had given; for the other, he would go through the form because God had commanded, but he would keep the best for himself.

And so through the ages this eternal conflict between the divine life of service and the earth life of carnal and sensual and selfish indulgence and ease continued. Millions lived and died believing that the whole purpose of life is to *get* and possess what earth has to give, never comprehending that the whole purpose of life is to *give*.

Then in the *meridian* of *Time,* came the Saviour of man, toward whose coming man in the morning of life had looked forward, and upon whose life man in the evening of life should look in retrospect. In the meridian of the Earth's history came the Son of Man declaring the eternal truth so opposed to the promises of the Earth, that

He that would save his life must lose it.

And in his brief stay upon earth, how perfectly he exemplified this truth. He owned no land. He owned no home; for he had not where to lay his head. "The foxes have holes and the birds of the air have nests but the Son of Man hath not where to lay his head."

His was a life of unselfish service—always helping those who were living incompletely to live completely—whether the incomplete living was caused by a physical defect such as blindness or deafness, or whether thru a moral defect such as the woman taken in sin—His mission was to give them life.

Now, my dear son, can you not carry this thought a little further and apply it even to the sacrificing of his life—to the shedding of His blood? His life—man's life is not dependent upon what this earth can give—his body yes, but that is only the house in which man lives—but the spirit, the real man is above the selfish and the sensual and seeks for its life and happiness the things which are eternal—faith, virtue, knowledge, temperance, Godliness, Brotherliness, charity.

In His life and death, therefore, Christ not only fulfilled the law of sacrifice but He fulfilled every conceivable condition necessary for man to know in order to rise or progress from earthly life to eternal life.

"And I if I be lifted up will draw all men unto me."

In this I think I glimpse, though ever so dimly, a reason for Christ's shedding His blood—in addition to the one generally offered for the redemption of man from the Fall. I confess that the latter has moved

David O. McKay and companion Hugh J. Cannon, front row, center, with missionaries in Japan

me less than the realization that in His life He lived for his fellow men, and in his death—he triumphed over all earthly elements, over the power of *Death*[,] Hell, and the Evil One, and arose from the *grave* an eternal Being—our Guide, Our Saviour, our God.

I am indeed proud and grateful that you are His servant, and sincerely pray for His protecting influence to lead and inspire you forever.

Affectionately,
Your loving
Daddy

In Japan, Father and Brother Cannon visited Joseph M. Stimpson, the mission president, and his family in Tokyo, held a conference with the 125 members of the Church and the missionaries, made courtesy calls on officials, and enjoyed ceremonial Japanese hospitality. With all of Father's duties, writing to Mother was a top priority. This letter is dated 24 December 1920, from Tokyo, within a day of their arrival:

My Beloved Wife and Sweetheart:

So many new and strange things have crowded themselves into my plane of consciousness since yesterday morning when we landed at Yokohama that it doesn't seem possible that only twenty-four hours have passed!

We have landed in a new world! The only familiar things are the sun, the *sky,* the *moon* and stars, and the dear old "honk, honk" of the automobile. The strange unfamiliar things are innumerable.

The *first* peculiarity that impressed me as we pulled into the docks, was the significantly marked coat worn by the workmen, the white stripes indicating the company or man employing the laborer.

The *second* were the "Jinrikisha" men and their "jinrikishas," two-wheeled, rubber-tired vehicles, drawn by a man who noiselessly paced along like any other beast of burden, while the occupant sits as comfortably as though he were in a rocking chair. These men crowd at the stations and wharves, crying "Rickshaw!" "Please, rickshaw," as our cab men at home. Their charges as given to us were, 80 sen (40 cents) first hour; 50 sen (25 cents) second hour, and 40 sen (20 cents) the third hour, and I suppose each hour thereafter.

The *third* was an old black Holstein Bull hitched to a four-wheel low baggage wagon. He had a collar on, was hitched between shafts, and was led by the nose by his driver. I think I got a snap shot of this curiosity. How I wished I could see my dear old Holstein friend at home, pulling one of these wagons! I'll venture a guess that there would have been a scattering of passengers on that wharf such as was never seen there before!

The *third* [fourth] were two beautifully dressed (and I'm pretty sure that I'm using "beautifully" correctly), Japanese maidens *clattering* along the pavement, making as much noise as Prince does on Washington Ave., just after he's been shod, shoes in both instances being the source of the noise, the only difference between that the women's shoes or rather *boards,* are made of wood. What a clatter, clatter, clatter, these boards make at a railway station! I do not include these clogs in the dress.

The *one hundredth,* happened this morning when a group of a dozen or more little Japanese girls came here to the Conference House to see the preparations that are going on for Christmas Exercises to-morrow. All their little wooden shoes were left outside the door, and each slipped on a felt-like foot covering before entering the house. When I was called in to see them, I naturally began to shake hands with them. Well, you ought to have seen the amusement this form of greeting created among them. As I went from one to the other, they almost convulsed themselves with laughter! I really became embarrassed; but having begun it, I went though with it.

I desire to get this note off on the "Russia" sailing to-morrow, so Good-bye, *Dearest, Sweetest,* Truest, and Best of *sweethearts, Wives,* and *Mothers!*

Kisses and love to the choicest children in all the world.

> Affectionately,
> Your devoted
> Dade

This letter had been written from the mission home, but the next was on the stationery of the Kanaya Hotel, Nikko, Japan, on 27 December 1920, where Father was delighted with the beauties of "this most romantic and interesting spot."

"I have not only never read about any place but cannot imagine one in which are combined more charmingly fascinating features in *nature, art, legend,* and *worship* than can be found in Nikko! Mountain scenery, unsurpassed in beauty, may be seen all around—lofty pine-covered peaks, verdure-filled ravines, beautiful waterfalls, a mountain river plunging and roaring through rock-walled embankments are the first to hold the tourist's attention upon the glories of this little part of Japan. . . .

"It's all very interesting, Sweetheart, but I should be far happier at my humble though ideal home enjoying the loving companionship of the sweetest and best of women and the loveliest children in the world, and I shall be the happiest man on this old globe when my encircling trip is over and I'm with you once again."

Mother wrote me on 30 December, recounting the Christmas news and including notes dictated by the children. I know that she would have sent something similar to Father:

My Dear *Dear* Boy—

Your Daddy's cablegram that he had arrived safely in Tokyo on the 23rd of Dec., and your letters, cards, and photograph arrived about ten o'clock Xmas morning. Maybe you think we were not glad to get them.

The best presents of the day! Oh, Lawrence, any word at any time from you makes your mother so happy and that message on Xmas morning was especially welcome, I assure you.

On their wedding anniversary, Father wrote Mother a reflective, tender letter from the mission home in Tokyo that mused over scenes of their past life, including their first meeting.

January Second,
Nineteen Twenty One –

My Sweetheart:

You were my sweetheart—twenty years ago this day; you are twenty times twenty times my sweetheart now!

It doesn't seem possible that a score of years have passed since you and I covenanted to walk side by side and heart in heart along the Pathway of life through Eternity; yet the reckoning of Old Father Time says such is the fact!

There are three great epochs in a man's earthly life, upon which his happiness here and in eternity may depend, viz., his Birth, his marriage, and his choice of vocation. With the first he has little to do, so far as we know; but he is fortunate indeed who can look back upon his birth as a truly regal one . . . pure, untainted blood, a strong body, and nobility of soul—a birth that furnishes the environment in which these gifts may grow in unrestricted development. Such a birth was yours, Dear; and such was mine.

It is generally conceded that American men and women, unlike the Japanese, have the right to make their own marriages, the right or privilege of each one's choosing a mate being almost inviolate. With this thought in mind, I pride myself in having manifested for once in my life perfect wisdom. But when I analyze the conditions I find that very little credit is due to me, for it required no superior, or discriminating judgment on my part to choose my life's partner when once I had met her. No other girl—and you know my girl acquaintances were not a few—possessed every virtue with which I thought a sweetheart and wife should be endowed. All these you seemed to have. I thought so, even when I met you for the first time, in the doorway of your old house, when a country lad, I paid you our first month's rent, and half acknowledged as much when I returned to our rooms, but was told by Jennette that 'There was no chance.' Later, one afternoon after Thomas E. and I had greeted you and Bell [White, her cousin] on the porch of one of the little cottages, I remarked to him as we drove away, that you were my ideal, possessing every grace and virtue. So, after all, it was not my judgement, but your superior endowment to which I am indebted for my first interest and choice.

But I give credit this Twentieth anniversary to even a higher source. When I think of the varied circumstances that brought us to-gether; of the nearness with which we both came several times to making a mistake; of the hundred and one little experiences that combined to draw us together rather than to separate us, I am willing to acknowledge the guiding influence of a Divine Power.

As long as Memory and Feeling shall endure, I shall always hold in sacred remembrance the absolute *trust* and *confidence* that hallowed my love for you — even before we were engaged to be married. It became in Courtship the foundation stone of our future happiness. . . .

January second Nineteen One marked the beginning of a new year, the beginning of a new century, the beginning of a new and happy Life!

I loved you that morning with the love and fire of youth. It was pure and sincere. You were my heart's treasure, no bride more sweet, and pure, and beautiful! But this morning, when I see you with these virtues and your many others crowned with the glory of perfect Mother-hood, when I see our seven precious boys and girls shining like heavenly jewels in the precious diadem that crowns these twenty happy fruitful years of your life, I think I didn't know what love was when I took you as my bride. It was but as the light of a star compared with [the] glorious sunlight of Love that fills my soul to-day. . . .

May twenty years hence find our love for each other and our chil-dren to-day twenty times twenty times sweeter and more precious!

> Your Devoted Sweetheart,
> David O.

After leaving Tokyo, Father and Brother Cannon went to Pusan, Korea, and then to China, which was suffering the aftermath of World War I. At Peking, on 9 January 1921, a Sunday morning, Father felt that he should dedicate China for the preaching of the gospel. His journal reads:

Sunday, January 9, 1921

We have traveled continuously since last Tuesday with the sole purpose in mind to be here in Peking on this Sabbath day.

. . . Every impression following our earnest prayers together and in secret, seemed to confirm our conclusions arrived at last evening, viz., that it seems that the time is near at hand when these teeming millions should at least be given a glimpse of the glorious Light now shining among the children of men. . . .

Accordingly, we strolled almost aimlessly, wondering where it would be possible to find a secluded spot for worship and prayer. We entered that part of the Imperial city, known as the "Forbidden City," and walked by the famous old buildings formerly used as temples. On we walked, until we came to a small grove of cypress trees on the edge of what appeared to have been an old moat running parallel with one of the walls. As we proceeded from east to west, we passed a tree with a large branch shooting out on the north side, and I distinctly received the prompting to choose that as the spot. . . .

Under the century-old limbs and green leaves of this — one of God's own temples, with uncovered heads, we supplicated our Father in Heaven . . .

Bro. Cannon, with well chosen words, and with a spirit of deep earnestness and humility, dedicated the chosen spot as one of prayer and supplication to the Almighty. . . . Acting under appointment of the Prophet, Seer and Revelator, and by virtue of the holy Apostleship, I then dedicated and set apart the Chinese Realm for the preaching of the Glad Tidings of Great Joy as revealed in this Dispensation through the Prophet Joseph Smith, and prayed particularly that the present government may become stabilized, if not by the Chinese themselves, then by the intervention of the Civilized Powers of the world.

With our souls burning with the assurance that we had acted in accordance with the inspiration given, we returned to the hotel.

From China, they went to Hawaii, where President E. Wesley Smith and a singing congregation of local Saints, some of the eleven thousand Mormons in the islands, greeted them. Father inspected the work of the Church school at Laie, then under the acting principalship of William T. Cannon, Jr., Hugh J. Cannon's brother.

Because they could not get a ship for the South Pacific from Honolulu, they decided to return to San Francisco and reembark. As the *Maui* prepared to leave, they were so smothered in leis that several passengers asked them to pose for photographs and one quipped, "Don't you fellows feel lonesome out in the world like this without any friends?" (Hugh J. Cannon Typescript, n.d., p. 67.)

On 20 February, Mother learned that Father and Brother Cannon were sailing toward San Francisco and wrote wistfully: "Wouldn't it be great if he could drop in and say Halloo! before starting out again? But of course he could not, using Church money & being known so well he would be besieged with questions. Oh, it makes me feel so lonesome to think of his being 'so near and yet so far.' But it's a comfort to know that two of the places to be visited are through with."

Then Mother got a surprise. President Grant arranged for Mother and Sister Cannon to accompany him to San Francisco to see their husbands, unbeknownst to Father and Brother Cannon, and I got this delighted note, dated 28 February 1921, from Mother:

My Darling Boy:

Wonders will never cease. Here I am on the train going to San Francisco with Pres. Grant, Bro. Ivins, and Sister Cannon & her baby to meet Papa & Bro. Cannon....

Pres. Grant phoned to us that he was going to have them come home until after April Conference and we were all tickled to death. But after receiving a letter from Papa telling him how conferences were all arranged and how thousands of people would be disappointed if they didn't go on scheduled time, he decided to have them go on and decided to invite the wives to go and meet them. They are paying all expenses so it is going to be a great treat.

The baby looks so sweet. I have shortened him [taken him out of long baby gowns] today and as Lou Jean says, "He looks darling!" ... He is crowing now and enjoying the train immensely.

Unsuspecting, Father wrote longingly in his journal, 1 March 1921, after his ship docked: "Our landing was not a very pleasant one; indeed, it was somewhat gloomy. Other passengers had friends on the wharf to greet them; but there were no smiling faces for us. Of course, we had sent no word as to our coming, so expected no one." Later that afternoon, when he heard that the Grant party was in town looking for them, he wrote exultantly: "I don't know of anything in my life that gave me more true joy than the realization of meeting my sweetheart and baby within the next few minutes!"

The meeting was all that he hoped for, and he fondly flattered himself that the baby "knew me." As matters turned out, President Anthon H. Lund died on 2 March, and the whole party, including Father and President Cannon, returned to Salt Lake City for the funeral. Father does not mention the funeral or the numerous public affairs that kept him occupied when he writes again. Instead he records "a joyous re-union" with the children and "two short, busy, happy weeks at home." When those weeks ended, and he and Brother Cannon left for San Francisco, bound for Tahiti, he wrote on 26 March 1921: "Parting from my sweetheart and dear kiddies was quite as difficult this morning as it was December 4, 1920 . . . even though nine-tenths of my time has been given to the public, and only one-tenth to my family."

Mother wrote her first letter to me that same night, with apologies for her tardiness: "I would have stayed up nights if I had not known that you would get word from home. But I knew that Daddy & Lou Jean were writing so I did not worry much." I was interested in every detail of her report:

"I heard Papa's voice over the phone before seeing him and Oh, it was sweet music to me! We had a joyful trip home together.

"Since coming home, he has had to go to Salt Lake every day. He has been missed so much by the organizations to which he belongs. They have all said, 'Oh we must have a meeting while you are here. So, hospital meetings, Weber board meetings, Sunday School meetings, Priesthood meetings, Quorum meetings and meetings galore where he has had to talk. Then company here every night that we have not been out. So you have never seen such a busy man. . . .

"It broke my heart to see him go away again. He looked so sick. The doctors have advised him to have serum for Typhoid Fever. So Dr. Joe has given him four doses and he has had the chills fevers pains & aches all night. His arm was all swollen and red this morning and he was sick but it will all be better in the long run down on those islands where so much Typhoid rages."

The typescript of Father's journal begins with his departure on the

Marama from San Francisco. He thoroughly enjoyed the voyage — no
seasickness, a "most sociable captain," a "good substantial group" of
passengers, no women smoking, and a Sabbath observed with a closed
bar, no games, and hymn singing. He read, rested, and enjoyed the
perfect weather and flying fish. A letter to Emma Rae, which he copied
into his diary, recorded the horseplay when the ship crossed the equator.
Neptune and his wife, with the assistance of some stout sailors,
"shaved" the men who had not crossed the line before with a "large
wooden razor about the size of a turkey's wing" and then forced them
to crawl through a tunnel made of benches while they squirted them
with a hose. Brother Cannon received this treatment, and so did a dozen
or so others. Father, wearing his white suit and holding his camera,
was simply sentenced to appear at dinner with his hair parted in the
middle.

They landed in Papeete, Tahiti, in early April 1921. Four elders
were waiting for them, but the mission president had been holding
conferences in the Tuomotos four hundred miles away with no means
of transportation but interisland schooners. Father, in addition to conducting meetings and observing conditions on the island, seriously re-
searched buying a schooner for the mission before they sailed a week
later for New Zealand.

Brother Cannon records an adventure of retrieving their passports,
which had been left with the customs officials. The arrival of a new
governor closed all government offices, and the *Marama* was due to
sail on Sunday evening, when all offices would be closed anyway for
the weekend.

"But Brother McKay instructed President Cannon to obtain them,
and as has already been stated, on this trip at least it was invariably
possible to follow instructions.

"The first official was awakened at six o'clock in the morning by
Brothers Cannon and [Grant L.] Benson [one of the missionaries], the
latter acting as interpreter. This gentleman promised to meet the brethren at the passport office at 8:30, a promise which he failed to keep.
Every officer connected even remotely with the passport department
was visited. All were helpless, or unwilling to do anything.

"Meanwhile, the *Marama* was preparing to sail at five in the afternoon. Brother McKay attended Sunday School and afternoon meeting
and President Cannon spent as much time in these gatherings as could

be spared from his apparently fruitless efforts. . . . Just before the after-noon meeting their troubles were explained to Brother Timmy, a prom-inent native Church member. He placed himself and his auto at their disposal. President Cannon went with him to the passport office. Two policemen were guarding the place, and to them Brother Timmy said:

" 'Two of my friends are here and must have their passes before the boat sails.'

" 'But we have no right to touch the passes,' was the answer.

" 'You show me where they are, then turn your backs, and I will be responsible to your superior officers.'

"The policemen pointed to a certain drawer and walked out of the room, and Brother Timmy secured both passes." (Cannon Typescript, pp. 81–82.)

Father's account of the voyage from Tahiti to New Zealand is en-livened by reports of albatrosses, gospel conversations with the other passengers, and shark-fishing. When he touched a "dead" shark on deck, he got "a blow on the legs that gave me a sensation I shall not soon forget. It's rather an unusual experience to come in contact with a live shark!" (McKay Typescript, p. 12.)

Father's next letter to Mother was written on the third day of a three-day conference:

Waikato District near Huntley, N.Z.
Sunday, April 24, 1921

My Darling Ray:

This morning, away out here in what the Minister of Native Affairs told us in Wellington last Thurs. is the "Wildest tribe of the Maoris," I was handed your Xmas letter, dated Dec. 26th., containing [a] card from Judge Rolapp, one from Mr. Fisher, and greetings from others. Also Llewelyn's newsy letter of Jan. 2nd., telling all about his trip to Huntsville last December. In it, I learned for the first time that he took his own money to buy my Christmas present to you. Bless his dear, unselfish heart! . . .

The letters, it is true, are several months old, but as I read them, not a few big tears dropped on the Maori mat covering the floor of my bedroom. One sentence, though, in your loving letter almost deserves a reprimand; it is this: "Sweetheart, if my letters are too long and wearisome, let me know." Why, you sweetest of all sweethearts, I would

David O. McKay, second row, center, with missionaries and Maori Saints in New Zealand, April 1921

wish your letters ten times as long, and then they would seem only one-tenth as long as I would have them. If you knew what joy just your handwriting on the envelope gives me, you would never hint that your letters might not be interesting. . . .

One thought and loving sentiment, you are with me every moment, even when I'm speaking, for I frequently find myself referring to home and Loved Ones in my addresses. With these thoughts, may my prayers bring to you and our boys and girls health and peace and sweet content until we meet again.

> Your loving husband
> Dade

His journal describes how, as part of the welcoming ceremonies, the Maoris lamented for those who had died since the last Hui Tau (conference). "Tears fell from their eyes like rain, on both sides. There was no 'make believe' about it—they were actually crying!" (McKay Typescript, p. 21.)

A problem of protocol arose when one of the visitors, a prominent member of another tribe, gave a speech of welcome. The king's aunt rebuked him as not being "of sufficiently high rank" to give a speech. He was going to trace his pedigree when another woman "put an end to the royal contest by saying, . . . 'We've met here to learn who God is, not who is the highest aristocrat.' " Commented Father, "I thought I detected in that little controversy a manifestation of the spirit that caused so many wars and contentions among the Nephites and Lamanites." (P. 21.)

The missionaries' testimony meeting particularly touched Father: "Few meetings have ever been held in the Church in which a richer outpouring of the spirit of the Redeemer was manifest. Every heart was mellowed, and tears flowed from every eye. Though we were together five and one half hours, the Elders wished we might continue longer!

"One young man, a Brother Jacobs, has lost his father by death since he left home; and he is now released to return home. At the conclusion of the meeting, Elder Gordon Young, having managed to get Brother Jacobs out of the room, proposed the collection of a purse to aid Brother Jacobs in his travels home. It was a wonderful demonstration of magnanimity and self denial to see that body of sixty men and boys, not a few of them in financial straits themselves, all of them with all they possess upon the altar of service, contribute of their scanty means to help a brother in need. They raised [thirty-eight pounds] which they presented with their love and blessing to their fellow missionary. . . .

"Having learned that the little Branch in this district was still in debt about $250.00 for the land on which their church is built, some brother [at the closing session of the Hui Tau] proposed that a collection be taken to liquidate the pending obligation. Notwithstanding the fact that nearly every Maori present had been put to great expense in travel, and in bearing his or her proportion of the cost of the Hui Tau; notwithstanding the further fact that the meeting house in question would never be of use to anyone outside the immediate district, and further, that the district had not really borne its proportion of the responsibility of the Hui Tau, within fifteen minutes after the proposal was made, Brother Duncan announced, 'Fifty pounds contributed and turned over in cash to President Taylor!' " (Pp. 26–27.)

Two of Father's letters written aboard the *Tofua*, en route from New Zealand to Fiji, have survived. The first letter was to Mother:

Wednesday night, May 4, 1921

My Own Sweetheart:

. . . Ten days or more before we reached Wellington, I suffered from a very tender tooth, loosened by *pyorrhea*. I couldn't chew my food properly, consequently my digestive organs began to rebel. However, I thought I could stand it alright until we arrived at Wellington, where I could go obtain the proper medical attention.

At Wellington, we learned that we had to leave at 8:30 P.M. that day in order to reach Huntley on time for the "Hui Tau."

A dentist informed me that he could not save the tooth, neither did he give me anything that lessened the pain. I was afraid to have it pulled for fear my speaking would be interfered with and the "Hui Tau" would probably be the largest gathering of our entire tour.

Coming into a colder climate, I had caught cold so that didn't make me feel any better.

However, if ever I prayed for help, I did that Friday night and Saturday morning of the "Hui Tau"; and we were certainly greatly blessed at that opening session. It was evident that the hundreds who had gathered with such high expectations were not disappointed. Many were in tears before the meeting closed.

The afternoon was equally successful—a wonderful spiritual feast! So also was the evening session.

But it rained, and I was so busy that I neglected to put on my rubbers. Result: aggravated cold, and a voice so hoarse Sunday morning I could scarcely speak. Fortunately, a Bro. Spencer, chemist, photographer, Florist, Dentist., etc. etc. was on the grounds, and gave me "just the thing for my tooth," and "medicine" for my hoarseness. Faith and works took us through the morning session; but at the conclusion, I wished I were home in the tender care of my darling wife. Without breakfast, and without lunch, we met at 2 P.M. in the greatest assembly of the Conference. While Pres. Taylor was presenting the Authorities, I turned so sick that I had to excuse myself, and go outside. One of those old "sick-at-stomach" attacks was on, and a thousand people assembled to hear the first member of the Council of the Twelve who had ever been in New Zealand!

After a vomiting spell, I rested a moment or two, prayed for strength to do my duty, and returned just as the last of a long list of local names were being voted upon.

After a song, I arose to speak. My voice was husky, and the tent large, and people standing in circles on the outside! . . . I didn't know I had a voice. I only knew my subject upon which I spoke with freedom for forty minutes. And then, I realized that my voice was not only filling the spacious tent, but was clearer than when I began.

Sunday night was equally successful, Bro. Cannon occupying most of the time, and I concluded. . . . Monday was a great day—my hoarseness better at night than when I began speaking in the morning.

Tuesday, no breakfast, and a five and one half hours Priesthood meeting. Though I had a severe headache, caused by my stomach, we carried through one of the most inspirational meetings I've ever attended!

A race or two in the afternoon, without lunch (I thought it best not to eat) a light dinner, and a grand concert at night concluded the "Hui Tau." It had been a success! Thank the Lord!!

As soon as I reached Auckland, Wednesday, I had that pestering tooth pulled, and took your castor oil—took it without lemon juice, oranges, or anything else. Indeed, it tasted so home-like, I almost relished it! I really believe my system craved it!

With the exception of a little lingering tenderness in my mouth, I'm alright again, and approaching the Tongan mission in pretty good physical condition.

I thought I would just give you these personal particulars because truly, Ray, I've never before in my entire public work faced such responsibility with such physical handicap[s]. It was no easy task! I freely and thankfully acknowledge divine help in its accomplishment!

Bro. Cannon says he has "never prayed so hard for anyone in his life as he did for me Sunday afternoon." "I did it," he confessed, "partly in self defense, but I was sincere in it." There is no doubt in his mind about the Lord's answering his prayer. . . .

O, Ray, but this is a long time to be away from you without hearing even an inkling as to how you are and what you are doing! Forty days, and it may possibly be nearly forty more.

The second letter, to Lou Jean, was written a day later. Father's loving letter paints an evocative picture of the Huntsville he loved so well:

Aboard the S.S. Tofua
May 5, 1921

My darling Lou Jean:

If you knew with what tenderness I have written "My darling Lou

Jean" this morning, you would have an absolute assurance that whatever else may come to you in life, you have a father who loves you dearly.

I'm feeling somewhat mellow this morning anyway; but it isn't just a mood that prompts me to tell you that you are very dear to your far away *daddy*. If this world tour does nothing else, it will imprint upon my soul everlastingly how dearly I love your sweet mother and you children. . . .

When you receive this letter, you will be preparing to go to Huntsville. . . . It's a beautiful place in June and July, and in September and October it's splendid! Of course, the crocuses and buttercups and other spring flowers are all gone before you go up there, but the "blue bells" and "pinks" and that tall white flower which grows in the meadow and fills the air with luscious fragrance, are in full bloom, and birds are singing their welcome to you on every tree and fence. Old "Spring Creek" with its crisp, luscious cress and speckled trout goes gurgling and rippling along the roadway and through the fields without ever dreaming that it is one of the dearest, coolest streams in all creation!

And there is Mike, too tender to do heavy work any more, but just strong enough and proud enough to "single foot" for hours with you in the saddle, and he would gladly carry you to where the meadowlark sings more clearly, and the dove coos as plaintively as any dove anywhere else in all the wide world!

Of course, the old house doesn't mean much to you, because you see only the big, scantily furnished and inconvenient rooms, and the bare, unattractive porch!

But to me, that old two-story residence is almost hallowed. The memory of a sainted mother makes it so. Her influence and beauty entwined themselves into the lives of her sons and daughters as effectively as a divine presence! There she lived and loved, and was loved— almost reverenced—by your grandfather, the best and noblest of husbands and fathers!

It was in that old house and on the old farm that together they toiled in self-denial and sacrifice, that their children might get an education, and if possible, amount to something in the world. They had their sorrow and suffering, and joy and happiness, anxiety and worry, as all parents do, but we children knew little about these things. We only knew that we had our marbles, our little wagons, our sleds, dolls and dishes and pretty dresses, that old Santa Claus never passed our

chimney, and that every present had a bit of poetry attached to it, which
he had written before he left the house; we only knew that everybody
was welcome, whether travelers, missionaries, or young folks, and that
we were always sure papa and mama would greet them with a smile
and appropriate words of welcome.

In memory, these and a thousand other treasures that are hidden
away where the world never sees them, make that old country house
a shrine to your sentimental daddy! The old rhubarb patch, the fruit
trees, and even the towering poplars, the barn, the old "tithing yard,"
the high board fence enclosing a half-block—all have memories entwined around them and about them that make them as cherished as
old friends.

Because of an outbreak of measles on Fiji, the captain did not allow
any of the passengers to disembark and then return to the ship. A brass
band serenaded them from the dock, however, and Father was permitted
to address the Saints from behind a barrier. Mark V. Coombs, president
of the Tongan mission, came aboard and accompanied them to Samoa.

After their meetings on that island, Father and Brother Cannon
visited Nukualofa in the Tongan Islands and Neiafu in the Vavau Islands.
Father's journal records that voyage and their memorable visit to Apia,
Samoa, in considerable detail. The voyage between the islands of Savaii
and Upolu had surpassed in beauty anything they had seen up to that
point; and when they docked in Apia harbor that evening, Father had
"a beautiful vision suggested no doubt by the scene last evening—
city—multitude led by Saviour—While radiant sign or motto: 'These
are they who have renounced the world—who have truly been born
again." (P. 40.)

A party of men with red headbands and white shirts rowed Father
and Brother Cannon ashore, singing. The customs officials threw open
the double gates usually kept locked and declined to inspect their luggage. "The streets were packed with people, and the Church school
band from Sauniatu, composed of native boys . . . played stirring strains.
. . . Business in the town was at a standstill. Stores, banks and offices
were closed and everybody was on the streets. All had heard of Apostles,
but this was the first opportunity ever given most of these people to
see one." (Cannon Typescript, n.d., p. 114.) Outside the Catholic school,
the children and their teachers stood at attention. At least fifteen

hundred people were gathered on the grounds of the mission home for the ceremony of greeting.

Father obviously appreciated the oratory and ceremony in the speeches and kava drinking which followed, regretting that he did not know more about local customs. About three hundred people were served at the banquet while the formal presentation of gifts, singing, and dancing continued until late. "We were literally buried in Samoan presents, many of them rare and costly," recorded Father. The consul's wife exclaimed in awe at one of the mats, "I've never before seen one of those presented to anybody," while a chief later told Father that he had not seen one made for forty-five years. (McKay Typescript, p. 45.) Father had the songs, composed for the occasion, recorded in both Samoan and English.

The next morning at 7:30 the natives began to build a bowery "without the use of spade, shovel, hammer, nail, rope or string," and by 9 A.M., meetings began. It was the beginning of a very profitable conference. Between the long sessions, entertainment continued and chiefs from other villages called to pay their eloquent respects. Father also inspected property, with a view to authorizing permanent locations and buildings. On 18 May, a week after their landing, the monthly mail arrived. For Father, there was only an *Ogden Standard* dated 26 March from Llewelyn announcing the death of Emmeline B. Wells. "I read and re-read jokes in the *Juvenile [Instructor]*," he wrote lonesomely, "and rehashed some old ones I remember to keep from realizing the fact that I might have had a letter which did not come." (P. 60.)

On 20 May, they sailed for Pago Pago aboard the *Marstal,* a little gasoline launch with no place for the thirteen passengers except a platform about six feet by eight feet built over the engine. They had ninety miles to travel, and it had been raining all day. In answer to their prayers, the rain stopped, just as the engine roared into life, and it did not rain again for the entire way. Father wrote:

"If it had kept raining, I think we should all have been half dead. As it was we were a sorry looking 'bunch' when we arrived at Pago Pago at 7:30 next morning. Eight of us crowded on the 6 x 8 elevation under the canopy, the four others lay out on the deck. We were singing until we sailed out of the reef. Then the boat began to interpret every movement of the sea. It pitched, it tossed, it rolled, it shivered! The sea was not rough either, but a little boat on the ocean is like a leaf in a lake—it responds to every slight movement of the surface.

"Sister Adams began it. I raised up with the intention of helping her, but suddenly decided to lean over the rail on the opposite side."

Only two in the party were not ill. Even Brother Cannon succumbed to the little boat's pitching. (Pp. 62–63.)

After a few hours' rest, they set out for the conference location inland. The rain came down in torrents, their unshod ponies were tenderfooted, and the women in the party, who were carrying babies, refused to ride; after trying the ponies, Father and Brother Cannon also started walking. Their umbrellas were no shelter, so they "trudged along afoot, mud and wet besmearing our shoes and trousers to the knees." Their spirits lifted when a band braved the rain to play welcoming music, and ranks of schoolchildren stood in order, drenched to the skin.

The conference was a fine one, and then they prepared to return to Pago Pago. Father indignantly "told the Elders, and President Adams particularly, that I didn't believe in teaching the gospel of love from the pulpit, and then persecuting and punishing God's creatures in life." They walked "six or eight miles" and "enjoyed [it] . . . far more than the ride." (P. 70.)

It would have been difficult for anything to have matched the warmth and spiritual outpouring of their first conference in Samoa; but when they returned the second time for a conference at Sauniatu, Apia, the conference, feasts, entertainment, and other meetings completely melted my father's heart again. Father described the farewell in his letter to Mother written 2 June when they were preparing to sail toward Tonga on 6 June:

"We were to leave Sauniatu, our Mormon village, at eleven A.M. following our inspection of the school. When we returned to the Conf. house about 10:50 A.M., several mothers were there with babies to be blessed. We blessed them, and in most cases the mothers too, and in several instances, the fathers also. Others hearing about it came with their babies, some of them as robust as health could make them but we blessed them all. It was 12:30 before we came out of our room, the last little infant having been blessed.

"The Relief Society had formed in two lines, reaching from our doorway through the parlor out across the lawn to the street, and the

Matars (heads of families) and best of all the children had continued the double column. The women asked if it would be alright if they sang a farewell song as we walked through the crowd to our horses, thinking that we could not spare the time to shake hands. Sister Adams led, followed by Bro. Adams, and Bro. Cannon, and I came last. When the women began to cry, and to pat and 'hongi' (kiss) my hand, and their sobs interrupted the song, I began to feel the tears spring in my own eyes. Half way down the lines, I came to old Brother Saimasima, whose one desire has been to live to greet an apostle, and as he fondly caressed my hand and sobbed his heartfelt farewell, I broke down too. . . . The entire assembly threw off restraint and cried and sobbed profusely. Old 'Papa,' the leading chief sobbed till his bowed shoulders fairly shook, and other men were equally shaken with grief. 'Kipen' our interpreter, threw himself on my neck, and sobbed aloud.

"As we neared the end of the crowd, where were grouped the boys and girls, the band struck up, 'Tofa My Felini (Good-bye, My Friend) Samoa e la galo atu.' It began to pour. We raised our umbrellas and waved our farewell to the people assembled on the porch and on the lawn. A turn in the road, in two minutes obscured them from view, but we could hear that never-to-be forgotten air which that day took equal place in our memories with 'Aloha oe.'

"We had no sooner turned the corner and crossed the bridge spanning the picturesque stream, than the rain ceased. Before we could mount our horses held in waiting across the stream, the people led by the band came hurrying towards us, and as many as could crowd around again shook our hands, amidst sobs that were no longer controlled.

"Then as we moved our horses slowly up the gentle slope along a vista embowered with beautiful branches and lined with stately, tropical trees, the band and the crowd of friends followed us as if they could not let us go. Those who could were singing, 'Good-bye My Felini.' We were a quarter of a mile ahead, when the picturesque solemnity of the scene began to dawn upon me! The silence and stillness of the woods, the green vines and foliage, the grass-lined trail, that group of friends — Brethren and Sisters — women in white and the band boys in uniform, their red head dress standing out in striking contrast to the white and green.

"Feeling impressed to give them a blessing there in 'God's first Temple,' I suggested that we return to them. When they were told why we had returned, their sobs almost drowned my shaking voice as I invoked God's blessing upon this genuinely true-hearted and loyal group and their kindred and race."

Father's journal recounts the same experience and then adds a few more poignant details:

"At this point I will record what happened later in the day, but which was not reported to us until the arrival of two of the Elders on the following afternoon. After they had watched us until we were beyond their sight, they returned solemnly to the village, and separated to their huts. Kippen, who had been our interpreter, immediately sat down, and wrote the prayer as he remembered it. He and some others then conceived the idea of burying a copy of it on the spot where I had stood, and erecting a pile of stones as a marking place. The suggestion, it seems, was no sooner made than acted upon. The town bell was rung, the people assembled, the plan presented and approved, and the crowd once more walked to the place of parting.

"Here the prayer was read, a hole dug, and the bottle in which a copy had been sealed, together with an account of the entire proceedings, buried underneath a pile of stones, each of the heads of families throwing a handful or two of soil to assist in the covering. The branch on which my umbrella had been hung was taken to the village to be kept as a souvenir, and steps were taken to erect a small monument on what seemed to them and to us to be a sacred spot.

"Following is the substance of the prayer offered on the occasion.

" 'O God, our Heavenly and Eternal Father, there have been many impressive partings between thy people and thy chosen servants in the days of the Saviour and in this day. Apostles Peter and Paul, with their associates, Timothy, Marcus, Luke and others, undoubtedly wept many tears in bidding solemn farewells; but on no occasion, we feel sure, was expressed more sincere attachment than that which is manifest here today. Thou seest, Heavenly Father, with what solemn and sorrowful feelings we bid one another farewell here in this beautiful grove, one of thy first temples.

" 'Holy Father, look down in tender love and mercy upon these good people. Protect them in their village from all evil influences. Bless the leading men therein that they may be indeed kind and wise shepherds to this little fold; and may no fierce wolves in the shape of enmity, ill-will, and indifference "enter in amongst them, not sparing the flock."

Bless the mothers, the young men and the young women, and especially the little children. Be merciful to the little ones whose eyesight is threatened, and others unto whom thy servants have administered. Heal the sick, we beseech thee, and restore to health and strength, through their faith and faithfulness, those who are afflicted.

" 'May thy peace abide here in the village of Sauniatu!

" 'Father, in thy love, prosper the labor of the hands of all who work for the necessaries and comforts of life, and may they possess in abundance, food and clothing. May their plantation be fruitful in the products adapted to local conditions; but above all, may Harmony abide in their hearts and homes. Our Father, may they have a clear understanding of thy truth, and make rapid progress in gaining a knowledge of thee and thy divine work!

" 'By virtue of the Apostleship and in the authority of the Priesthood with which thou hast endowed me, I seal these blessings upon these, thy Saints! May this parting and blessing prove, through thy power and mercy, a sacred blessing to them and to us, we humbly pray, in the name of Jesus Christ our Saviour, Amen.' " (Pp. 80–82.)

A year later, hundreds of Saints in white unveiled a thirteen-foot monument with a bronze plaque commemorating this event. On 15 January 1955, Father took Mother to that farewell scene to dedicate Sauniatu's new chapel. At the monument, a fifty-voice choir welcomed them with "We Thank Thee, O God, for a Prophet," and the rain that had fallen all week gave way to blue skies and warm sunshine. Standing next to Father, Howard B. Stone, the mission president, saw tears spring to his eyes and heard him whisper, "Truly, this is the most beautiful place I have ever seen!" (*Cherished Experiences from the Writings of President David O. McKay,* comp. Clare Middlemiss [Salt Lake City: Deseret Book, 1976], p. 73.)

The letter to Mother in which Father recounted his extraordinary experience at Sauniatu also contained his fervent birthday wishes and all the love and longing of his homesick heart:

From early boyhood days, I have always loved the month of June. Even before I realized its life-producing beauty, I had a fond interest in it because on June 15th, we could "go fishing." . . .

As I grew older, I began to appreciate June for her own vigorous, virginal beauty. Her copious streams, leafy trees, green grasses half hidden by taller plants capped by bright-flowered luxuriant fields of grain; singing birds, all mated, and nesting their broods of fledglings; — all awakened an almost unconscious feeling in my young mind, which just at about that time, fortunately found expression in those lines in "The Vision of Sir Launfal":

> *And what is so rare as a day in June?*
> *Then, if ever, come perfect days;*
> *Then heaven tries earth if it be in tune,*
> *And over it softly her warm ear lays.*

To-day, in the noon-day of life, to my boyish anticipations and fancies, to youthful glimpses of the beauty of June, and to my more mature appreciation of the glories and joys of this best of seasons, I add the treasured fact that June gave me my Sweetheart, my beloved wife! All my interest in 'June 15th' has practically faded, and if appreciation of all the natural beauties and glory of this favored month should likewise grow dim, your birthday, Sweetheart, would still make June the sweetest and best of all the year! I hope you will receive this letter near *June Twenty-third.* Therefore, I am wishing you now, with all the fervor of a lonesome, loving heart:

Many, MANY, Happy returns of the Day!

... Sweetheart, good-bye. May we be together next Birthday, and not have to be separated so long again! It may be June and it may possibly be July before I hear from you. I had hoped that my last cable would bring one in reply, but as yet none has come. ... Bro. Cannon received one here written April 18th; but your sweetheart and lover is still hungering and thirsting for a line of good news and affection from "one who loves him best."

Your loving Dade

Father and Brother Cannon sailed from Samoa, accompanied by President Coombs and four missionaries, on Monday, 6 June 1921. They reached Vavau in Tonga on Thursday, 9 June, but were prohibited from landing because they had come from Samoa where measles had been reported. Father and thirty other passengers therefore took up quarters in the quarantine area on Makahaa Island, only a short distance from Nukualofa, while Brother Cannon continued on to New Zealand. Father could have gone on to New Zealand himself and left Brother Cannon

in quarantine to conduct the conferences in Nukualofa but did not want
to disappoint the Saints who had been anticipating seeing an apostle.

Although irked by the delay and expecting to be bored, Father wrote
in his journal:

"Monday, June 13, 1921. It is truly surprising how many interesting
things one can find around this little island! At first, I thought that all
I could do would be to write articles and letters and read; but now I
find interest in searching for beautiful shells when the tide has gone
out. Then Brother Coombs and I began to examine the various forms
of life hiding or crawling around the coral, some evidently in their native
habitat, but others left stranded by the ebbing tide. I have never before
realized with what myriads of forms of life the old ocean must teem!
Crab-like things of all sizes, shell fish, jelly-like creatures, some beautifully colored like poppies, and others black, snakelike and loathsome,
star fish, some with a center smaller than a one cent piece, and thread-
like tentacles, two or three feet long! Little fish stranded in pools among
the coral reef, some gasping on the sand. How gratefully they swam
when I helped them back into the ocean!

"Men sometimes get stranded, and the current of human life flows
on without them! . . .

"Wednesday, June 15, 1921. . . . The nights are beautiful, the beams
from the half-full moon in the northwest, casting on the ebbing waters
around the shore a mellow dreamlight that fills my soul with a longing
to have my sweetheart and kiddies around me to share the romance
and beauties of these ever-satisfying and pleasure-giving south seas. . . .

"After writing a report to the Commissioners of education, I read
to four of the Elders . . . half of 'As You Like It.' One of the boys 'never
liked Shakespeare,' so after I had read one or two scenes, I would stop
and inquire, 'Are you getting tired?'

" 'No, go on,' they would answer.

"When the lunch *rap rap* was sounded, Brother Phillips said: 'Please
finish it tomorrow, Brother McKay, will you?'

" 'I think I heard one of you say,' I replied 'that he did not like
Shakespeare.'

" 'Well, that's the first time I ever liked him,' confessed Brother
Parkin.

"Just another example proving that interest can always be awakened
by producing mental pictures of personality and action."

David O. McKay, second row, center, with missionaries in Tonga, 25 June 1921

Released from quarantine on 22 June, Father joyously met with the Tongan Saints and "shook hands with everyone, not missing even a tiny baby and bade each 'Malo lile.' " (P. 101.) Father squeezed out time to send a cable to Mother, "my sweetheart who is one year older and sweeter and dearer tomorrow." (P. 102.) It was a wonderful conference, and Father records, "The requests for administrations and blessings exceed the power and time at my disposal to grant them." (P. 106.) In fact, a few days later on Monday, 27 June, Father's strength was ebbing: "Meetings, concerts, impromptu entertainments, administrations and disturbed sleep had their effect upon my physical strength. I was about as weary and exhausted this night as I've ever been." (P. 113.) The next day he received a cablegram from Mother and wrote exultantly in his diary:

" 'Everything and everybody all well. Letter received—have written—I miss you very very much.'

"As this was the first word from my loved ones since I left home, March 26th, it seemed the dearest message I've ever received in my life. 'Everybody all well!' What more comforting words would a traveler have than these? Unless it be those from his sweetheart, 'I miss you very, very much'!! I felt it no weakness to let tears of joy express my appreciation." (P. 113.)

Father's journal for the next several pages is filled with eloquent letters of love, joy, and blessing from the Saints and his own reports of giving blessings and bidding sorrowful farewells. Friday, 1 July 1921, he left on a little gasoline-engined ketch, its decks loaded with seventy people, to visit the northern islands of Haapai and Vavau. He reported the quite alarming voyage to Mother in his next letter, on 4 July:

Captain Doughty seemed to be a very congenial sort of man, and judging from his promptness in leaving port, an efficient officer. However, I learned from him during our first conversation that he had not sailed this route before and he was rather fearful of reaching the *reefs* before daylight. As we sailed out of the harbor into the choppy sea, I surveyed our situation—seventy people on an open deck—each one huddling, kneeling, or lying in a little space scarcely large enough for a medium-sized dog to lie comfortably in. . . .

At sundown, a heavy wind came up, and the waves dashed the little bark up and down and sidewise as if it had been a shell. Passengers became very sick, but I stood the tossing pretty well, *at first.*

The captain had very considerately tendered his berth to Sister Coombs who was desperately ill; and about dark, the engineer graciously insisted that I occupy his berth, opposite the captain's. Thus we two were favored above the sixty eight others. . . .

At 11:30 P.M. when the captain came down to examine again his charts, I thought I noticed unsteady movements not entirely due to the rocking of the boat. But I dismissed the thoughts; for it seemed inconceivable that any man would so far forget himself as to drink whiskey to excess when he had such a responsibility as the Captain was carrying that night—seventy people aboard a light craft; a high wind and an angry sea! Surely he wasn't becoming intoxicated!

A few minutes later my fears became a reality when I saw him thrown to the floor by a sudden lurch of the ship. My seasickness was replaced by actual horror when I detected him hugging a full quarter bottle of whiskey—*full* excepting what he had drunk of it! Then flashed through my mind a combination of evils that would be difficult to duplicate for danger—a *mad sea, midnight* and pitch darkness, seventy people aboard a small vessel, sixty-eight of whom were exposed on the open deck, dangerous reefs ahead—and the commander intoxicated! My heavens, sweetheart, I became alarmed! . . .

Soon, without his knowing what had become of it, I had the whiskey under my pillow. At 1:30 A.M., he awoke, felt for his bottle, held his head as if trying to remember where he put it, and then began to search for it. Finally, he lit a cigarette, and scrambled up on deck. He was soon down again, and began to fumble behind some packages. Then, I surmised that he had another bottle! I spoke to him, and he pretended he was getting a towel to wipe his face, for it was raining on deck! I knew, by that subterfuge that he would not drink while I watched him; so my duty for the night was plain—I must keep an eye on him until morning. Oh, but I was sick! and my gloomy forebodings and fears for the poor people exposed to the storm only aggravated my sickness. . . .

At 3 A.M. the lad called down, "Three o'clock, captain" and "We tacked the ship" in answer to which the captain, half aroused from his stupor gave a sort of half audible "umphm-m," and drowsed again.

It was at that hour that we were in our greatest peril! It seems that some blunder was made in turning the ship "windward" to "tack," the result of which was the overwhelming of the boat by a gigantic wave. "Lui" Wolfgramme, a native weighing 215 lbs. was floating on deck. He thought he had been carried completely overboard and was in the sea. Elder Clark of Eden was washed from the top of the cabin, and hurled against the rail—saved from going overboard only by his catching a rope! Everyone, excepting only the native sister who was holding Sister Coombs' nine months old baby, was drenched. Fortunately, only one native woman was bruised, and no lives were lost! I acknowledge Divine Care over us that terrible night.

At daylight the captain again assumed command, and we continued our course, arriving in Haapai at 6:30 P.M. Friday, twelve hours late!

Notwithstanding our sickness, sleeplessness, and exposure, we held meetings from nine P.M. to ten-thirty P.M. with 116 people in attendance. The school children gave an impromptu concert after dismissal of meeting, and accompanied me to the house where I was to sleep, sang two more songs, and joined in evening prayer. . . .

[Then, en route to Vavau, came] another night at sea. . . . The gale was still on, the sea tempestuous, the weather cold; but the captain was sober, and we were at no hour in immediate danger, although we were blown several miles off our course, "tacked" and bobbed up and down in the wind and waves till morning. . . .

Just before going ashore, I called the captain to one side and said, "Captain, did you lose a bottle of whiskey Thrs. night?"

"Yes, but that's alright!"

"Well, I want to tell you that when I saw your condition, I concluded that if I took *good* care of your bottle, you would take *better* care of us!"

"I surmised you took it," he said, "and it was alright. But I wouldn't have gone too far!"

"I didn't throw it overboard, because I did not want you to think that I had confiscated your whiskey."

"It would have been alright if you had."

However, his face lit up when I told him where he would find it, and we parted friends. . . .

Bro. Cannon had given the Purser all my New Zealand mail, so at 11 P.M. I sped on wings of lightning from Tonga to my loved ones at home. From the large packages, I selected my sweetheart's letters, and Lou Jean's, apologized to a gentleman room mate for keeping the light on, and read all your April letters before touching my head to the pillow.

Oh how I enjoyed the news of our children's successes at school, and elsewhere! I will write to Lou Jean and congratulate her upon her excellence in her studies, and to Llewelyn, upon his leadership! I do hope I shall get word at Samoa of the result of the school election! And Emma Ray, "Bro. McKay's little girl" — Bless her dear heart, how I should like a hug! And Neddy boy, too, an accomplished singer and clever as the rest of them! and baby "the sweetest in all the world!"

And the mother of these fine children! What of her? — The *purest, noblest, sweetest mother, the truest wife* and most *beautiful sweetheart* in all the world! How I wish I could fly with my thoughts and embrace her! . . . My soul is hungering for just one loving look into your eyes, and one fond embrace!

Good night — Dearest — Sweetest and Best!

Loving and longingly,
Dade

When he returned to Samoa where he had the enormous satisfaction of presenting new instruments to the Sauniatu brass band (he had discovered that the musicians had been playing on borrowed instruments!), Father also took the opportunity of visiting the grave of Robert Louis Stevenson. When the boat stopped over in Suva, he read in a local newspaper some attacks on the Mormons, promptly went to the office, sent in his card to the editor, and pointed out some of the errors. The editor instantly invited him to write a reply and Father, with one eye on his watch for the boat's sailing, sat down and wrote it. The editor "chuckled, seemed pleased, and promised to publish it the next day." (P. 136.) Father had plenty of occasions aboard ship to provide information about Mormonism as well: "One [passenger] said today that Joseph Smith founded Mormonism in England, and then took it to America. Another wants to know if Utah is a very large city." (P. 136.)

Father docked in Auckland "and met once again, in a most joyous and reciprocal greeting, my companion, brother, and friend, Hugh J. It seemed like meeting one of my own folks! I think we'll not separate again. . . . At the Mission House I received a welcome letter from my rosebud, Lou Jean, and one from my missionary boy, David L. Two or three others also, from friends, but none from my Sweetheart." (P. 137.)

They held their first conference in Whangarei on 21 July that lasted for several days, another in Poirua on 26 July, and a third in Dannevirke on 27 July where they were royally entertained by the Napera family. Then they went on to mission headquarters at Hastings where they visited the Maori Agricultural College at Kronogata. Father's farming eye critically noted the poor soil: "There are approximately three hundred acres and they cannot raise sufficient garden stuff to supply the needs of the school. Branches send them tithing potatoes from other districts!" (P. 147.)

The weather was consistently stormy on their voyage to Australia — "the worst storm of the voyage. It became impossible even to sit on deck, let alone walk on it." The pitching of the vessel hurled dishes from the table and once threw Father "against the door which swung open, and I dashed against a young man, pinning him to the stair case." (Pp. 152–53.) Even under such adverse circumstances, he did not become seasick.

Father's next letter to Mother was written on Australian Mission stationery and dated 8 August 1921, the day after they landed:

My Darling Sweetheart:

Do you know that it is twenty-four years since we plighted each other our love, before I left for my mission, Aug. 7th, 1897? I thought of it yesterday, as I wrote the date in my diary. My accomplishments during those twenty four years are very insignificant, but there are three possessions I prize most dearly, viz., my *Loved Ones,* my *Standing in the Church,* and *my friends;* and the great joy of my life is the fact that my Sweetheart of a quarter of a century ago, has made this earth a heaven—much more so for me than I have made it for her. But, we are true to each other, we love each other, we have children of whom we may be justly proud so why shouldn't we be happy! and happiness is only heaven!

In Australia, Father made a three-day trip to the Blue Mountains, literally the only pleasure excursion of the trip that far. The Jenolan caves, famous for stalactites and stalagmites illuminated by electricity, were impressive. Father wrote: "Those subterranean passages with their groups of grotesque forms; their stalagmites and stalactites, their massive pillars and curiously shaped figures . . . present surprises and thrills at nearly every turn." (P. 155.) Although Father's stops in Australia were brief, he was impressed by the country and the people. The Perth missionaries who attended the conference in Adelaide had traveled sixteen hundred miles to do so.

Back in Sydney, Father received more word from home: "Delighted with photographs of Ray and the three babies. They are lovely. The sight of their sweet faces gave me a longing desire to fly over land and sea to join them in our little home." (P. 166.) On Sunday, 4 September, in Brisbane, "was surprised and very much delighted to be handed a letter from David L.! Received just in time to make me happy before sailing from Australia." (P. 173.)

Father and Brother Cannon pulled away from the wharf at Sydney, on 6 September 1921, their visits to the missions in the western hemisphere complete. The last words in the typescript of Father's journal are: "Now, I'm ready for home. Every hour but intensified my longing desire to see my loved ones. If it weren't for the Holy Land and David L., I should be tempted to take a boat to San Francisco." (P. 176.)

No holograph portions of his diary beyond that point are in my possession. His letters to Mother, a typescript of his journal, and Brother Cannon's typescript journal record their voyage to Java, then on to Singapore and India.

Father posted a letter en route to India to Mother, written aboard ship on 13 September 1921:

Sweetheart:

. . . I'm homesick.

While on the South Sea Islands, in New Zealand and in Australia, I was kept so busy with meetings, entertainments, conversations, and traveling, that time passed very quickly; but now that our mission is practically over, I want to get home.

We are on an elegantly furnished vessel, and thus far have had calm seas and delightful weather; but I have too much of a yearning to see you and the children to enjoy a long sea voyage under the most favorable conditions.

Of course, I realize that the sensible thing to do is to make the best of it, and to enjoy things as they come along; but the fact remains that I am surfeited with sightseeing and associating with strangers; and want to be home—home with the dearest, sweetest wife and the most darling kiddies in the world!

Brother Cannon's journal reports a tourist's interest in Java, where the only known member of the Church in the nation of thirty million was Frank W. Beecraft of Ogden, an official with the Krain Sugar Company and a former student of Father's. He placed himself and his automobile at their disposal, and they visited many sites of interest during their short stay.

In Singapore, Father and Brother Cannon discarded their travel-worn garb for four linen suits, ordered late in the afternoon from a Chinese tailor. Two were delivered the next morning at 6 A.M. with the other two arriving before evening. The bill for the four came to about $15. (Cannon Typescript, pp. 171–72.)

The itinerary included Calcutta, the Taj Mahal at Agra, and Delhi, a journey of 902 miles, and then they sailed from Bombay toward Aden and Port Said. Near Cairo, they briefly visited biblical sites, Memphis, and the Sphinx; and Father sent Mother this letter:

Egypt
Oct. 24, 1921

Dearest:

. . . We are now moving noiselessly and unquiveringly through the

Suez Canal. Trenches and piles of sand bags—grim reminders of the recent war are on our right. Just beyond them lying lazily in the sun amidst the sand, some of them with loads already on their backs, are about sixty camels. In the distance starting across the sandy waste are three camels and a man. Around a little mud hut in the foreground are some Mohammedan women, dressed in typical far east costumes.

Away off in the distance are Moses' Wells, still sheltered from the hot rays of the sun by palm and date trees, which a sailor just now told me "Moses planted." Pretty old trees, aren't they?

Yesterday, just as we entered the Gulf of Suez, we saw Mt. Sinai on our right. Truly from now on during the next four or five weeks, we shall be treading on historic ground. . . .

I still say of this tour—Wonderful! *Wonderful!* and still more wonderful!

When we were in the Orient, we would meet globe trotters who made us feel that our few thousand miles of travel were truly insignificant; but now we meet fewer and fewer who have visited more lands and people than we.

I feel that I'm not getting out of the trip all I should but one thing I'm sure of: it has saved me from a threatened physical break-down, for which I'm mighty grateful, indeed!

I sincerely hope and pray my gain has not proved to be your loss in this respect.

Love and kisses to the truest wife, the sweetest sweetheart, the dearest mother and to the choicest children in the world, from

Daddy

Riots in Jerusalem on 2 November 1921 over the Balfour Declaration, affirming that Palestine should be set apart for the Jews, brought out armed British soldiers. Recorded Brother Cannon:

"Mohammedans and Christians, united in their hatred of the Jews if on no other point, stoned these unfortunates in the streets, and naturally where their numbers warranted it, the Jews retaliated. At one place Brother McKay, in righteous wrath, ordered a number of Christians to desist in the assault upon some helpless Jewish women and children, and with such sternness that the offenders were convinced he would, if necessary, follow his orders with physical force." (Cannon Typescript, p. 196.)

Of the commercialism surrounding the traditional sites of Christ's life, Father recorded in his journal on 4 November 1921:

"I'm not *disappointed* but *grieved* — grieved to see the manger, the sacred cradle, profaned by the contentious spirit of the jarring, selfish creeds — grieved to see the spot desecrated by lavished wealth — grieved to learn of the feuds and fatal quarrels that have occurred upon the very spot where the Son of God was born — grieved to see the keys of the Holy Sepulchre kept by a follower of Mohammed because the professed Christians cannot trust one of their number with them! Grieved to witness these same so-called Christians uniting with Mohammedans in opposing the return of the Jews to the Holy Land!"

As a result of experiences like this one, Father and Brother Cannon found "a secluded spot under a fig tree" on the Mount of Olives, knelt and prayed:

"1. That the seed sown during our visits to the various mission fields on this tour would be blessed and multiplied many fold;

"2. That the Lord would accept our gratitude for the privilege of visiting the Holy Land at this time when the prophecies concerning it are about to be fulfilled — that we are witnesses to the beginning of the great movement that will eventually restore Palestine to the Jews.

"3. That the form of worship, the outward semblance of devotion without the true spirit of the Redeemer, which we have seen manifested at nearly every spot made sacred by the footsteps, teachings and prayers of the Redeemer, might be replaced by more appropriate memorials and the places themselves surrounded by keepers who are imbued with the spirit of tolerance and love and true Christian service.

"4. That the spirit of opposition and hatred which we witnessed yesterday by Moslems and so-called Christians in opposition to the return of the Jews to this land may be overcome. By the power of the Priesthood this antagonistic bitterness was rebuked that it should not prevail.

"5. That the members of the Church of Christ might more earnestly manifest in their daily lives the genuine fruits of the true Gospel of the Redeemer, and thus convert the world, who, seeing their good deeds will be led to glorify their Father in Heaven.

"6. That the Church and our Loved Ones may receive special protection and guidance.

"7. That we may be led by inspiration on our trip to the Armenian Mission." (3 Nov. 1921.)

This seventh point involved a special problem: how to find Joseph Wilford Booth, the last missionary to labor in Syria and the surrounding country. This faithful elder had been recalled on another mission to take money collected in the United States to the suffering and persecuted Armenian Saints. But he did not know where Father and Brother Cannon would be, and they did not know how to find him. A cable of inquiry to President Grant had simply brought the unhelpful news that Brother Booth was on his way.

They had planned to drive from Jerusalem through Samaria; but at the conclusion of the prayer, they both had a strong impression that they should go by train to Haifa on the Mediterranean coast. For the first time on the trip, Brother Cannon had forgotten to secure accommodations in a hotel; and while they were occupied in the Haifa train station in trying to find a hotel, "a man suddenly rushed up with an exclamation, 'Isn't this Brother McKay?'

"The inquirer was Brother Booth. Leaving Utah nearly six months later than the others and traveling in the opposite direction, he had met them exactly at the spot where it was absolutely necessary for them to meet in order properly to perform their work. Had they not met at Haifa, it is doubtful whether they would have done so at all, for Brother McKay's intention was to go to Damascus, while Brother Booth planned to proceed to Beirut. His passport entitled him to go to this point and no further." (Cannon Typescript, pp. 198–99.)

Father added in his diary: "We had no doubt but our coming together thus was the direct result of divine interposition!" (4 Nov. 1921.)

They drove eighty miles to Beirut and then on to Aleppo. The brethren needed to meet with the little group of Armenian Saints further on in Aintab and in a Turkish-dominated zone; but a general in the British army who was well acquainted with local conditions advised Father: "Unless you are prepared to leave your head behind, you should not go to Aintab." Father was determined to go and wrote a deliberately casual note to Mother on 8 November 1921:

My Beloved Sweetheart:

While waiting for the auto to call to take us to Aintab, I have concluded to drop you a note merely to state that I'm well, and about to the end of the special mission.

We have been advised not to go to Constantinople; indeed, we've been cautioned not to go to Aintab, but we'll venture the latter, and forego the former.

When we leave Syria, we shall begin our homeward journey in earnest, and, believe me, Sweetheart, intervening cities and noted places between me and home will hold very little attraction!

A few days with Lawrence, and then Home!

Brother Cannon continues the story:

"It is 80 miles from Aleppo to Aintab, and with no railroad connection. This trip, therefore, had to be made by auto. It was arranged to leave one afternoon, but the spirit of the Lord indicated that they should not go, though their baggage was already in the car when Brother McKay decided to postpone the trip. Next morning was different. All were eager for the journey, and, though their driver was manifestly nervous, he alone was thus affected. Other autos were on the road, and one noticed a disposition on the part of drivers to keep close together as a matter of mutual protection, but the trip was made without interruption. Many wrecked cars were seen whose occupants had been robbed and the cars burned.

" . . . The very day they passed over this road a company of people traveling with carriages and wagons was held up and robbed of everything worth carrying away, including sixty horses. No lives were reported lost, but these unfortunates were left, helpless, with vehicles but with no means of propelling them.

"One cannot conceive of more heart-rending stories than those to which the brethren listened, related by the Saints in Aintab. Having suffered for food and shelter, they clung to the visiting brethren as they would to angels from heaven. Not a person was present but had lost some relative at the hands of the merciless Turks. One mother, with tears streaming down her cheeks, told of having become separated from her husband and three-year-old daughter in one of the raids made upon them. Later she learned of her husband's violent death, but had never heard a word from her babe and did not know whether it was alive or dead.

"The money being distributed by these missionaries was raised for this purpose by a special fast day held in all stakes of the Church. It is not too much to say that every man or woman or child in Utah who fasted on that occasion would be willing to abstain from food for a week, or longer if necessary, could they have seen the good which their money was doing. Before Brother McKay left Syria, arrangements had been made to transplant all our members from the danger zone to Aleppo or Beirut, where their lives at least would be safe, and where opportunities could be created for them to earn a livelihood." (Pp. 201–2.)

When Father returned to Aleppo after this visit, he wrote Mother a much more explicit account on 9 November 1921:

"Inasmuch as all cause for worry or anxiety on your part will have passed several weeks before you receive word that we've been in danger, I will tell you now that we have visited our Armenian Church members in the face of advice of U.S. Consuls not to try to go to Aintab.

"The U.S. Consul at Cairo told us not to attempt to enter Syria, and a soldier there, who seemed to know what he was talking about, said 'on no purpose risk going to Aintab,' as it means an eighty mile drive by cab or auto through a country infested with Brigands. It was near Aintab on this same road that two Americans and their chauffeur were killed, about 18 months ago, and their auto burned.

"Well, I have felt all along that if any of our missions needed visiting and encouragement, it was this same Armenian Mission; so we concluded to go as far as we could in safety, and then trust to inspiration as to what would be best.

"[At Beirut], the U.S. Consuls there after examining our passports informed us that we had come as far as our passports would carry us under U.S. protection. . . . The more I learned of our people's condition, the more I felt the necessity of our seeing them. . . . After about three hours drive, we passed the skeleton of a burned auto, and knew we were in the neighborhood of the Turkish brigands. And an ideal neighborhood it is for them! Rocks, hills, gullies, and other secluded spots so suitable for their concealment!

" . . . It was three o'clock before any of our Saints knew of our presence; but at 5:15, there were seventy people assembled in the room chosen in which to hold a meeting, only half of whom are members of the Church.

"Their joy at meeting Bro. Booth knew no bounds! I never felt so richly repaid for an effort in my life. The appreciation of these sorely stricken people was beyond expression. One sister, as she grasped my hand and held it in both hers, said, 'We've been in hell seven years, but now we are in heaven!'

"We had arrived on the very day that the French officials had given official notice of their intention to evacuate Aintab within thirty days.

"Do you know what that means to these Armenians who gathered around us, and to the other five thousand Armenians in the city? Abandonment of their homes or massacre! The Armenians fought with the French against the Moslems, and the latter have threatened revenge as soon as the French withdraw!

"We held a two hours meeting, and for three hours more listened, through an interpreter, to their heart-rending stories, which I will tell you when I come home.

"With Brother Booth, we have planned to get all our members out of Aintab, perhaps within ten days.

"How fortunate Bro. Booth has that six thousand dollars back of him which the Church contributed last March! Wonderful Church! Wonderful people!! The Lord's Church! The Lord's People!!

"Have you noticed that I have twice used the phrase 'when I come home'!

"Well, if we can get a boat from Port Said on the 16th inst., I think I shall be *home — home December 14th, 1921!* (You will understand what this means to me when I tell you that writing the above line has brought the tears.)"

Father and Brother Cannon left Haifa on 16 November, traveling via Port Said and Naples to Rome. Father had written, telling me that they would be on the 8:15 P.M. train from Milan on Saturday, 26 November 1921. I'm afraid all of my missionary plans went by the board, and I could think of nothing but seeing him again. President Ballif came down to Lausanne from Basel on the day Father was expected.

I was at the station well in advance of the train's scheduled arrival and was much taken aback when station personnel informed me that it was not scheduled to arrive until 4:50 Sunday morning. Dejected, I walked up to President Ballif's hotel, informed him of the news, and then had a very peculiar feeling. "I'll go back down and see whether that schedule has been changed," I told him. I went back down the hill.

The train had, in fact, come in. Father's journal records: "Just as we stepped out onto the sidewalk and began to wonder where we should go, I saw a straight, dignified young man walking down the hill about a block away, whom I recognized as my boy! In a moment or two we were in each other's embrace!"

Brother Cannon, the most sympathetic of onlookers, wrote: "If no other reward were ever to come to [Lawrence] for his devotion to this work, he would be repaid in the pride and love written on his father's face as they sprang into each others arms." (P. 209.)

We took a cab up to the hotel and, with very different feelings, I knocked on President Ballif's door and announced, "We have some visitors here."

I was then the only missionary in Lausanne, but we had rented a large hall and had a group of about a hundred, including our fifteen or so members. I translated Father's addresses, anxious to do the very best I could. President Ballif and I then accompanied Father and Brother Cannon to mission headquarters in Basel, where we held another meeting with members, to Frankfurt am Main, where I enjoyed spending some time with Howard Stoddard, one of the missionaries in our original party, and then to Liège for the last conference via Cologne, Brussels, and Waterloo. Near Waterloo, at Herstal, we visited the Fabrique Nationale, which manufactured Browning firearms. Father's explanation that he was a fellow townsman of John M. Browning, inventor of the Browning automatic rifle, secured our party a deluxe tour.

After the conference in Liège (Father noted, "David L. bore his share of the speaking commendably"), I was allowed to accompany them to Paris with President Ballif. Attending the opera and visiting the Louvre with my father were prized experiences. When we parted on 7 December 1921, he wrote in his journal: "It was almost as hard to say good-bye to Lawrence at the station as it was one year ago when he left home for his mission. Our most memorable ten days together have served only to make him dearer to me than ever, and I would keep him near me always."

When I returned to Lausanne, a letter from Mother was waiting for me:

Ogden, Dec. 7, 1921

My Darling Boy:

... I can hardly wait until Papa gets home to tell me of his visit with you. I know that you both enjoyed it and I know you must have

David Lawrence
McKay,
missionary in
Switzerland

felt pretty lonesome when he had gone. But the visit will strengthen you & do you good in many ways.

We are all so happy to know that Daddy will be home for Xmas.

I also received a letter from Father, written 10 December 1921 from mission headquarters in Liverpool:

My beloved son David: —

. . . Thursday I spent a most delightful day visiting a few old friends [in Glasgow] who [were] in the Church when I was a young missionary distributing tracts from door to door. I called on our old housekeeper, a Mrs. Noble, now 72 years of age. When she saw me she broke down and cried saying, "When they telt me ye were comin', I kent ye'd call and see me," but when she looked at my gray hair she said, "Ah, but ye're nae my bonny laddie, you've changed." However she accepted my word that I was still her laddie and we lived again the experience of twenty three years ago. . . .

We have spent our last night on foreign soil and in a few hours we will be on the good ship "Cedric," sailing for the land of the Stars and Stripes. While I look forward with true delight to meeting loved ones and friends at home, be assured my dear Boy that I am leaving with you a heart full of true love and a Father's blessing. What happiness your Mother will have when I tell her all about our happy week together. I shall ever treasure that week as one of the most blessed experiences of my life.

I must confess that my thoughts followed Father across the Atlantic, then across the American continent, and finally home. He arrived on Christmas Eve. And what a Christmas that must have been!

In President Cannon's summary, he notes: "During this trip which required 366 days, the missionaries traveled on 24 ocean going vessels. They spent the equal of 153 days on the water, traveled a total of 61,646 miles not counting trips by auto, street cars, tugs, ferry boats, horseback, camels, etc. Of the miles traveled, 23,777 were by land and 37,869 were by water." (P. 213.) I suppose it would be impossible to derive even a rough estimate of the number of people they addressed, administered to, gave blessings to, and who, in turn, ministered to their needs. I am not the appropriate person to comment on how this year of travel to the far-flung missions of the Church affected the later President of the Church. But in 1952, when Father was president of the Church, my wife and I accompanied him and Mother on a tour of the European missions that gave me some sense of what the presence of a prophet among his people could mean.

Chapter 8

EUROPEAN MISSION PRESIDENT 1922-1924

• • • • • • • • • • • • • •

Getting letters from home about that Christmas of reunion between Father and the rest of the family was far different from being there, but they gave solid images to supplement my longing imagination. Lou Jean wrote on New Year's Day:

"This last week has been simply wonderful! Having Papa home has made this Christmas almost the happiest we have spent. If you had been home it would have been the happiest. I have never in all my life seen or heard anyone so interesting as Papa. For eight days now, we have been traveling in strange countries, seeing naughty and good people, seeing their queer habits and costumes, hearing their jib-beyabbering (Bobby beats them there, however) and best of all receiving the gifts or souvenirs from the many countries. Did Papa show them all to you? Aren't they gorgeous, exquisite, beautiful, 'chic,' lovely, queer, etc?...

"Papa is a slave to Bobby, already."

Mother wrote two weeks later:

15 Jan. 1922

My Darling Boy:

... We are all so happy to have Papa home with us again. All the folks, or nearly all, were at the station to meet him but they would not come to the house because they thought the main family should be alone for awhile. On the way up from the station Papa talked of you with tears in his eyes & love in his voice.... I told him that was the part of his trip I envied most, to see our beloved first-born again.

Papa has been dined and entertained continuously by his relations and friends.... He has given some wonderful talks & the halls are so crowded that the aisles cannot be used for the passing of the sacrament.

The first letter I received from Father after his arrival was written 4 February 1922:

My beloved Son, David:

... Coming home has been even more glorious than I anticipated, so you may know that we have had a most glorious reunion. Your sweet Mama has done remarkably well in attending to all the home duties and financial affairs during my twelve months' absence. Llewelyn, too, has assumed responsibility, and carried his end of it most manfully. Lou Jean has blossomed into a beautiful young woman, with talents and accomplishments that place her easily among the first in her class. Emma Ray [sic] is still the same sweet sunbeam, Neddie Boy, the same loving, lovable, sensitive Daddy's boy; and Bobbie, *all* and even more than Mama and Lou Jean have said he is! He is truly a treasure!

I haven't been up to the farm yet, so cannot tell you how the horses and cows are faring; but Thomas E. says that everything up there is alright.

Llewelyn was elected student-body president "2 to 1" in the spring. Father received an honorary master of arts degree from Brigham Young University, the first of many honorary degrees, and had two vacation trips — one through southern Utah and another to Yellowstone Park.

President Grant appointed John A. Widtsoe Church Commissioner of Education, but Father retained ties to another educational institution by taking up his duties on the board of regents of the University of Utah, an appointment he had received just before being called on his mission.

My only letter from Father during the summer was written 21 July 1922:

Llewelyn and his parents, David O. and Emma Ray Riggs McKay, on an outing at Fish Lake, Utah, about 1922

My beloved son, David L.:

...Time flies so swiftly that I can scarcely realize that several months have passed since I last wrote to you; but such is the case. Please forgive me, and show your true Christian spirit by returning "good for evil"—by writing two letters for every one I have *intended* to write to you.

I left Huntsville at 4:30 A.M. this morning in order to get to my office here in Salt Lake at 7:30 A.M. to attempt to clear my desk of accumulated correspondence. I am now ready for my stenographer and am seizing the interim to assure you that you are not forgotten....I think you and your brothers and sisters make an ideal family. With such children and the sweetest wife and mother to guide you, I feel proudly happy and thankful. I am sure you will all do your best, as I desire to do, to bear our name in honor.

Church duties are keeping me busy as usual. There is so much to do, so many appointments to fill that one wishes one might turn night into day and not get weary. But after all, such a wish is foolish; for rest and relaxation are just as essential to success as work. In fact, I have just about reached the conclusion that one might accomplish twice as much in one's work if one will take twice as much rest. Recuperative power and reserve force are vital essentials.

I congratulate you upon your appointment as conference president and pray that the Lord will sustain you, and guide you constantly by the light of His Holy Spirit. Your grandpa used to say, "Keep a high head, but a humble heart."

Llewelyn's desire to graduate from Weber may keep us in Ogden another year, so our plans to move to Salt Lake are no further matured than when I met you in Switzerland. . . .

With a heart full of love and blessings, I remain,

> Affectionately,
> Daddy

In my birthday letter in September, Father sent this exciting news: *"Your Mama, the kiddies, and I shall leave for Liverpool about Oct. 15th! . . . What do you think?"*

As a matter of fact, I had already heard the news. Fred J. Pingree, a missionary in London and a former classmate at Weber, had telephoned to say with studied casualness, "You've probably heard that your father's been called to the presidency of the European Mission?" To say I was very pleased and excited is quite an understatement!

The task included presiding directly over the British mission as well as supervising the Swiss-German, the Austrian, the French, the Swedish, the Norwegian, the Danish, and the Netherlands missions. Father's little diary for this period does not mention receiving this appointment or how he felt about it, although he recorded, on 26 September, "Quarterly Conf. of Twelve. Bro. Widtsoe prophesied that Bro. McKay will return and declare in this room that his mission was a joy to him." I also never heard or read any reaction from Mother that was not totally cheerful and positive while this experience was happening; but in an undated notebook in which she made pencil drafts of personal letters, she confided to a Sister Sorensen, whose husband was a mission president in Brazil, that the European mission had been "a great experience. The hardest I ever went through but very interesting." (10 Nov. 1959.)

On 8 November 1922, my parents, brothers, and sisters were bidding goodbye to friends and relatives at the Ogden train depot. "Almost a benediction," recorded my father. Llewelyn, called on a mission to Germany, accompanied the family. They sailed from Montreal on 17 November, arriving at Liverpool on 25 November and settling into Durham House, 295 Edge Lane. Father recorded contentedly that day: "Arrived in Liverpool docks—just 25 yrs., 3 mo. after my landing in the same place on my first mission. How different my circumstances and feelings to-day from then! The welcome received to-day and greetings awaiting us made this almost a homecoming."

Father wrote proudly of his brother: "11 Dec. 1922. Letter from Thos. E. giving conditions at home. He has attended to my personal affairs better than I could have attended to them myself. He is a true loyal brother and a noble man! I read today in a scurrilous sheet an attack on 'Mormonism' in which our traducer says, 'There is not a Christian among the Mormons.' If Thos. E. is not the finest Christian gentleman in the world, there is none to be found."

Father's journal on New Year's Day records: "I have made no *new* resolutions, but sincerely desire to make 1923 a successful part of my life. I am facing some difficult problems but hope to solve them, if the Lord will help me."

Some of those difficulties were family problems. Mother wrote: "We went over to Liverpool College to register [the children] but when they found that we are 'Mormons' they told us that they had reserved the right to accept or reject whom they choose & they would not receive us. Lou Jean's face was a study. Papa thinks they are more bigoted and ignorant than they were twenty-five years ago when he was on his first mission." (Undated; first page missing.)

Again Mother wrote: "Lou Jean . . . was refused both at the Church of England School and at the Catholic school. The head mistress of this last-named school held our hands for fifteen minutes and told us how she liked us *but* 'although we accept people of other denominations, this is such an exceptional case, isn't it? People just shudder when a Mormon is mentioned and we must consider our people.' " (21 Jan. 1923.)

The McKay family in Liverpool, England. Children, left to right: Emma Rae, Robert, Lou Jean, and Edward

Eventually Lou Jean was registered at Queen Mary's public school and the younger children at another. Mother wrote proudly:

"She had been dreading a bit letting them know who she is but she threw the bomb yesterday in a grand way. In Scripture class, the teacher was describing a man who was claiming to be the Christ. Said he had a long beard. 'Oh, like a Mormon you know.' One of the girls said, 'Oh, and does he have a lot of wives like the Mormons?' Lou Jean immediately arose and said, 'You are mistaken in thinking that the Mormons have a lot of wives.' 'And how should you know?' asked the teacher. 'For the simple reason that I am a Mormon myself,' said this brave little girl. Then the grand confusion. They all talked at once asking a hundred questions, among them being, 'Does your father wear a big black hat?' One girl said, 'Isn't this awful!' and the teacher rapped upon the desk & said, 'I do not know why it should be awful. We should not say such things about people that we do not know anything about.' After class, Jean says she was never so popular in her life before."

In Cardiff, South Wales, Father found "opposition to church very intense. Impossible to rent suitable hall for worship. Friends and sympathizers seemingly hunting cover." (3 Jan. 1923.) His journal shows a keen awareness of the administrative and public relations battles he was fighting:

"Fri., Jan. 5, 1923. Ray and I called on U.S. Consul, Mr. Washington. Cordially received. Pleasant consultation. He said that during his many years of service here, 'No member of your association has ever given the Dep't. one moment's trouble or concern.' He wished he 'could say the same of other organizations.' . . .

"Sun., Jan. 7, 1923. Liverpool. S.S. Service at 11 A.M.. I conducted theol. class. Fast service at 1 P.M. Gen'l meeting at 6:30 P.M. Few attended Fast meeting, but the hall was fairly filled at night. Prejudice is very intense against the Mormons. People really believe us unchaste and lawless."

Father scheduled conferences virtually every weekend. In January, he was in Holland. In February, he and Mother went through Paris, Zurich, Basel, Dresden, and Berlin, holding meetings as they went. In March, they held meetings in Wales and Grimsby, near Hull. Just before Christmas 1923, he records concluding a five-session conference in London—"the last of fourteen successful conferences in as many weeks." One reason he put so much energy into maintaining contact with each district was for the missionaries' sake. Some had been slothful and others indiscreet. For Father, it was doubly difficult to deal with elders who forgot the purpose of their mission, especially when their indiscretions brought the Church into disrepute.

He felt a desperate need for more missionaries and, to my delight, wrote in early March asking if I could edit the *Millennial Star* at the close of my mission. I responded immediately on 13 March 1923: "There is nothing that would please me more than to help you there in the office, to be with you and to do that kind of work, and I shall do all in my power to be worthy of the confidence you place in me."

I arrived in late March and worked with Father for the next five months, until the end of September. Durham House combined both living and working quarters. On the first floor were most of the offices

President and Sister McKay with missionaries in England. Future Church president Elder Ezra Taft Benson is seated at right

and the meeting hall for the branch. Family quarters were on the second floor. On the third floor were the offices of the *Millennial Star* and those of our printer, James Foggo. (Two-year-old Bobbie discovered that he could turn the key on Mr. Foggo's door and delighted in locking him in.)

The conference presidents sent in their reports during the week, which took up about one-third of the issue. The other two-thirds consisted of articles from contributors, speeches at general conferences by General Authorities, and occasional reprints from various sources, including the *Christian Century*. Father wrote an editorial for each issue.

It was a great privilege to be with my father daily and see him administering the affairs of a complex unit of the Church. When I first arrived in Liverpool, a large chiffonier drawer was full of articles from different newspapers supplied by our clipping service, all of them fantastic stories about the Mormon elders bewitching young girls into conversion and then sending them to Utah to lead debased lives. I recall one astounding tale based on the affidavit of a man who swore that he rowed a boat from San Francisco to Salt Lake City but could not get inside the wall around Salt Lake City. Another told about the chopping block behind the Beehive House that Brigham Young used to get rid of his unwanted wives. The elders had been trying to fight back by writing articles of rebuttal and submitting them, but they were not published.

Conditions must have reminded Father very much of his own mission experiences. When he realized that even forums for presenting the Mormon perspective were limited, he called on Lord Beaverbrook, owner of a chain of newspapers, and appealed to his British sense of fair play. It was a cordial visit, there was a decided change in the atmosphere, and the dialogue continued on a more even footing, with the worst excesses stopped.

During those months I spent at Durham House, Father taught me one of the most important lessons of my life, which was to teach by praise rather than by criticism. Our local branch president was a faithful soul, but he had an overpowering weakness—he liked to talk. Oh, how he liked to talk! Sometimes, we complained, he spent more time introducing the speaker at sacrament meeting than the speaker had time to speak. One weekend, Father visited a conference on the Continent. When he returned, he asked, "How did things go at sacrament meeting?"

"Just fine," I reported with relief. "The branch president stood up, introduced the speaker in a few words, and sat down."

"Did you compliment him?" queried Father.

"No."

"Oh, if you had complimented him, you would have found the best way of criticizing him. He would have felt happy at having done the right thing and, at the same time, would have realized that he had been doing something wrong." It was a memorable lesson.

Father's brief but consistently kept diary contains little introspection, but I find those passages most valuable:

"20 June 1923. 'Flanders Front.' A day at Ypres and vicinity. Cities entirely rebuilt and yet even the remains of the war are ghastly. Oh the horror of it! How useless! How diabolical! . . .

"23 June 1923. Sweetheart's Birthday—forty-six years today and she is sweeter and dearer far even than when we married. She's a jewel! . . .

"26 June 1923. When I reported to our Consul, Mr. Washington, that I had informed the Royal Swedish Consul that I thought Mr. Washington would give me a letter of introduction, he interrupted me by saying, 'Now, Mr. McKay, if ever you say that again, I shall be very

President and Sister McKay with missionaries of the Swiss-German Mission, Hannover Conference, 6 July 1923

much offended. You should not say you *think* Mr. Washington will give you a letter, you should say you *know* he will be delighted to.' . . .

"6 July 1923. At Hannover . . . Elders went in body to station and gave us a memorable farewell. . . . To Frankfurt. At 11 P.M. welcomed by Llewelyn and 12 other missionaries. . . .

"9 July 1923. [Cologne] After a few hours rest, Mama, Llewelyn and I spent the day shopping. Didn't enjoy shopping but was delighted to be with Ray and our son. . . .

"10 July 1923. . . . Tears came freely as we left our boy in the station."

In July, Father accompanied his two fellow apostles, Senator Reed Smoot and John A. Widtsoe, to Rotterdam, Copenhagen, Göteborg, and Stockholm, where they met with several United States and Swedish officials in an effort to resolve the opposition to granting visas to elders. Because of scheduling problems, Father found himself with a free day, which he spent alone at Saltjobaden, "a very delightful swimming and boating resort." Then this most sociable of men added candidly, "The most lonesome day I've spent in the mission field!" The journey continued through Kristiania, then back to Stockholm, Rotterdam, London, and Liverpool. In each city, Senator Smoot's political credentials gave them entry to government officials with whom they could then profitably discuss matters pertaining to the Church.

In August, Father combined a conference in Lausanne with a stop-over in Paris, Mother and I accompanying him, where in one herculean day we visited the tomb of Napoleon, the Arc de Triomphe, and the Louvre. (17 Aug. 1923.) This mission tour covered much of the same ground Father had earlier gone over with the two visiting apostles: Berlin, Kristiania, Bergen, Oslo, Copenhagen, Chemnitz, Leipzig, Frankfurt am Main, Brussels. Finally home again, on 13 September, Father spent the next day "wading through accumulated correspondence" and wishing for more elders: "102 released and only 65 appointed to fill their places!"

Father then gave me a choice of going home to start school at the University of Utah or going to school in Paris, Geneva, or even Lausanne. Paris was my first choice and, on 29 September 1923, seventeen-year-old Lou Jean and I left together. Father's diary records: "Pretty sad parting especially between Mama & Lou Jean and Lou Jean and Bobby!" Lou Jean studied piano with a private teacher and was also enrolled in French language and literature classes at the Alliance Française, while I took psychology classes at the Sorbonne. In Paris, we found ourselves meeting trains to give bewildered tourists and missionaries directions, hosting departing missionaries, providing information and references for friends who were thinking about coming to Europe, and occasionally running errands for my parents as they requested. Letters from my family and about my family bring back wonderful memories of those times.

My first note from Father, enclosing some money "for incidentals" and some instructions about my passport, ended warmly, "We love you dearly. Our hearts are with our six *Treasures*, especially with my Rosebud, and my two fine sons who are away from us. God bless you always! Lovingly, Daddy." (29 Sept. 1923.)

The ugly French-German feelings that later resulted in World War II were already evident. Traveling between Stuttgart and Berlin, Father recorded: "Hatred of French intense. A German school teacher expressed this by saying, 'In about ten years when Germany goes to war with France, I will enlist and fight to kill every man, woman, and child that speaks the French language.' " (23 Aug. 1923.) When a new mission president was chosen to replace President Ballif in the Swiss-German mission, Llewelyn wrote me candidly from his mission in Germany, "You say it is too bad he is a German. I thank my stars that he isn't a Frenchman. The Saints here would only remember an eye for an eye and would never bother about salvation for the dead." (13 Mar. 1923.) That spring he also reported "one of the biggest [Socialist Democrat] demonstrations I've ever seen. . . . The streets were absolutely packed with marching men waving red flags, singing and yelling. . . . The large square by the Opera House . . . looked like a mass of sardines. People estimated that over a hundred thousand were assembled, besides the people standing in the many crowded streets leading to the square." (2 May 1923.)

In the fall, conditions were no better, though he described them with his usual verve: "Last week . . . the feelings were made mostly with knives, bricks, bullets and fists among the Germans. . . . It was hard to dodge a mob around a corner because one bumped directly into another on every turn. It wasn't so bad here in Frankfurt as not more than four or five (at an average) got killed a day but in several of the other cities it was quite serious. . . . It isn't dangerous for foreigners unless we get in the mob and as we make it a habit to be where the mobs aren't, we're alright. . . .

"One can't blame the workers for striking though, because the mark drops continually, the wages they earn amount to nothing and 2/3 of them have only 2 or 3 days work or none at all. . . . Yesterday morning I priced some coal and found it to be 42,000,000,000 marks for 100 pounds. In the afternoon, I went back to buy it and it cost 180,000,000,000." (3 Nov. 1923.)

Mother wrote on 18 October urging us in the first paragraph to be sure we ate nutritious meals and reassuring me in the third paragraph: "Papa and I have the greatest confidence in that judgment of yours and know that everything you do is for the very best. We feel just as content with Lou Jean in your hands as though she were in our own." Her letter to Lou Jean, enclosed in the same envelope, was a tender one:

"Your sweet loving letter to your Daddy & Mother made us both cry. Then we read Lawrence's letter & cried some more, then Llewelyn's where he said not to send him so much money as we have been sending because you two would need it more (and we have hardly been sending him anything) and we surely had the 'weeps.' You children are all so appreciative and it all goes to our tender hearts and makes us 'feel good all over.' "

Father's letter 3 December 1923 gave this tender vignette:

"Wee Bobbie has been ill during the last few days, so Mama did not accompany me to Birmingham. He seems better today. He fell asleep in my arms about an hour ago, and when I started to lay him on the bed, he awoke and said, 'Please lie down with me.' 'Alright,' I answered, 'as soon as I finish opening my letters.' He awoke just now, and the first thing he said was, 'You didn't come to lie down with me!' My explanation that he was asleep when I finished my letters hardly convinced him that I hadn't broken my promise. O these baby minds! They understand more than we think!"

Lou Jean and I were more than ready to join the party at Durham House for our family Christmas. Llewelyn "sent a cable that he could not come. Branch duties detained him at Frankfurt. We were disappointed but proud of him for faithfulness to duty," Father recorded in his journal on 25 December 1923.

May Booth, the wife of Wilford Booth, had reached London just before Christmas to join her husband. Father and Mother decided to escort her to Syria, Lou Jean agreed to stay out of school "for six weeks to take care of the children," and I reluctantly returned to Paris alone. "It seemed harder for him to leave us this time than when he left for his mission," Father noted in his journal on 4 January 1924.

Father, Mother, and Sister Booth traveled by train to Marseilles, then sailed to Beirut via Alexandria, and then went on to Aleppo. "Though no word had been sent of our coming, there were at the station at 3:50 P.M., a crowd of eager members of the Branch," Father recorded on 19 January 1924. The conference and testimony meeting next day was held in Turkish, French, English, Armenian, and Arabic. The farewell was an emotional one with Mother and the younger women sobbing their good-byes.

At the end of February, Father took Lou Jean to Paris on his way to conference in Liège where eleven converts were baptized in the Meuse. "Although there was a flurry of snow, and the weather [was] bitterly cold, every one of the eleven applicants entered the water without a murmur, an elderly woman included. It was a beautiful ceremony," Father wrote on 24 February 1924.

From Liège, Father continued to Konigsberg, Stettin, Berlin, Dresden, and Frankfurt. Llewelyn accompanied Father for part of this journey, and Father wrote on 11 March 1924: "We have had a most enjoyable trip to-gether. He is a fine boy, and will succeed, if he remain as clean and energetic as he is to-day."

On 14 March 1924 in Basel, Father summarized: "From Mar. 1 to 12, I travelled 2000 miles, held 15 meetings, each ranging in length from 2 to 10 hours, met 228 Elders in special, inspirational meetings, and addressed in the aggregate over 7,000 people not including Elders' meetings, spent 64 hours in meeting and 68 hours on trains."

Father's diary until early April is a blank. He had caught a cold in Lausanne; and his next entry eighteen days later shows him ill, either still or again, this time seriously enough with "a cold" and "lumbago" to spend a day in bed at Mother's insistence. Father was mortified, during this period, to have one of his elders "jailed and fined" for some unspecified indiscretion.

Father's journal becomes sporadic after this point, but from his conference notebook, it is possible to reconstruct the weekly conference schedule that he again imposed upon himself between March and June: Birmingham, London, Bradford, Rotterdam, Hull, Birmingham again, Dublin, Sheffield, Leeds, Newcastle, and Glasgow, Norway, Paris, and Switzerland. (In Glasgow, on 8 June 1924, he recorded, with obvious relish, a homely saying: "Ye micht as weel try to have a coo climb up a tree backwards as tae try tae get into heaven withoot love," 8 June 1924). He and Mother were gone five and a half weeks this time and, after only a week at home, set off again. Father was still writing a weekly editorial for the *Star* and "wading" through correspondence every day he was in the office. His appreciation for the members and missionaries and his zest for travel seem to have remained undiminished despite this grueling schedule.

Lou Jean and I cherished a little note written on 3 June 1924:

I am just in the mood to write you a long letter; but Mr. Foggo is waiting for an Editorial. . . .

Ned just came from school. Bobbie met him at the front door, and, with face beaming said, "O Ned, guess what we have upstairs." Ned bounded up, and later reported to Mother as follows: "I hurried upstairs expecting to have a baby sister or something good to eat, and found only an old rope!"

Lovingly,
Daddy

The first week in September, Father's journal notes: "The American mail contained a letter from the First Pres. announcing my release to take effect about two months hence. Elder James E. Talmage has been appointed to succeed me as pres. of the European Mission. My trip around the world visiting foreign missions counted in my three years mission, so the letter states."

Father may have hoped to stay longer to see the fruits of reorganization, a reinfusion of dedicated spirit, and more vigorous efforts to combat public prejudice; but characteristically, he made every remaining day count. He had already scheduled three months' worth of conferences from 7 September to 23 December 1924, and kept them up to the very eve of his departure: Manchester, Norwich, Liverpool, Sheffield, Ulster, London, and Liverpool. On 5 December, the family sailed for home.

Between these dates, he had squeezed out time to write a year's outline for the course of study for the European Mission MIAs (24 Sept. 1924), escorted Emma Rae to the birthday party of a friend, entertained several American guests at Durham House, listened to a concert by renowned pianist-composer Sergei Rachmaninoff, shopped for linens and china, traveled to Holland to administer to Elder Zappey, "who has become broken in health thru overwork for the Church," dedicated the Amsterdam meeting hall, made one last visit to Llewelyn in Berlin, spent a day shopping in Paris with Mother and Lou Jean ("a pretty tedious, tiresome job for a man!" he grumbled privately to his journal), attended two operas and two plays, continued writing his weekly editorials, and fulfilled a promise to a Maori woman to find and dedicate her husband's grave in France where he had died during World War I.

A partial draft of an undated farewell letter to the missionaries at Durham House has survived the ocean voyage:

Beloved Associates:

We are now in mid-ocean—about half way across these angry, old waves. We've pitched, we've tossed, we've rolled, we've quivered, we've walked, we've sat, we've strained, we've shivered. . . .

Bobbie was the first to proclaim the fact that he was sick. He accepted the condition as a distinct achievement *at first:* "Ned!" I heard him call: "Are you sick yet? I am. . . ."

Ned . . . came into the room where Mama and I were quietly, O so quietly, lying in our respective berths, and said, "Daddy, are we in the ocean?"

"Yes, Ned, we certainly are."

"O, that's too bad," he whined. "I wanted it to be rougher than this!" . . .

All join in sending best wishes to you and to all associated with dear old Durham House.

Father records on 21 December, four days before Christmas: "Arrived home. Weather cold but welcome at station warm and heartfelt."

On 12 January 1925, he met with the Quorum of the Twelve Apostles and suggested "that Swiss and German mission be divided. (2) that foreign missions be visited by General Authorities each at least once a year. (3) That a pres. of British Mission be appointed independent of European Mission presidency." All of these suggestions were later adopted.

Chapter 9

PREPARATION FOR THE FIRST PRESIDENCY 1925-1934

* * * * * * * * * * * * *

Father marked his fifty-second birthday in 1925. He was the sixth senior apostle, experienced and tempered in Church administration and acquainted with the affairs of the Church both nationally and internationally. The First Presidency consisted of Heber J. Grant and his counselors, Anthony W. Ivins and Charles W. Nibley. Preceding Father in the Quorum of the Twelve Apostles were Rudger Clawson, Reed Smoot, George Albert Smith, George F. Richards, and Father's beloved "Jonathan," Orson F. Whitney. The other six were Joseph Fielding Smith, James E. Talmage, Stephen L Richards, Richard R. Lyman, Melvin J. Ballard, and John A. Widtsoe, then the junior apostle. Hyrum G. Smith was presiding patriarch. The Seven Presidents of the Seventy were B. H. Roberts, J. Golden Kimball, Rulon S. Wells, Joseph W. McMurrin, Charles H. Hart, Levi Edgar Young, and Rey L. Pratt. The Presiding Bishop was Sylvester Q. Cannon and his counselors were David A. Smith and John Wells.

I turned twenty-four in 1925, Llewelyn, still on his mission, was twenty-one that summer, Lou Jean nineteen, Emma Rae was eleven going on twelve, Ned turned ten, and Bobbie was five. Thus, although three of us were fairly well launched, Mother still had a family of three young children to tend.

Father was even more in demand as a speaker than before, especially for funerals, baccalaureate services, and conferences of young people. He also honored as many requests as he could that he perform

Elder David O.
McKay, about
1925

temple sealings for young couples. His stake conference schedule remained much the same during the next few years. He averaged three weekends out of four away from home with a longer absence, usually two weeks or more, about three times a year. Mother did not accompany him on any of these longer trips; but every two or three months, especially as the decade advanced, she went with him on a conference assignment that was within a day's drive.

One of Father's longer trips that year occurred in September when he visited the Eastern States Mission, then presided over by B. H. Roberts. He wrote Mother on 3 September 1925:

My Darling Ray:

. . . I have missed you every moment of the four nights and four days that I have been away from you. So many things recalled my association with you and the children on a similar trip nearly three years ago. . . . Even William M's [his brother's] welcome and courtesy could not keep me from *wishingly* and *longingly* associating everything I saw with our last two visits to that city. . . . Niagara Falls had little or no interest, except at every point—the American Falls, the Suspension Bridge, the rapids below the bridge, the walk on the Canadian side, the Horseshoe Falls—even the waiting room where you left your purse for five minutes—recalled a happy visit with you and our darlings.

I told you once before that either you must stay home altogether or you must accompany me on all my trips. This trip has only added confirmation to that *necessity.* Well, I am glad that I do miss you; for wouldn't it be miserable to be married to one from whom it would be a relief to get away! The whole point of this is that you and I must scheme some way to take these long trips together.

In the fall of 1926, he was sent to tour the Southern States Mission, a trip that lasted from 17 November until just before Christmas. The itinerary, via Chicago, included conferences in Louisville, Cincinnati, Richmond, Durham, Raleigh, and Atlanta, where he celebrated Thanksgiving at the mission home and wrote Mother:

6 Dec. 1926

My Darling:

Saturday morning we arrived in Atlanta. . . . I was met by your telegram, conveying the disappointing news that you will not meet me this week. No other word nor letter from home, although there are three girls and four boys, there, each of whom ought to send at least one little random thought to their husband and daddy who thinks of them so many times every day of his life. So I felt. So I thought; and so I was thinking when one of the sisters in the office handed me your sweet letter of the 27th ult. It dissipated all clouds, and let sunshine fill my heart. It was full of good news, and radiated the love that makes you my cherished sweetheart. . . .

I must thank you for putting "Lorna Doone" in my satchel. In the absence of my own true darling, Lorna was an interesting, sweet companion. In fact, when the author praised Lorna, I just substituted *Ray* for *Lorna,* and saw portrayed the beauty and virtues of my own true love, of *Ray,* "of my lifelong darling, of my more and more loved wife. Year by year her beauty grows with the growth of goodness, kindness, and true happiness—above all with *loving.*"

Of note in 1927 was Father's visit to the Alberta Stake in August. He attended stake conference and then visited the temple, scheduled for dedication later that month by President Grant. Father had laid the cornerstone in 1915 and was deeply stirred by the beauty of the building. "The temple is magnificent!" he wrote hastily in his conference notebook. "Spirit of peace—harmony—spirituality." After conference, Father much enjoyed the opportunity to spend a few days at beautiful Bertha Lake—fishing, boating, and riding—before conducting another conference in Taylor Stake, and a third in Lethbridge; but on the weekend of the temple dedication, he was almost three thousand miles away in Los Angeles, presiding at another stake conference.

As in the previous year, Father spent most of November and part of December on a mission tour, this time of the Central States, which then covered Kansas, Missouri, Texas, and Oklahoma.

It was in late 1925 or early 1926 that Mother and Father decided it was no longer practical to make the long commutes from Ogden. Mother's cousin, Bell White, suggested they try the Miller Apartments, directly across from Temple Square on the north and under the management of the Presiding Bishopric. A large apartment—fully half of the fourth floor—was then vacant, so Father was able to procure it for the family.

I had been enrolled since the fall of 1924 at the University of Utah in political science and history, while also teaching in the French Department. During my last year at Weber, I had taken college courses, and I also received a year's credit for my work at the Sorbonne, so I began as a junior. I had decided to pursue a legal career and continued teaching French and taking law courses after my graduation in June 1926.

I met an attractive young woman named Mildred Calderwood at a university dance, and one of our early dates was to accompany Mother and Father, at their invitation, to Weber State, where a large portrait of Father was being hung. As Mildred recalls:

"Lawrence told me, 'Don't be late! Father likes to be on time.' Well, I was ready *early* and we had a very pleasant drive to Ogden. My mother and Sister McKay were both on the Relief Society board of the Salt Lake Stake, but I had never met the McKays. I particularly noticed President McKay's solicitude for Sister McKay. A large party was waiting to welcome him, but he did not shake hands with them until he had opened the car door and helped Sister McKay out. He brought her into the hall on his arm, helped her off with her coat, made sure she was seated comfortably, and 'fussed' over her a bit in the tenderest way before he allowed himself to be taken off to the rostrum.

"I always felt completely welcomed by the family. I can imagine how intensely interested Lawrence's parents must have been as the courtship progressed, but never once did I sense being 'under inspection' or having the faintest feeling of anything but interested, friendly concern. Our relationship was our private affair and we were not pestered with advice or pressure of any kind."

Father's sisters were less reticent. Aunt Kitts told me frankly that fall, "Lawrence, you're going to see someone else walk off with Mildred if you're such a sluggard." I was already quite sure that I didn't want that to happen. After the Chi Omega formal near Christmas time, Lou Jean, Russell Blood, Mildred, and I were sitting by the fireplace in the Calderwood home. Russell and Lou Jean were already engaged, and Russell was being inconveniently obtuse, so I had to resort to pretty brisk action to clear them out of the living room.

Mildred did me the honor of accepting my proposal. Several days later, Mother, a model of courtesy and patience with my quite extraordinary reserve, asked:

"Lawrence, are you still seeing Mildred?"

"Yes."

"Do you love her?"

"Yes."

"Does she love you?"

"She says she does."

"Are you engaged?"

"Yes."

I think she said, "Oh, how nice," or something of the sort. The next day when I saw Father, he said, "Your mother tells me you and Mildred are engaged. Congratulations!" They recognized Mildred as an exceptional young woman and were very pleased.

Father performed our wedding ceremony on 28 June 1928 in the Salt Lake Temple. I'm sure he gave us very good advice, but I was much too taken up by the occasion to pay it the kind of attention it deserved. Looking back from the perspective of a parent who has seen four daughters married and knowing how profoundly I wish them a loving, united partnership, I can understand a little better some of the feelings my own father must have had on my wedding day. One little indication of his feelings showed up in his unexpectedly shaky signature on our marriage license.

Mildred and I had the "middle" McKay wedding. Lou Jean and Russell had been married six months before, just after Christmas in 1927, and Llewelyn married Alice Kimball Smith the next month, July 1928. A tender letter from Father to Mother, written a few weeks before Lou Jean's wedding, captures some of his feelings on that occasion and also gives an indication of how he felt about the marriages of subsequent children:

Nov. 22, 1927

My Own Sweetheart:

I have just finished a letter to Lou Jean. Tears began to blur my eyes so I had to bring it to an abrupt close. As I began writing, the full realization of the fact that the first one of our darlings to leave us to make a home for herself flooded my soul to overflowing. I confess that this first break in our lovely, charming family group gives me a feeling in my heart akin to a pang. . . .

Your sweet letter of the 11th . . . was received at Dallas, Texas; . . . Just the hand-writing on the envelope, as it is handed to me, gives me today even a sweeter thrill than it did when it made my heart go "pit-a-pat" in Scotland, thirty years ago, when I wondered if you would ever be mine.

Mildred and I established our own home in Washington, D.C., where

I attended George Washington Law School, an institution with a fine reputation favored by many of our Utah attorneys because classes began at four or five in the afternoon, permitting us to work during the day. We were in Washington for seven years, until 1935. I received my J.D. in 1932, but because of the depression and because we both had good teaching positions, we stayed on in Washington. Our first two daughters, Midene and Teddy Lyn, were born there.

We maintained contact with home through Mother's frequent, newsy letters and Father's less frequent but equally welcome notes. Father also tried to arrange conference visits so that he could stay overnight, although sometimes it was a matter of snatching an hour between trains. Occasionally, as a very rare treat, Mother was able to join him.

All of my brothers and sisters and their children have wonderful stories to tell about Father and Mother. Father and Mother unabashedly and unreservedly adored children. Seeing them with our daughters gave me a glimpse of how I must have been welcomed, loved, and petted as a child. Mildred's parents were also exemplary grandparents, equally loving and generous with their time and means.

The grandchildren all called my parents Papa Dade and Mama Ray. Lou Jean's son, Russell, hearing my parents refer to each other by these names, had adapted them in a combination so happy that all of the grandchildren followed.

When Midene was six months old, Mildred paid a visit to Salt Lake City to display our treasure to our parents. In a letter to me on 6 October 1929, she reported the generosity of her parents and the success of both visits:

"Mother bought a little bed for Wumps [our affectionate baby name for Midene] because night before last, when she slept with me, . . . the poor little thing was on a hill all night. I wish you could have seen how delighted she was to get into the little bed. She patted the sides and felt the little bars as if she had met an old friend. She kicked and gurgled and spit to her heart's content.

"Friday evening I took her down to your place and introduced her to the family. They surely are nice, Lawrence, I don't blame you for liking them so much. Your mother was so sweet with the baby and your father held her and sang a little tune to her. . . .

"Saturday I took her down in the afternoon right after her nap &

she laughed and pulled at your father's face and tongue and got your mother's hair, in fact, did about all of her tricks. . . . Your mother held Wumps who went to sleep with her little cheek up against your mother's. She said she had often dreamed of holding 'Lawrence's baby in her arms' like that. It was so sweet."

Father's conference notebook is blank between 15 May and 28 July 1929; but during that time, he made another protracted trip east for one of his long mission tours, this time through eastern Canada. He wrote to his "dearest sweetheart" aboard the Continental Limited on 22 May 1929, reporting the trip and then urging her to buy a new hat: "Be sure to get a hat that is becoming. I'm afraid you will buy something that isn't just because it doesn't cost much. Get something you like. That is the main consideration."

The next letter came from Montreal on 3 June 1929:

Sweetheart:

"For ye see your calling, brethren, how that not many wise men after the flesh, not many mighty, not many noble are called:

"But God hath chosen the foolish things of the world to confound the wise; and God hath chosen the weak things of the world to confound the things which are mighty; and base things of the world and things which are despised, hath God chosen."

This saying of Paul's came to my mind last Thursday night at the opening of our meeting in Amherst, Nova Scotia. There is not a member of the Church residing in that town. Excepting the six missionaries, there was not a member present at the meeting. A dingy, old stairway led us up one flight of stairs to an unattractive, low-ceiling hall used, I think, by the W.C.T.U.

As we entered, a man was playing the piano. He was a stranger, but a friend to the Elders. I was surprised when he changed from the more difficult selection that he was playing to "An Angel from on High." Then I noticed that he had no music before him.

He was blind!

Just then two people came in—a man and his wife—The man was on crutches.

He had only one leg!

Later an old but intellectually alert woman took her seat in the small audience—

She was paralyzed in the right arm!

Near her on the same seat sat a young girl about 23 years of age. *She is the mother of two illegitimate children!*

I did not become intimately acquainted with the other twenty- eight who had accepted the invitation of the Elders to attend that special meeting.

When I looked at the hall, and observed the good, honest, though unfortunate people in that humble audience, as I say I was reminded of I Corinthians I:26, also of that hymn we sing,

> *Ye Elders of Israel, come go now with me,*
> *And search out the Righteous, where-e'er they may be,*
> *x x x x x*
> *"We'll go to the poor, to the halt and the blind,*
> *And bring them to Zion, rich treasures to find—*

or something to that effect. I forget the exact words.

Alice's father, Ella and Heber [Smith], accompanied by a Mr. Eddie drove ninety miles last Friday to attend our meeting in Burlington, Vermont, where we held an excellent meeting. I returned to the memorial cottage with them, and spent a very enjoyable time in their company. Tell Alice [Llewelyn's wife] the folks are all well, and feeling happy, until someone mentions Alice and the baby; then Sister Smith gets home-sick.

When I arrived in Montreal Saturday night, I found your letter of May 26th awaiting me — the first word from home since I left. We haven't as yet been near Toronto, nor shall we be there until to-morrow. So I am looking forward to letters from you, Emma Rae, Ned, Bobbie and Llewelyn.

News from home gives me a far greater thrill than the most interesting thing offered to the sightseer.

I am wearying of meetings! meetings, meetings, from one to five every day, but one, for ten successive days, and the end not yet in sight! I will not accept another such schedule. It's really too strenuous.

The next day, he wrote again:

Toronto, Ontario
June 4, 1929

My Darling Sweetheart:

Once again you have made me happy when otherwise I should have felt depressed. Again, as you have ten thousand other times, you have proved to be my darling Ray of sunshine.

After traveling all night by train from Ottawa to Toronto, I approached the Mission house in high anticipation of finding awaiting me at least four letters from Loved ones at home, as I have had only one since I left two weeks ago. Though the sun was shining brightly, yet the air was cool; the city seemed to have an unwelcome aspect, an incident happened on our way to the street car, which impressed me as foolish, the mission house seemed rather still and undemonstrative, to say the least—no Elders to meet us. . . . These and other things combined to keep my feelings just a little below par; but interjecting itself constantly like a ray of sunshine through the clouds, came the thought—"There are letters from home so I'll be content." I was shown my room, but there were no letters on the table awaiting me. Later, I met the mission secretary, but he said nothing about mail. Breakfast was announced, but no letters given me. As we were eating, the postman came. The little girl brought in papers and letters, wondered which one was for her, handed the bundle to her mother, who glanced through it, then handed it to the secretary, who also looked at each envelope and wrapper, but handed me no letter. Thinking that he did not want to disturb me while eating, I asked, "Any for me?" In answer, he handed me a long letter from the Beneficial Life, but not a line from a *chic* or a child at home!

Well, Toronto became a gloomy old place! Cold in climate and every other way! "Kiddies don't give a rap, anyhow." "They are cold in their feelings also." "It will be a cold day before I write to them again!"—These cold, somewhat rebellious thoughts threw the thermometer of my feelings down to near the freezing point. I don't know whether I radiated chilled feelings or not, but Sister Hart turned on an electric heater, and later Bro. Hart lit the gas radiator!

I was in a good mood to write a letter to the assistant superintendent of the civic hospital at Ottawa, who, I thought, treated us in an ungentlemanly not to say contemptuous manner when we called, yesterday, to administer to a sister missionary. I wrote the letter, and read it to Brother Hart, who seemed a bit frightened, and mildly suggested some gentler terms instead of "insult," "ignorance," "bigotry," etc.

Well, by the time that letter was modified and another written to

"His Excellency, the Mayor of Ottawa," the postman came with the afternoon delivery of mail. *I was handed your letter of the 31st inst.*

Toronto is not an unpleasant city at all. The Mission house is really a cheerful home! Sister Hart is just as considerate as a hostess can be! The outlook of the Branch here is favorable! Everything that hour seemed to take on a different aspect! Yet everything was just as it had been before; but my sweetheart's letter had put sunshine into my heart, and made all things gladsome! I've given you this peep into my innermost feelings, just to assure you again that *I love you!* My life's sunshine!

Hamilton, Ontario
June 7, 1929

My Own Sweetheart:

Last night we held our twenty-fourth meeting, and in one half hour shall be in the twenty-fifth, with seven more in four different cities awaiting us! Traveling thousands of miles, and attempting to keep speaking powers on "high speed" on an average of twice a day for two weeks requires an expenditure of more nerve energy than some people think. . . .

Home! Blessed haven of happiness and contentment! I would not exchange our ties of companionship and true affection for each other — our ideals as exemplified in the lives of our children, for all else this old world can offer! . . .

Lovingly,
Dade

I cherish the next letter in the collection, from Father for my twenty-eighth birthday in September 1929. Mildred and I were carefully watching our pennies; and that summer in Salt Lake City, I had sold my beloved violin. It was a considerable sacrifice for me, because I dearly loved my music; and it had provided both recreation and companionship for me on many occasions when I had been far from home. Father did not remonstrate with my decision, but he quietly took action of his own. He sent me a little handwritten note: "Your old violin is on its way to Washington and you" and this typewritten poem:

> *As I looked at your old violin to-night,*
> *I heard sweet tunes that you played at sight,*

When you were a growing boy;
I saw Lou Jean, Llewelyn and you
Playing trios as you used to do —
A memory of treasured joy!
The thing I know isn't the best of its kind,
But it's won a place in my heart and mind,
  Which no Stradivarius can fill;
So I've bought it again for counted joy,
And the tones it gave forth at the touch of our boy —
  I recall them e'en now with a thrill.

So accept it, dear son, as a memory of youth
(For its purchase, you'll say, if you speak the real
  truth
    Is not an example of thrift)
But we're sending it not for its intrinsic worth
But for memories as precious as any on earth
  With love, as a birthday gift.

O we love you as only fond parents can love
And invoke choicest blessings from Heaven above,
  On Mildred and darling wee Dean;
May each coming year find you happier than last
With a rich store of memories of incidents past —
  There's no greater blessing, I ween.

Affectionately,
Daddy and Mama Ray

When I opened the case containing that familiar old instrument, my vision blurred and my hands fumbled as I picked it up. I tuned it by touch, unable to speak past the lump in my throat. That night, I played everything I knew by heart — played for hours into the night with tears of joy and gratitude for my beloved parents streaming down my cheeks, and Mildred wept with me. No matter how straitened our circumstances in the years that followed, I never considered parting from it again, and it still has an honored place in our living room as one of my greatest treasures.

Our next letter from home came a few days before Christmas from Mother:

Salt Lake City, Dec. 20, 1929

Dear Lawrence and Mildred:

... We were delighted to hear that baby is succeeding in great accomplishments — turning over in bed and knowing so much. We should like to hear about every new thing that she does. ... I certainly learned to love the little pet while she was here and missed her and you, Mildred, so much when you were gone. I shall never forget the picture she made in that pink outfit as we said goodbye to her at the station. How I wish we lived near you that we also might watch her develop! What a fine specimen of babyhood she is! Just perfect!

... We have sent you a box the contents of which are small but our best love goes with the little gifts. You must enjoy Bobby's especially. He earned his money by eating clabber. He was broke and wishing he could make some money some way. Daddy said, "I'll give you a quarter for every bowl of clabber that you will eat." You should have seen his face while he was downing that stuff — full of dislike and yet determination to get through with it. Daddy's eyes were twinkling. He was enjoying it to the full. He would like to get somebody in this family to enjoy clabber with him since now he must eat it alone. Bob has eaten three bowls now and has received some quarters for practicing so well. He is really enjoying his music. Goes regularly to the piano three or four times a day *without being told.* But *Ned, dear me.*

Two months later, in February 1930, when Father was in Moscow, Idaho, on a conference assignment and Mother was ill, Father had a dream depicting the "chaos" that would result in his life were anything to happen to Mother:

My darling Ray:

This has been the most gloomy day which I have spent for years. Indeed, part of the time, I concluded that I have never before felt quite so downhearted.

Early in the morning, the jerking of the train started me off on a dream in which the car I was in became detached from the others and started down the highway on its own accord, tearing down fences, smashing wagons, and finally bumping into a self-binder. I awoke just before the binder struck two men on the opposite side of it! ...

My worst concern and anxiety have their source in your sickness. It was no easy matter for me to leave you yesterday, just after our coming in from that siege in the testing laboratory. My imagination has run somewhat riot to-day, and I've been anxious about you.

Sweetheart, your health is of first importance, and everything must bend to its restoration. You must regain your strength. Why, darling, if anything should happen to you, our home, our lives, our all would be chaos!

How in the world you can so undervalue yourself and your ability as you sometimes do, when you make up the most important part of your husband's and your children's lives is more than I can understand! However, no matter how much you modestly subtract from your own virtues, we know that you are the sweetest sweetheart that ever made happy a fortunate husband.

I feel a little better, now that I have talked to you.

> Affectionately,
> Your loving Dade

During this period, national interest focused on child welfare and recreational programs for youth. Father often found himself called upon to represent the Church at such conferences. On 20 November 1930, he wrote enthusiastically to Mother from Washington, D.C.:

My Only Sweetheart:

This White House Conference on Child Health and Welfare is undoubtedly one of the most important conferences, if not the most important conference, ever held in the United States. To be an appointed delegate to it is one of the greatest opportunities and privileges of my life.

Yesterday I sent you a telegram suggesting that you hear President Hoover over the national broadcast. I hope you listened in. It was a good address, though he did not speak with much force or enthusiasm. Mildred, Lawrence and I had excellent seats in the Constitution Hall where the address was delivered. From eight thirty to nine, the U.S. Marine Band gave a concert. As President Hoover entered in state, he was given a hearty and prolonged ovation by the great audience. Mildred said it was "thrilling," and Lawrence and I agreed. . . .

This afternoon between five and six o'clock at the White House, he and Mrs. Hoover gave an informal reception to the delegates at the conference.

At 9:30 this morning Honorable James J. Davis, Secretary of Labor, gave an impassioned address on the subject for, or to consider which the conference has been called.

Just before this meeting, I had the honor of meeting Dr. H. E. Barnard, Director of the entire Conference — a very fine and able gentleman. I have been introduced to a number of other men and women prominent in governmental and educational affairs, among whom I will mention Miss Bess Goodyboontz, Assistant Commissioner of Education in the U.S., and Mr. Wm. D. Boutwell, editor of public documents and publications of this Commission. . . .

This morning as I stepped out of an elevator in the Interior buildings, I suddenly discovered that a lady's scarf had become entangled in a link in the dangling chain by which I hang my overcoat. The coat was on my arm, but her scarf was around her neck. We were pretty securely *hooked* together. As I vainly tried to extricate the two articles without injuring her beautiful neck piece, she said, "O, it's all right if you do tear it." "No, indeed," I said; "I can get it. I'm only sorry that you seem so eager to dissolve this sudden union." This provoked a laugh among her friends and mine who were watching the proceedings. Prof. Peery G. Holden of "International Harvester" fame — you remember his visits to Utah — said as the lady and I became disengaged, and referring to my remark, "If she had only known to whom she had got attached! I could hardly refrain from telling her that one of the dreadful Mormon leaders had her in his toils!"

It will soon be meeting time, so I must sign off. Every minute, I wish you were by my side enjoying this great treat and privilege!

Love to the children and to the sweetest and best of wives and sweethearts!

Lovingly,
Dade

On 24 and 25 November 1931, he attended the Idaho State White House Conference on Child Health and Protection, and another in Helena, Montana, in December. He was also very concerned about the movement to repeal Prohibition and spoke eloquently – though to little avail – against it.

Additional entries that give family glimpses for this time period continue:

"2 Jan. 1932. Thirty one years ago to-day, Ray and I were married in the Salt Lake Temple by Apostle John Henry Smith. During that time I cannot recall that she has spoken a cross word to me. She has been an ideal sweetheart, a charming companion, and a loving wife . . .

"4 Jan. 1932. Began writing new handbook for the Melchizedek Priesthood. . . .

"5 Jan. 1932. 9:30 A.M. Meeting with Gen'l Sup'ey, of Sunday Schools. 10 A.M. Meeting with Missionary Committee. 11 A.M. With the Board of Advisors Gen'l Ch. Bd. of Ed. 2 P.M. With Auxiliary Executives until 4 P.M. 4:10 P.M. Meeting of Gen'l S.S. Sup'ey. 5 P.M. Gen'l. Board S. S. Union. 7 P.M. Instructed missionaries. 8:30 P.M. Took Ray to a picture show. [This meeting schedule was, as nearly as I can tell, typical of every Tuesday unless Father was traveling on a conference assignment.]

"6 Jan. 1932. Drove to Huntsville in the morning. Went to the farm, and rode two horses one at a time to the blacksmith shop. The valley was beautiful under a blanket of pure white, newly fallen snow. . . .

"8 Jan. 1932. . . . One of a committee of three to consult Gov. Dern on the personnel of the Executive Committee of the State Council on Child Health and Protection. [Father was selected to chair this committee.] . . .

"March 11, 1932. Held a meeting with the Committee on Priesthood Course of Study and the Presiding Bishopric to consider the establishing of a Ward Correlation Committee, the duty of which would be the accounting for every person in the ward. A plan has already been adopted to account for all young men between the ages 12–20, but the broader plan includes everybody in the ward. . . .

"Monday, April 4, 1932. Went to the office at 8 A.M. intending to study, but callers came so consecutively that I could not get time to read even a paragraph. Called to the hospital to administer to the sick. . . .

"Tuesday, 19 April 1932. [He lists five meetings that lasted from 8 A.M. until 5 P.M., then notes wearily:] I had to preside at every meeting. . . .

"Thursday, 25 August 1932. Mama Ray underwent a Tonsillectomy — a severe shock to her nervous system. Much *worried* all day. . . .

"Sunday, 2 Oct. 1932. . . . Took my sweetheart to the L.D.S. hospital to prepare for what seems inevitably necessary to the best interests of her health — a thyroidectomy. . . .

"Friday, Oct. 7, 1932. . . . Patriarch Nicholas G. Smith, Bishop of the Seventeenth Ward (our ward) opened the Conference by prayer. In asking God's blessing upon President Heber J. Grant, who is ill in Chicago; upon Elder Melvin J. Ballard, convalescing from an operation for appendicitis, the Bishop also kindly included Ray as one worthy of united appeal and of Divine help. I appreciated his kind thoughtfulness, but I knew how Ray would feel when she heard of this publicity, for she did not want anybody but her closest friends to know that she was in the hospital. All the same, I thanked the Bishop for his remembering Ray in his prayer.

"Monday, 10 Oct. 1932. Visited Ray several times. . . .

"Wednesday, 19 Oct. 1932. Ray left the hospital today. Much improved . . .

"Monday, 14 Nov. 1932. . . . Drove to Huntsville in the afternoon, accompanied by Ray, her first long auto trip for months. . . . My sweetheart stood the trip so well, we went to the theatre at night."

Father left the next day to tour the East Central States Mission and wrote to Mother on the train on 16 November 1932:

Sweetheart:

It was very considerate of you to accompany me to the train last night, but I fear you overexerted yourself — shopping all day, and then sitting in the car in the chilly night air. In your thoughtfulness and unselfish love for others, you forget yourself entirely. Thus may the attributes of a beautiful soul react adversely on the health of the body. If you feel any ill effects, if your pulse is running high again, please keep Mabel [Kelsen, a maid] at least another week. Do not let your keen sense of economy warp your judgment as regards to your health. . . .

I have noted particularly this morning how natural it seems to be on a train. I have traveled so much that the pullman seems to be a second home — sort of a bachelor's home, plenty of comfort and convenience but devoid of loving company.

On this particular expedition, Father was able to come through Washington, D.C., and we were delighted to drive him to his next appointment. In his conference notebook, he jotted laconically: "David L., Mildred and Midean drove me to Alexandria through a dense fog." I recall it as quite a harrowing journey. The "dense fog" grew steadily thicker as we started out before 8 on the morning of 25 November 1932. We crept slower and slower and eventually had to stop and stay in a hotel overnight because it was simply too dangerous to proceed. We got up very early the next morning (the fog had lifted) and got Father to his meeting on time. Father was never tense as a passenger, which made a difficult situation much easier.

In that year's conference notebook, Father carried in a special envelope at the back two letters from Harold B. Lee describing the various work projects and policies then employed in Pioneer Stake in Salt Lake City to deal with the unemployment and suffering caused by the deepening depression. I do not know what use Father made of these materials; but from other notations in his conference talks, he stressed the need for economic cooperation and, perhaps as early as the fall of 1932, was describing principles of mutual assistance that would, the next year, be formalized as what we today know as the welfare plan.

During the spring of 1934, we learned that Mildred was pregnant with Teddy Lyn. Mother responded delightedly on 4 May 1934, sharing our happiness and unself-consciously revealing some of the difficulties with her own pregnancies that she had borne so uncomplainingly:

"How wonderful to know you are going to have another beautiful baby and how thrilled Midean will be when she knows. Have you told her? People nowadays say babies should know most everything. How are you feeling, Mildred? Have you had four months of misery as I always had? I hope not. Lawrence says that you are as thrilled and nervous as you were five years ago. Yes, a new baby is never an old story. It is a thrill each time though you have a dozen — at least it was to me. When we told Bobby he grinned from ear to ear & said, 'Gee, isn't that great!' We all think it great and offer congratulations."

About a month later, she wrote from Huntsville, thanking us for the birthday present of handkerchiefs that Midene had helped select and adding: "I forgot all about my birthday this year until Daddy came in and said, 'I didn't know it but fifty-seven years ago my happiness began.' Wasn't that sweet of him?"

Then she gently chided me: "You mention, Lawrence, about talking so much about Midene. You know the most interesting things in the world to me are the thoughts and doings of my own children. Next come the doings and sayings of my grandchildren, so you can never weary me of telling about darling Midene. The more you do it the better I like it." (June 1934.)

Our second daughter, Edna Marilyn (Teddy Lyn) was born in August 1934. Father wrote a warmly welcoming letter, expressing both his and Mother's pleasure with our baby: "Mother and I are both anxious to see that sweet baby girl. . . . When Mother read Lou-Jean's letter yesterday telling how sweet and cute the baby is, her face lighted up and she said, 'Oh dear, I must see her.' "

Mother's own letter followed three days later, on 18 September 1934:

My Dear Lawrence:

We are so very happy to hear that all is well with Mildred and the new babe. I wish I had glasses that would permit me to look as far as Washington that I might have a glance at the little thing. There is nothing I like quite so well as a tiny baby. And I do like to cuddle one to touch its soft flesh! There is nothing so sweet.

. . . It is nice that Lou Jean could help you. I hope her husband isn't too lonesome.

You speak of our coming back. I do not see any opening for me to come. We have no money and no one to take care of the boys. Of course they are not babies any more but I do not like to leave them alone. It would be a wonderful opportunity to see the South and to see you all a few minutes. When Daddy goes anywhere he is like a whirlwind and doesn't stay long in one place.

When the baby developed colic, she wrote sympathetically, "Have I told you that nearly all my babies had colic for nine months? And does the care they must have spoil the little midgets! I used to get daily scoldings for taking them up when they cried but I just couldn't stand their crying when a change and a little patting or jolting would move the wind." (25 Nov. 1934.)

Mildred and I can be forgiven, I hope, for believing that Teddy Lyn's birth was the most important event in the family for the entire year, but events were to give us all a surprise. Anthony W. Ivins, first counselor in the First Presidency, died 23 September 1934. When the funeral was held on 27 September, Father was one of the speakers. Then he records:

"After the return from the cemetery, Pres. Heber J. Grant called me by telephone, and requested me to call on him at his residence. On this occasion, he informed [me] that he had chosen me to succeed Pres. Ivins in the First pres. The call coming so suddenly, I was entirely overcome. After an extended interview, when I arose to leave, he put his arms around me and kissed me."

Mother wrote, sending me birthday wishes, three days later on 30 September, breathing never a word of this great news. I honestly do not know if she had been told, for if a matter was told Mother in confidence, it remained confidential forever! Instead, she commented glowingly on Father's funeral sermon for President Ivins:

"It was wonderful! Everybody was delighted with it. Daddy's office was full of people for two days congratulating him on his talk and everybody I met stopped to tell me how fine it was. Dr. Rich said, 'Tell David he has outdone himself.' Llewelyn says everybody at the U is talking about it. . . .

"Daddy's very hard work starts this week with conference coming on. [President Grant had gone to California to recuperate from his cold.] There will have to be a new president chosen and a new President of Seventy because President [Charles S.] Hart has just passed away. What a change is taking place in the general authorities!"

On 6 October 1934, in general conference, Father was sustained as second counselor to President Heber J. Grant, while J. Reuben Clark, Jr., the former second counselor, became his first counselor.

The very evening of the conference in which Father was sustained, Mother sent us a newspaper clipping and this note:

Salt Lake City
Oct. 6, 1934

Dear Lawrence and Mildred:

The enclosed will tell you what a wonderful honor has come to your father.

David O. McKay
about the time
of his call to the
First
Presidency,
1934

The people seem to be overwhelmed with joy. Men and women come to him, fall in his arms and weep for joy. They cannot speak. People by the dozens have told him they have been praying for this to happen, in fact that it has been the universal prayer since Pres. Ivins died that David O. should be chosen the new counselor. Many people have sent telegrams of congratulations.

Your missionary companion's father, Bro. A[lonzo] A. Hinckley, has taken your father's place in the Quorum of Apostles. Isn't that lovely? Daddy thinks he is a wonderful man.

When Father himself had a chance to write to us children a few days later, his letter said very little of his new assignment or his feelings about it but instead turned with full and affectionate regard to pay tribute to the beloved woman beside him:

Salt Lake City, Utah,
October 25, 1934

To my beloved Sons and Daughters—

David L. and Mildred,
Llewelyn R. and Alice,
Lou Jean and Russell,
Emma Rae,
Edward R. and
Robert R.
—children, not one of whom has ever done a thing to cause their parents sorrow, but who in their consideration, devotion and achievement have filled our hearts with justifiable pride and gratitude.

Dear David L. and Mildred:

Recently there came to me the highest honor and greatest responsibility of my life. I am not unmindful of what this appointment to the First Presidency of the Church means to us as a family. I am sure you also appreciate this and share willingly and conscientiously whatever added responsibility the Call may place upon you.

Aptly it has been said that, "Often a woman shapes the career of husband, or brother or son. A man succeeds and reaps the honors of public applause, when in truth a quiet little woman has made it all possible—has by her tact and encouragement held him to his best, has had faith in him when his own faith has languished, has cheered him with the unfailing assurance, 'you can, you must, you will.' "

I need not tell you children how fittingly this tribute applies to your mother. All through the years you have seen how perfectly she fills the picture. There is not a line or a touch but is applicable. For over thirty three years, I have realized this and each of you has known it to a greater or less degree as many years as your ages indicate; but like the Scotchman who "cam' near tellin' his wife ance or twice" that he loved her, we have not told mother of her loving worth and inspiration to us.

Recently, since October 6th particularly, I have had a yearning to see my father and mother just to tell them what their lives, their daily example, and willing sacrifices for their children have meant to me. I want to acknowledge to them my unpayable debt of eternal gratitude. But they are not here, and I must await an opportunity in the distant Future.

Your mother is here — well and happy and as sweet and charming in life's afternoon as she was in the morning of beautiful womanhood. I want to acknowledge to you and to her, how greatly her loving devotion, inspiration and loyal support have contributed to whatever success may be ours.

Willingly and ably she has carried the responsibility of the household.

Uncomplainingly she has economized when our means have been limited — and that has been the case nearly all our lives.

Always prompt with meals, she has never said an unpleasant word or even shown a frown when I have kept her waiting, sometimes for hours.

If I had to take a train at midnight or later, she would either sit up with me or lie awake to make sure that I should not oversleep.

If duty required me to leave at five o'clock in the morning, she was never satisfied unless she could prepare me a bite of breakfast before I left home.

It has been mother who remembered the birthdays and purchased the Christmas presents.

Since January 2nd, 1901, the happy day when she became my bride, she has never given me a single worry except when she was ill and that has been, with few exceptions, only with the responsibilities of motherhood.

Thus my mind has been remarkably free to center upon the problems, cares and requirements incident to my duties and responsibilities.

In sickness, whether it was one of you or I, her untiring attention night and day was devotion personified; her practical skill, invariably effective; and her physical endurance, seemingly unlimited. Many an ache and pain she has endured in uncomplaining silence so as not to give the least worry to the loved one to whom she was giving such tender care.

Sometimes I have come home tired and irritable and have made

Emma Ray
Riggs McKay

remarks provocative of retaliating replies; but never to this day have you heard your mother say a cross or disrespectful word. This can be said truthfully I think of but few women in the world.

Under all conditions and circumstances, she has been the perfect lady.

Her education has enabled her to be a true helpmate; her congeniality and interest in my work, a pleasing companion; her charm and unselfishness, a lifelong sweetheart; her unbounded patience and intelligent insight into childhood, a most devoted mother;—these and many other virtues combined with her loyalty and self-sacrificing devotion to her husband, impel me to crown her the sweetest, most helpful, most inspiring sweetheart and wife that ever inspired a man to noble endeavor.

To her we owe our happy family life and whatever success we may have achieved.

I know you love her and, oh how she loves each one of you!

Hundreds of letters and telegrams from friends, acquaintances and even strangers — members and non-members of the Church in all walks of life have brought congratulatory messages, prayerful wishes for success and assurances of confidence and loyal support for which I am indeed sincerely grateful.

I have noted with joy that in many of these messages your loving mother is included in the congratulations and commendations expressed. I want at least her loved ones to know that she rightfully shares in *all* achievements and honors.

> *Happy he*
> *With such a mother! Faith in womankind*
> *Beats with his blood, and trust in all things high*
> *Comes easy to him, and though he trip and fall*
> *He shall not bind his soul with clay.*
> *But one on earth is better than the wife;*
> *that is mother.*

With loving devotion and appreciation of your love and loyalty, I remain as always

Your affectionate
Daddy

Chapter 10

"PAPA DADE AND MAMA RAY" 1934-1952

◆ ◆ ◆ ◆ ◆ ◆ ◆ ◆ ◆ ◆ ◆ ◆ ◆

When Father accepted the calling to the First Presidency, he was just a few days past his sixty-first birthday and was the fourth senior member of the Quorum of the Twelve Apostles. He served as counselor first to Heber J. Grant and then to George Albert Smith for the next sixteen and a half years.

Father's little pocket diary for 1935 comments very little on the changes that the new calling brought into his life; however, another meeting joined the list — First Presidency meetings — and he was obviously not traveling so much. Not infrequently, his diary entry simply reads, "At the office all day," even Saturday. I smiled, then, to read this entry for Sunday, 10 February 1935: "Had a day of rest, prepared two manuscripts, Wandamere Ward at 6:30 P.M."

In February, he and Mother took a genuine, though strenuous, vacation. They took the train to Detroit where they were "met at Michigan Central station by car from Graham-Paige Motor Co. While waiting for new car, we visited Green Field Village and Edison Memorial, Dearborn. Drove to Toledo." (19 Feb. 1935.) It was very cold and became colder as they drove farther east to Ohio and Pennsylvania. They reached Philadelphia where Lou Jean and Russell were living while Russell was in medical school, spent an evening *en famille* with Russell, Lou Jean, and "master Russell," their little son, then drove on to meet us in Washington, D.C. Father arrived in time to address a large crowd of 533 in our chapel.

It snowed for two days while they called on Senator Elbert D. Thomas, visited the Senate Chamber, the LDS church, and the Lincoln Memorial, and attended an organ recital and the theater. To avoid the storms, they returned home by the southern route, driving across Florida, Alabama, Mississippi, and Louisiana, where they arrived in time for part of the Mardi Gras celebration ("parades *spectacular!*"). Then they angled up from Texas, through Denver, and home.

Just before April conference, Ned came down with scarlet fever. Father moved into Hotel Utah so he could continue his duties, and Mother was quarantined with Ned for almost three weeks. Father filled us in on the details on 16 April 1935:

"I came to the hotel, Mother, of course, stayed with her boy, and Bobby, on his own insistence, moved into the garage. There the janitor's wife furnished him meals. With Scotty [the dog] and the radio (until the battery ran down) Bobby had a pretty good time for the first two days. After that time dragged heavily. Poor lad! But he stayed with it uncomplainingly until the end of the 'incubating' period (seven days).

"Fortunately, he did not take the fever, and last Friday, he returned to School. Thursday night and Friday night he stayed with me here, and since then he has been living with Llewelyn and Alice."

Possibly the most telling detail about Father's busy schedule was his note in April that he had hired someone to break the three-year-old filly. "To think that I cannot take time even to train a colt makes me feel pretty sad! She is a choice animal, too!"

Father had an attack of lumbago in May. In July, he and Mother accompanied President and Sister Grant and their party on a visit to Palmyra, where they held a dawn meeting in the Sacred Grove. An August weekend at Fish Lake with Ned, Llewelyn, and Mother, a chokecherry expedition in September in Huntsville, a day of fishing in the Snake River after Teton Stake conference in October, attendance at one of Emma Rae's high school plays at Granite High School in November, and several entertainments in December were virtually all their social activities for the year. Father seems to have dropped no official duties. He was still serving on the missionary committee and writing Gospel Doctrine lessons.

In a New Year's letter to us in January 1935, Father wrote:

One of our greatest disappointments this year is our failure to get back to see you. If we do not realize this desire soon we shall find two young ladies in the David L. McKay family instead of a little baby and a young girl. . . .

I am going to write a letter to my sweet Midene, and as I hear voices gathering for a meeting to be held here in a few minutes, I will sign off, with purest love and heartfelt wishes that the New Year will bring to you in abundance joy, prosperity and contentment.

Affectionately,
Your loving Daddy

The note to Midene was warm and loving:

January 17, 1935

My darling Midene:

Before Christmas, 1934, when I had occasion to use scrap paper or a note book, I had to use the blank side of letters that had been thrown away; but now there lies before me on my desk a beautiful package of clean sheets, well-bound, in a most useful scrap book. And every time I look at it I think of my little girl in Washington. It is just what her Granddaddy wanted and needed for Christmas. Thank you a hundred times for sending me that lovely present. Every time I write a note on a sheet of the paper, I think of the little girl who sent it to me. . . .

. . . We love you sincerely and send sweet kisses to the baby and to Mother and Daddy.

Affectionately,
Grandpa "Dade"

In 1935–36 I completed my law education by spending an intensive year in Harvard Law School. Mildred and our daughters returned to Salt Lake City to live with her parents, who generously made this arrangement to free us from some financial worries and enable me to concentrate full time on my studies. It was very lonely, but I worked hard and was greatly encouraged by Mildred's cheerful, supportive letters.

Winter conspired to make it difficult for Mildred and the girls to see much of my parents. Both girls had repeated colds during the winter, Mildred, worn down by long nursing, also became ill, and my parents' schedule had become even busier. Mother tried to accompany Father to as many assignments as she could, and she was also suffering that year from abdominal pain that she refused to have diagnosed. Mildred's letters to me during that year contain numerous references to my parents, however; and each reference simultaneously exacerbated and soothed my homesickness:

Oct. 18, 1935

... Last night Midene went with your father and mother to the Seventeenth Ward to see Emma Rae in a Mutual Stake play. I had this psychology class so had to go late. I thought I would take Midene from the show early but when I got there I found a seat at the back and finally saw Midene way up towards the front sitting on your father's lap enjoying the play thoroughly. During the intermission she sat on the bench between your mother and father and they all were having such a good time I didn't have the heart to disturb them. They said, after, that Midene seemed to understand every bit of it. I believed they enjoyed having her with them very much. It was eleven o'clock before the little rascal was in bed.

Oct. 28, 1935

... Father and Mother [Calderwood] drove up the canyon yesterday and just as Midene and I were feeling rather lonely — who should ring our bell but your mother. She said she just felt as if she would like to see us so she got Emma Rae and her young man ... to drive her up. She visited quite awhile. She invited Midene and me to dinner at the Lion House next Wednesday at six o'clock. She is having the family there for Aunt Nettie.

Nov. 23, 1935

... Your mother phoned and invited us all to dinner on Thanksgiving and asked me again to go to that movie with her. I went this afternoon and had a lovely visit with her, too. . . .

Continued — day after Thanksgiving.

We had a very nice time at your house yesterday — even Teddy Lyn [fifteen months old] behaved. . . . Your mother had prepared a delicious dinner — pumpkin pie and whipped cream for dessert! She has promised to show me how to make pie. I have never tasted such pie — but then you know all about it.

Dec. 5, 1935

... Your folks had a lovely party Monday night. I helped Emma Rae serve — as I told you. After the dinner was over, your mother asked us if we didn't want to use their tickets and go over to hear the symphony Concert at the Tabernacle. Did we! ... I wish you could have heard the concert. It was marvelous. Teddy Lyn is walking all over the paper and climbing to the top of the desk — hence the wrinkles.

Mother wrote on 4 December 1935: "[Midene] certainly is doing well with her music. Mrs. Ure [her teacher] just raves about her. Says she not only has a perfect hand and a love for music but she has intelligence behind it and is bound to succeed. She had told Emma that Midene is the brightest child she has ever seen. Thanksgiving afternoon I read to her for about two hours and she combed my hair nearly all the time. I enjoyed it as much as she did. She doesn't come down half often enough since the cold weather."

During the bleakest part of the year — January and February — Mildred took the girls and went to visit her sister in California, and Father had business that took him and Mother to Hawaii:

February 5, 1936

My dear son Lawrence,

Your mother and I arrived in Honolulu two weeks ago tomorrow morning.... During the last twelve days, we have held twenty-four meetings besides attending a number of receptions, three luaus and many entertainments. We have traveled over 3000 miles throughout the various islands.

You will be surprised as I am, to know that your mother has been flying on airplane[s] from island to island, across water, over mountains and fertile valleys. Yesterday on our return from Kauai, the plane ascended 5000 ft. above the clouds and flew with a fifty mile gale. It was one of the most beautiful and thrilling experiences of our entire trip. To see the clouds below us and through them occasionally the blue ocean beneath was a most unusual and inspiring experience....

Your mother joins me in sending truest love and heartfelt wishes and continuous success in your studies at Harvard.

Affectionately,
Daddy

This trip had not been a good one for Mother. She wrote to me on 21 February 1936, apologizing for her shaky penmanship and making light of the fact that she was nauseated during the entire stay in Hawaii. This condition did not go away when she returned home, and it was then complicated by a bad cold and "weakness." Instead, she concentrated on the positive aspects of the trip:

"Daddy held twenty-five meetings in thirteen days, travelled three thousand miles by auto, rode in airplanes six times, the first for nearly two hours, besides feasts . . . and other entertainments. . . .

"Everywhere we went, we were covered with beautiful wreaths or flower leis made of roses, carnations, the rain flower, little white bell-like flowers & the royal yellow flower of the islands. The women who brought the leis were dressed in long trains and always sang and danced to welcome us. There are fourteen thousand native Saints on the islands and I guess we shook hands with every one of them. Daddy gave them some wonderful talks and they just about worshipped him."

I returned to Salt Lake City in the summer of 1936 and set up my law practice in the offices of Henry D. Moyle and Lynn S. Richards. Two more daughters, Catherine Jean and Margaret Joyce, were born to Mildred and me. We were both active in our wards and stakes. I also served for several years in the general superintendency of the Sunday School, and Mildred was on the Primary General Board.

People have sometimes asked me if I ever mentioned matters of Church or professional business to my father that others had brought to my attention. Such an idea was unthinkable to me. Father was always upset if any details of the Church's internal workings got into the newspapers. He was absolutely scrupulous about never mentioning meetings or decisions. Occasionally a friend who was a member of the Twelve or the Seventy would tell me of an action being taken, but I never heard it from Father.

Certainly the good opinion of Father and Mother was very important to me. I am sure that unconsciously I appraised all of my decisions in light of their effect on Father and the family. My parents were unstinting and consistent in their praise and affection; these qualities, along with the warmth and affection of my own wife and children, were the sunshine of my life. Our conversations dealt with family matters, the farm, music, plays, books we were reading, and other topics of shared interest.

I seldom consulted my father for financial advice. I recall once asking him about a particular stock investment. He observed, "I wouldn't invest in that." "I already have," I said. He smiled but said nothing. I sold it a few months later at a loss.

Father's recreations were few. If he had any spare time, he went to Huntsville where the farm was both work and pleasure to him and where his horses were a constant joy. He traveled so much in the line of duty that, except for family vacations or a few days when he could slip away with Mother, a traveling vacation probably was not too appealing to him. In reading over his diaries and conference notebooks for those years, I marvel at Father's energy and commitment — and also at the constant refreshment he found in Mother's presence. "Still sweethearts," he wrote on New Year's Day, 1937, but it would have been true any day of any year. That same day he reported on family whereabouts: Lou Jean and Russell were in Cleveland where Russell was completing his medical training, I had passed the Utah Bar and had begun practicing, Llewelyn had received his Ph.D. from Stanford in German and was teaching at the University of Utah, Emma Rae was teaching in Granite High School with "an excellent record," Ned had been on his mission in Germany for three months, and Bob was president of his high school senior class.

Father was involved in many more meetings close to home, due to the frequent and extended absences of both President Grant and President J. Reuben Clark. His journal is replete with notations of "answered First Presidency mail"; mentions of marriages solemnized in the temple; the selection, interviewing, and setting apart of mission presidents and their wives; calling, instructing, and setting missionaries apart; hours every day spent with callers; weekly meetings of the Church Security Committee; addressing just-endowed missionaries in the temple on the significance of temple ordinances; and taking part in ceremonial occasions such as dedicating the Springville, Utah, Art Museum on Independence Day, 1937, or this one: "Dropped letter addressed to Mayor San Francisco into Pony Express mail pouch, carried by Lincoln Zephyr. Letter extended congratulatory greetings of First

David O. McKay and his sons, left to right, Llewelyn, Edward, David Lawrence, and Robert

Presidency to the people of S.F. on the opening to traffic of the Golden Gate Bridge." (10 May 1937.)

Here are some items of historical and personal interest from his journal for these years:

"Feb. 19, 1936. . . . Consultation with Nephi L. Morris and Dr. George F. Middleton, representing Sons of the Utah Pioneers, on an eleven year-program preparatory to and culminating in a great celebration July 24, 1947 . . . Many others called on different matters, so occupying my time that I had difficulty in signing letters. . . .

"Feb. 29, 1936. . . . Pres. Grant left . . . for Los Angeles. Pres. Clark is in the East, so I am again alone with the duties of the First Presidency. . . .

"Sunday, March 8, 1936. This day I kept free from all appointments in order that I might start on the second half of the course of lessons I am preparing for the Gospel Doctrine class of the Church. Spent a very satisfactory day in contemplation, study and writing. . . .

"2 Jan. 1937. . . . Met a few minutes with Pres. J. Reuben Clark Jr. and Bp. David P. Howell in consultation about a proposed site for the Temple to be built in Los Angeles. . . .

"8 Jan. 1937. Only one of the Presidency at the office—heavy mail and important decisions to render. . . .

"26 Jan. 1937 . . . With a number of other invited guests, saw the preview of the "March of Time' [newsreel] depicting the church Security Plan [Church Welfare Program]. It is very good, and will undoubtedly wield a helpful influence throughout the world wherever it is shown. . . . Was one of the speakers at a Regional meeting of the Ch[urch] Sec[urity] Plan held in the Granite Stake House. Crowded hall—a very important meeting! . . .

"Feb. 24, 1937. . . . Wilford Wood called in regard to the purchasing of part of the Temple lot in Nauvoo. . . .

"13 March 1937. . . . M. Ramm Hansen, the architect, accompanied Ray and me to Huntsville, where we attempted to choose a site for a summer cottage. The snow was over two feet deep on the level.

"20 March 1937 . . . .Received encouraging news . . . regarding our son Ned's work as a missionary. Parents are amply rewarded when their children make a success in life.

"21 March 1937. . . . Prepared new plan for ward teaching through-out the Church.

"12 April 1937. Arbor Day. I went to Huntsville and with four hired men transplanted and planted about two hundred trees . . . .Came home in the evening so stiff I could hardly straighten up, but I thoroughly enjoyed the day.

"24 April 1937. This morning as for several mornings this week, I went to the office about 6:30 A.M., and dictated letters. . . .

"Sunday, 25 April 1937. No appointment. Attended to daily duties. Had a good *restful* day of *rest.*

"27 April 1937. . . . Jeannette, Anne, and Katherine called—sweet, darling sisters.

"1 May 1937. . . . Midean and Dickie boy, two grandchildren were baptized in the Tabernacle font by David L. Later in the Reception Rm. in the Ch. Office bldg, I confirmed them. . . .

"18 May 1937. . . . Mr. H. C. Mortensen, mgr. of the Deseret Gym convinced me that I should take exercises regularly. Will start tomor-row—perhaps. . . .

"31 May 1937. Decoration Day. At 7:30 A.M. Lawrence, Llewelyn, Bobby, Dickie and I left Salt Lake for Dry Hollow farm. Although the ground was damp and the grass wet, we had an interesting forenoon plowing ditches and doing other necessary work. Four other men repaired fences and cleared dead trees from grove. I received a knock on my right knee while driving the team on the plow, that nearly laid me up. Afternoon met members of the family in the old Home. Annual meeting of the David McKay Co. Had nervous chill when I got home — nerves pretty well shattered by blow on my knee.

"Tuesday, 1 June 1937. Usual duties from 7:30 A.M. until 1 P.M. Ordered off my feet by doctor because fluid and swelling stiffening my knee. . . .

"Thursday, 3 June 1937. . . . Kept three secretaries busy until 6 P.M. . . .

"19 July 1937. . . . Set apart Thos E. McKay as president of that portion of the Swiss-German-German-Austrian Mission to be designated later, and Sister McKay as Pres. of Relief Society. . . .

"August 24, 1937. . . . Meeting with the following architects to discuss plans for the erecting of the new Temples: Edward O. Anderson, Ramm Hansen, John Fetzer, H. C. Pope, Lorenzo Young. [Presiding] Bishop Sylvester Q. Cannon was also present. . . .

"Sunday, 12 September 1937. . . . Welcomed [President Grant] home from a 3 months visit to the European Missions.

"Tuesday, 28 Sept. 1937. . . . Pres. Grant returned to the city this morning . . . has been in New York for the past ten days. Pres. Clark also returned this morning with Pres. Grant, after several months' absence in New York and Europe."

In June 1939, Mother and Father bought a fine large house at 1037 East South Temple, just across from Holy Cross Hospital. Father and Mother were on the best of terms with their Catholic neighbors and enjoyed hearing the bells from the convent chapel. Father told with relish a story of visiting John Fitzgerald, who was ill, and having a priest in the hospital tease him, "What are you doing in my bailiwick?"

Father also numbered among his friends Arthur Wheelock Moulton, bishop of the Episcopalian diocese from 1920 to 1947. I recall once when Father, while recuperating from an illness, was upstairs resting on his first day home from the hospital. Bishop Moulton stopped by to pay his respects, and I explained that the doctor had recommended rest and that I would prefer not to disturb him.

"Oh, of course, of course," said Bishop Moulton. "Please tell him that I called."

When Father woke later that afternoon and came down, I told him of Bishop Moulton's call. He was more upset than I've ever seen him. He immediately put on his hat, got in his car, and drove up to Bishop Moulton's apartment, walked up the stairs, and returned the compliment.

From 1938 to 1940, Father suffered the longest stretch of ill health in his life up to that point. He had a kidney infection in the spring of 1938 and then an operation for a double hernia in November 1939, complicated by pulmonary embolism while he was recuperating. He spent six weeks in the hospital; but the winter air of 1939–40 did not help his recovery, and he went to California for a month. Returning to work too soon, he had to spend another month in Arizona and California, returning to work just before April conference. By then, President Grant was seriously ill from a stroke he had suffered in February. Although he recovered to lead the Church for another five years, his health was seriously impaired. President Clark was able to devote more time to responsibilities at headquarters and, with Father, bore the burdens of the First Presidency. In retrospect, it seems clear that Father's experience as a counselor was a thorough grounding in the administrative tasks of running the Church.

World War II tried our family as it did almost every American family. These were especially difficult years for President Clark. His son-in-law Mervyn S. Bennion was killed during the 1941 Japanese attack on Pearl Harbor, and his wife died in 1944 after a long illness. We were spared such sorrow. Ned was a doctor in the Navy, attached to a destroyer on convoy duty; he and Lottie Lillace Lund were sealed in the Salt Lake Temple by Father on 10 June 1945. Bob returned home from his mission to Argentina in February 1944 and was inducted into the army in March but was home often enough to develop a warm "understanding" with Frances Ellen Anderson. They were married after the war on 28 June 1946. Dr. Russell Blood enlisted in the Navy and served in the Pacific, and Lou Jean returned to Salt Lake City with young Russell to live with Mother and Father while he was gone. Llewelyn was in Europe as a civilian interrogator for the Army, and his wife Alice stayed in Salt Lake City with their three children. Father had married Emma Rae to Conway Ashton in the Salt Lake Temple on 16 August 1939, and they spent the war years in Provo, Utah, where Conway was employed at Geneva Steel, a defense plant.

I know that Father was very concerned about the servicemen and also that missionaries have opportunities to serve both their church and their country. One of our family treasures is a hardbound composition notebook in which Mother wrote penciled drafts of letters to the children before she did final drafts. It covers between 1941 and 1949, though most of the letters are concentrated in 1945 and 1946. Father's pocket diaries and appointment books for this period are extremely sketchy and consist mainly of notes for his addresses, lists of appointments, and "to do" items. Consequently, Mother's letters, though sprinkled over the period, give a warmly illuminating insight into their steady faith and affection for each other and for the rest of the family. (Mother frequently used abbreviations in these first drafts; for greater clarity, I have spelled them out.)

                                                                Aug. 23, 1941
Dear Lou Jean:

. . . Daddy has had his stomach x-rayed and they find it with no ulcer. Tomorrow he will have it pumped to see if there is [illegible]. If there is he cannot take the medicine they give for Meniere's disease, an attack of which all the doctors think he has had.

Last Friday we had Lawrence's family down to noon dinner in honor of Midean. Daddy ate a good dinner of trout, corn, and apple pie, etc., talked to the folks until three o'clock and then went to the office. He went to bed rather tired but no more than usual. I went out on the porch to sleep. About three o'clock I heard some very difficult retching. . . . He had gone to the bathroom, became dizzy, slumped to the floor, and almost passed out. With great difficulty and will power he got back to bed and into bed. He told me to call a doctor. Ned was in Yellowstone so I called Leslie [Dr. Leslie White was the son of Bell White, Mother's cousin]. Les said he had seen Daddy sick many times but never so "out" as he was that night. He finally threw up a pint of blood and after that some bile several times and between times seemed almost unconscious. About nine Les ordered him to the hospital. He still seemed almost unconscious and had to be put on the stretcher and put off at the hospital, too weak to help himself. Dr. Viko, the heart specialist and Dr. Bauerlein, the stomach specialist, consulted with Les & they all thought at first from his last x-ray that the stomach had ruptured the diaphragm and that the part there had ulcerated. But after

Bauerlein ordered him to a sitting posture in bed and he didn't vomit blood again, he decided it was something else. Then since his heart and blood pressure were very good they decided it was Meniere's Disease. The dictionary says that it is a hemorrhage in the canals of the inner ear. It sometimes causes complete deafness and vertigo (dizziness). Usually the room whirls around to the patient but Daddy was himself dizzy, if you know what I mean. Daddy had been a little deaf this year; thank goodness this attack hasn't seemed to make his hearing worse. Oh I hope he has no more attacks. The doctors say it isn't likely but the books say differently.

He had a really hard trip in Palmyra, shaking hands with hundreds of people, giving three talks, examining farms and places of worship to buy in Rochester. . . .

Oh, I've been so worried about him and so thankful he seems better. He held three meetings in his room today. He *cannot* be held down. The minute he feels a little better, he *must* work.

There are no letters from 1942 or 1943. The next letter is dated 10 January 1944:

Dearest Bob:

Congratulations on your very successful mission! Bro. Barker wrote us a letter telling of the fine things you have accomplished and of your excellent Spanish—the best in the mission. Are we proud of our son! Brother Barker certainly didn't hesitate to sing your praises. According to him, you have done wonderful work.

Daddy had your three articles in your magazine translated and I think they are very fine. So does your father. Daddy sent the one about Pres. Grant to the president who was thrilled to get it.

June 12, 1945

Dearest Ned:

Your letter brought us closer to this dear fact that you are safe notwithstanding your extreme nearness to death, and I know from what Lottie said that you were even nearer in the risk to your own life trying to save others. You haven't said a thing about that and we want all the details—please! . . . You know we are not going to even *think* that your

David O.
McKay,
second
counselor
in the First
Presidency, 5
October 1934

life will be lost even if you do have to go to the Pacific. We must have the strongest faith always that you will be protected, and I know you will, for you deserve it. You have always worked for the right, and our Father takes cognizance of those things. We are grateful to Him that you are alive! . . .

Daddy has been suffering several days with pain over his left hip. He thinks it came from getting his feet wet. I can't get him to do anything except take aspirin and apply heat. . . .

There is to be an annual Sunday School party on the 19th and Lawrence is bothering his brain writing up funny stories in rhyme about some of the members. It's a hard job. Some people are too dignified to let out funny stories about themselves. Isn't that silly?

June 27, 1945

Dearest Bob:

. . . You say you hope that on my birthday I might have rest. Of my own volition, I went to Huntsville to clean up the place for the fourth of July, so that some of us might sleep there if we wish. Jean and Russell were with us. Daddy cut the grass in the lot with the mower. Russell cut the croquet lawn, and Jean and I cleaned the house. We were all tired, but it was fun, and I enjoyed it. . . .

Llewelyn sent me a birthday letter, the saddest ever. He met with Saints in destroyed Frankfort and one of them offered Llewelyn his slice of bread, only one slice of which he can have in a day. Each gets one loaf of bread a week. His old Hausfrau and daughter were buried in their cellar when a bomb blew their home to pieces. You know how tender you feel toward your mission mothers and you know how Llewelyn feels when he sees and questions the innocent among the guilty. But if anybody thinks the bombings have stopped their meetings, he is sorely mistaken. They go on as usual and in tip-top shape. Those are services that one can be proud of. Sunday, thirty were present.

Soon after V-J Day, Mother wrote exuberantly to Robert:

Aug. 16, 1945

Dear Bobby:

Ain't life grand! Ain't the news wonderful!!! To think that the wars are over! . . . Oh, we are so happy for all the boys, and of course especially for our own. We are so grateful to our Heavenly Father for his wondrous help. And now the question is, When can you come home? Over the radio yesterday we were told that international censorship is all over so I suppose you can say what you please now without your letters being snooped at. . . .

Ned . . . has a ten day leave and then will be sent to the San Diego Naval Hospital. Isn't that fine? . . . Ned is now a full-fledged Lieutenant, made so after his second citation.

Llewelyn arrived home on the 14th looking fine and dandy. He flew across the ocean. . . .

Daddy is now talking at the funeral of Sister Collet. Yesterday he spoke at the funeral of Preston Blair. . . . That's the way your father spends our two victory holidays – comforting others. He is a most wonderful man. Do you know that?

Sept. 29, 1945

Dear Ned and Lottie:

... We went to the Idaho Falls Temple for four days [for the dedication ceremonies] and ... enjoyed the meetings in the temple very much indeed. The brethren all spoke very well indeed, and Pres. Smith is surprising all of us. He seems to have much added power since becoming president. The Lord is blessing him exceedingly. ...

On the road home we came upon a terrible collision. Daddy stopped and I waited in the car while he went up to it. He saw Sister Neslen sitting straight up in the car dead. Her husband [Clarence Neslen, also a bishop], the former mayor of Salt Lake, has two legs broken and a skull fracture. Sister [Norma] Romney has both legs broken near the hip, Sister Marba Josephson, editor of the *Era,* is blinded in one eye, and her husband [Newell Josephson] died about 10:15. He had two broken legs and a skull fracture. He was given blood transfusions but couldn't be saved. His wife with one eye must care for five children and all because of a drunken driver in the other car. It is the saddest case. We were making for home that afternoon, but Daddy was needed so we stayed in Pocatello all night.

On 15 December 1945, Mother was taken unexpectedly to the hospital where she had an appendectomy. A few weeks, later, she wrote cheerfully to Lou Jean and Russell, making light of her illness:

7 Jan. 1946

... The last two days I have spent answering cards and flowers that were sent to the hospital. There were 19 floral offerings sent to me and now when flowers are so expensive, too. ... Besides those flowers, eighteen Christmas gifts of flowers were sent here. Azaleas, poinsettias, begonias, cyclamen, chrysanthemums, asters, heather, and roses. Six or seven boxes of roses, white, pink, and red. More every year. Poor Daddy! He has had to get up an hour earlier to take care of all these flowers. I am just beginning now to help him. Notwithstanding my age and many operations, our Heavenly Father has blessed me and has brought me out on top.

Jan. 17, 1946

Dearest Bob:

... I am getting stronger every day but still can't turn the world over.... It's a wonder Daddy didn't get down. He had a very bad cold but he wouldn't give in to it and go to bed. He stayed home an hour or two each day until he was better. He is working harder than ever. Today he has a meeting with the commissioners telling them what the committee has planned to do for the 1947 celebration.

Between Christmas 1946 and New Year's, Father and Mother drove to California to stay with some friends, Soren and Anna Jacobsen, on Balboa Island. Sister Jacobsen was an excellent cook, and Mother described the menu for every meal. After one breakfast of tender sea bass, she noted in her little travel journal: "We sat around the table and Dade told story after story much to the delight of Bro. Jacobsen. The tears came quickly to his eyes at any tender bit. Dade is a wonder at story telling. People sit enthralled and as many times as I've heard them I still enjoy them."

Part of their trip was to see the Rose Parade in Pasadena, something Mother had longed to do for years. But even though they had tickets in a grandstand, it was no use. "I was never so disappointed in my life," she wrote, "because I could not see the floats properly being short. I had wanted so many years to see this parade and then to be so disappointed. My blueness lasted all through the game which was a perfect bore to me. I was too tired to enjoy any of it. Was glad I was on the other side of Dade so I could pout to my heart's content!"

Another of the trips they took that spring reveals Father's idea of a "rest." According to Mother's entry on 15 May 1947:

"Dade was in great need of a rest so made arrangements to attend the dedication of the new Klamath Falls church. ... We started at 7:30 Friday morning & drove 500 miles over desert and stopped at Sparks, just out of Reno."

The next time Father needed a "rest" was even more comical in retrospect, though not at the time it was happening. Mother recorded:

Nov. 5, 1947

Left in the auto for Los Angeles for a rest which David O. badly
needed. The first snow of the season was coming down rather heavily
and Dade expressed the opinion that perhaps we'd better not go. We'd
better heed that premonition next time because since we didn't he had
a strenuous time battling with the snow all the way to Cedar [City,
Utah]. Several times he had to get out and wipe off the window because
the wiper would freeze. He consequently took cold which settled in his
back and gave him lumbago. . . .

The snow was so heavy in Springville he turned back as far as
Provo but since it abated a bit he decided to go on. The snow continued . . . and the car began to skid and Dad couldn't stop it. He was afraid
to put on the brake until just before the car decided to go over a precipice
and then he put it on quickly. It worked and the car stopped very
fortunately. Were we frightened!

It is unfortunate that we do not have Father's own record of the
long-awaited centennial in 1947 of the Saints' entry into the Salt Lake
Valley. Certainly it had occupied a great deal of his time and attention
as chairman of the Centennial Commission, and his personal involvement contributed significantly to its success in bringing both Mormons
and non-Mormons together in a spirit of community. Fortunately, Loren
F. Wheelwright, manager of the Arts Division, recorded memories of
two particularly outstanding events related to the creation of *Promised
Valley,* a full-scale musical with music by Crawford Gates and book and
lyrics by Arnold Sundgaard.

Only three weeks before opening night, Brother Wheelwright
showed the committee proofs of the souvenir program, one side of which
had already been printed. Father, as chairman of the committee, complimented their work but pointed out that a photograph of "Brother
John" (John Fitzpatrick, Catholic publisher of the Salt Lake *Tribune*
and vice-chairman of the Centennial Commission) was missing. Determined on anonymity, Fitzpatrick had refused to supply the necessary
photograph. Father's counsel, in Fitzpatrick's presence, was tactful but
clear: "Even if you have to reprint 40,000 copies, I request that you
give official and proper recognition to our distinguished vice-chairman.
And John, I trust that you will find it possible to instruct your paper to

find that picture." Brother Wheelwright recognized "our chairman wants a printed record of the fact that here, in our time, on this occasion and for this purpose, we are one as a community and old resentments of any kind are hereby buried and forgotten."

Promised Valley turned out to be a smashing success, and word of mouth brought people streaming in from out of town to obtain tickets. Two performances had been rained out, and the play was scheduled to close after two weeks on a Saturday night. The pressure to extend the performance raised the question of holding a final performance on Sunday night. Brother Wheelwright discussed the pros and cons with Father who, after a day's deliberation, authorized him to have a final performance on Sunday at 8:30 P.M., after sacrament meetings in the valley wards would be over.

Brother Wheelwright recorded: "No sooner is the word published than I receive a phone call from another high Church official who says, 'Brother Wheelwright, I see you are going to break the Sabbath and run that show.' I respond by thanking my caller, and then observing, 'You flatter me to think that I possess the authority to make this decision alone. The fact is, it was made by our chairman, David O. McKay. His office is not far from yours. I suggest that you discuss the decision with him.' Then I call our beloved leader to report the conversation. Here is a sensitive problem, and I wonder how he will respond. After a moment's pause, he says simply, 'I have given this matter full consideration, and *I am willing to face my Maker on this decision.*'" (*Instructor,* Jan. 1963, center section.)

Chapter 11

"I'LL NEED A SECRETARY": THE 1952 EUROPEAN TOUR

◆ ◆ ◆ ◆ ◆ ◆ ◆ ◆ ◆ ◆ ◆ ◆

In August 1950, George F. Richards died, leaving Father the senior apostle. When President George Albert Smith died on 4 April 1951, Father was seventy-seven years old and had been an apostle for forty-five years almost to the day. He was sustained president of the Church. He selected Stephen L Richards as his first counselor and J. Reuben Clark, Jr., as his second counselor.

Father confidently left his two experienced counselors in charge of much of the day-to-day administration and traveled vigorously to strengthen the Saints, conduct conferences, and get direct impressions of the needs of the Church. No record from Father of that first year has survived in family hands, but Mother's little travel notebook records some details. On 4 May 1951, while Father was recuperating from prostate surgery, surrounded by "200 short-stemmed pink roses," she wrote rhetorically, "Bro. Richards wants [Dade] to take a ten-day or two week rest but will he?" Of course, the answer was no.

At his bedside, Mother jotted down notes for a biographical sketch, doubly precious now since many of these details, even in sketchy summary, have been lost to us. For instance, she specifies that Father proposed to her "under the umbrella tree" in Lester Park, in Ogden, and that she was "putting up fruit" in the summer of 1922 when Father came in and told her that the First Presidency had called him to preside over the European Mission. I wish she had been able to complete her own story in her own words.

David O. McKay, ninth president of The Church of Jesus Christ of Latter-day Saints

As soon as Father felt strong enough that summer, he set out again on a cross-country trip with Mother to the Hill Cumorah Pageant. Mother wrote:

"Aug. 8, 1951. . . . I've never seen such delighted people as these were to meet the new president. People who had never seen a church president before, newcomers and converts to the church were thrilled. There were hundreds of Kodaks and people everywhere wanting to shake hands. Dade gave a . . . talk that thrilled everyone."

Father, after concentrating so closely on managing the affairs of the First Presidency, seemed to want to experience the needs and strengths of the Saints in the field. After traveling within the United States and Mexico for the first few months after his ordination as president of the Church, he then decided to visit the Saints abroad.

On Mother's Day, 1952, Mother and Father had dinner at our home.

Just as Mildred was bringing in the dessert, Father announced, "I'm going to tour all of the European missions this summer, Lawrence, and I'll need a secretary. The Brethren said that I can ask you, if you're free to accept; and if you can 'scrape up' enough money for Mildred, she can accompany us, too."

Mildred confessed, "I almost dropped the dessert." Both of us were thrilled with the opportunity. Midene was married, and a dear friend, Lucy Millfred, lived in to care for our three younger girls while we were gone.

Both of us feel that those sixty-four days — one day more than nine weeks — with my parents are among the most precious of our adult lives. We were able to see what commitment to building the kingdom meant, day in and day out, under a variety of circumstances, many of them very strenuous for a couple in their late seventies; and it made us think sober thoughts about the purity and love that actuated such commitment. Both Mother and Father kept diaries in pocket-size, wire-bound books, as did Mildred; it is from these diaries, plus our own vivid memories, that we have reconstructed the events of that tour.

In those nine weeks, we visited nine countries, several of them more than once, and attended scores of meetings. Father gave numerous interviews to journalists, selected two temple sites, and conducted much private mission business. A little note in the back of Mother's diary observes, "45 meetings in 50 days," but a last four-meeting Sunday in Scotland after the tour was officially over had not happened yet, nor does that number include the dozens of meetings Father held with small groups, mission leaders, service men, and individuals.

Father's diary concentrates mostly on events, appointments, and decisions. Mother typically noted items on the menu, the weather, and what people wore, in a life-long habit of capturing and preserving vivid details.

They left by train on 19 May 1952. Although flying would have been faster, both of them liked the train. Not only did Mother dislike flying, but those hours in a train were a precious time for Father to relax and rest in comparative peace. Mildred and I saw them off and then flew a day later to meet them in New York, where Lou Jean and Russell were living.

In New York, they checked into the Waldorf Astoria and visited with Lou Jean, Russell, and grandson Russell M. for the afternoon. They had been given a lavish tower suite, and Father promptly instructed the travel agency to secure much more modest accommodations for the rest of the trip. "It would be ridiculous for the Church to receive this kind of exclusive treatment in Europe," he commented. On Sunday, "we went to Sunday School at the Manhattan Ward," Mother recorded. "A very good class was held. Afterwards fast meeting at which beautiful testimonies were given. Daddy's short talk was a gem."

The flight via Gander, Newfoundland, was, as Mother wrote, "very smooth and uneventful. . . . I wasn't the least bit frightened." In fact, after the frequent flights within Europe, Father asked Mother if she wanted to fly home or take the ship back. After thinking about the relative merits of both cases, including her almost inevitable seasickness, Mother decided she'd rather "fly and get it over with." As far as I know, Father always enjoyed flying—both the achievement of the machine and the sensation of speed.

Our itinerary included Glasgow and Edinburgh in Scotland; London; Switzerland; Rotterdam and Svestdyke, Netherlands, where they met Queen Juliana; Copenhagen, Denmark; Oslo, Norway; Stockholm, Sweden; Helsinki, Finland; Hamburg, Berlin, Hannover, and Frankfurt, Germany; and then back to Switzerland for six days that took the party through Zurich, Basel, Lucerne, Wengen Scheidegg, Lausanne, Geneva, Bern, and Interlaken. From Switzerland, the party went to Paris and then to Great Britain, where Father went to Grandmother McKay's birthplace in Merthyr Tydfil, Wales, attended Queen Elizabeth's garden party at Buckingham Palace, and left for home via Glasgow.

These memories are dear to us, of course; but the full journal accounts and our own memoirs are far too lengthy to recount here. Many elements of the visits were the same in each area: in those few weeks, we heard "We Thank Thee, O God, for a Prophet" sung in English—including Scots and Welsh accents—French, German, Finnish, Norwegian, Dutch, Danish, and Swedish. Virtually every party that we met during the entire tour had flowers for Mother and Mildred and a presentation gift for Father, usually something reminiscent of the locale. One of the secretary's duties, I discovered, was to arrange to have the gifts sent home. I also recorded each public speech he gave, lugging around a large reel-to-reel recorder, locating the proper adapters, and stringing endless extension cords in the various meeting halls. I sent these reels home to Father's secretary, Clare Middlemiss, daily;

and she transcribed them, both for the official records and also for the *Deseret News*, which followed the European tour with interest. I also tried to take care of the routine duties for Father—packing, assembling notes, arranging schedules, and making sure that travel arrangements were adequate. Since airplanes did not have reserved seats at that time, Mildred and I tried to be in line well ahead of time so that we could locate four seats together and fairly forward in the cabin to reduce the amount of vibration for Mother and Father.

In general, the Saints seemed pleased that President McKay had brought part of his family with him; and Mother never failed to win delighted smiles by her modest statement: "President McKay came to represent the Church, my son came to represent the Sunday School, his wife came to represent the Primary, and I came to take care of my husband." And she did! When Mildred once asked if she could help wash out a few items that needed to be laundered, Mother responded firmly, "*I* can take care of my husband." She unobtrusively encouraged Father to get more rest and tried to see that he got enough to eat—not always successfully.

Father never gave the same sermon twice, although he had virtually no preparation time. Instead, he drew on his well-stocked memory and understanding of gospel principles to address the Saints on such subjects as divine authority by direct revelation, by their fruits ye shall know them, and the greatest thing in the world: a Christlike character. He tailored his addresses to each national audience and delighted his hearers with appreciative quotations from their own literature. In England, he quoted Charles Dickens's appraisal of Mormon emigrants aboard the *Amazon* as "the pick and flower of England." In Berlin, he quoted Goethe; in Paris, Victor Hugo. He insisted on scheduling special meetings for servicemen ("They're missionaries, too"). Father spoke easily with a translator, adapting the rhythms of his speech to convenient units for translations, but occasionally overestimating the translator's capacity to deal with his eloquent and versatile vocabulary.

He also gave numerous interviews to reporters. His journal does not always specify the number of reporters present at interviews, but he gave at least thirty-two. His charm and courtesy had an almost magical effect on these individuals. I attended nearly all of these sessions and recall no hostile challenges. Father completely won over one reporter by quoting Othello's charge, with twinkling eyes, "Speak of me as I am, nothing extenuate, nor set down aught in malice."

Father's stamina was extraordinary. He seldom got more than six or seven hours of sleep a night, and almost never slept in the same bed twice. Meals were often irregular, depending on travel schedule. Father thought nothing of making up time by missing a meal or even two and had a remarkable ability to move from public presentation to intimate counseling sessions without losing his intense focus. He was never inattentive nor distracted, no matter how fatigued, when he was in personal interviews. He understood intuitively that his visit was the experience of a lifetime for the Saints and willingly stood in line, shaking hands for hours with entire congregations after nearly every conference.

I recall at one point in Wales when we were quite worried about him. We had been traveling during the day and arrived just in time to go straight to a missionary meeting where he spoke, and then he and Mother attended a Welsh musical. After that, the mission president asked if he would consider visiting a sick elder in the hospital who would otherwise not see him. Mildred and I gently remonstrated, "You just can't keep this up. It's already midnight." With even greater gentleness and a good deal of firmness, he reminded us, "This is what I'm here for if they have to carry me out on a slab."

Our health, too, was remarkably good during the entire nine weeks. We joined Father and Mother in their hotel room for prayers each morning, and the petitions for health and strength were answered literally. Mother came down with a cold in Finland but shook off its effects in a day or two. Father was immune to everything. And those moments together, when Father supplicated the Lord on behalf of the members of the Church in Europe, were some of the sweetest and most powerful memories we have of that trip.

Here, then, are highlights, selected from many precious memories and events, of those nine weeks.

Scotland. Mildred noted in her diary as we flew in to Glasgow: "Tears in eyes as Papa Dade looked from plane to shores of Scotland." (2 June 1952.)

The plane was three hours late in landing, so we rushed straight to the first meeting, the dedication of Glasgow Chapel—the first LDS-owned meetinghouse in Scotland. Afterwards, recorded Mother, "we shook hands with 300 people. 12 asked for baptism."

Next morning at the hotel, Father joked with the waiter, "This isn't like the Scotch porridge I remember fifty-four years ago," and the waiter quipped back, with such a straight face that we weren't sure he was joking, "Oh, *that* cook! He just died a fortnight ago."

Father had scheduled that first full day in Scotland as a special day to visit some of his beloved sites in Scotland—Loch Lomond and the Trossachs. Father regaled the party with his vigorous recital of the classic duel of James Fitzjames and Roderick Dhu and other passages from Sir Walter Scott's *The Lady of the Lake.*

On 4 June 1952, we took an express bus for Edinburgh, where Father dedicated the new meetinghouse, a remodeled four-story home, freshly cleaned, painted, and papered. Ceiling murals in the chapel area in the Greek style had featured naked cherubs that a mission artist had modestly painted trailing draperies on. At the services, Mother wrote, "Lawrence & Mildred gave very good short talks and I had to say a few words. Daddy's talk was marvelous for those people. He told about his grandmother's friend, the old lady who thought Scotland a Heaven. ... The people were thrilled when he talked Scotch. His talk & prayer were wonderful." It was typical of Mother to be reluctant to speak and thrilled with Father's speeches.

Father noted in his journal that we then "greeted entire congregation" and caught the 10:30 P.M. train for London.

At some point during this day, we had found time to visit Argyle Archives, seeking a published history of the McKay clan that, as I recall, Father had heard about on his mission. The archivist knew the book in question and explained, "It's out of print now, but we frequently receive collections of genealogical works. If one were to come in, would you like me to inform you?" Father said that he would, indeed. Twenty-five years later, in 1977, after Father had been dead for seven years, a letter was forwarded to me from this stationer, stating that the book had come in. It is now carefully preserved in our family.

London. Thursday, 5 June, was not only Queen Elizabeth II's official birthday but also that of Llewelyn. "I hope the dear boy had a good time & hope the new hat we left him will suit him," Mother wrote. Father "spent the [next] day investigating a temple site" with President Stayner Richards. I accompanied the party and recall, as one of the more interesting possibilities, a large historic home with a secret room, entered through the fireplace, where the Cavalier owner could hide from

Cromwell's Roundheads. Another historic property had been a home owned by Henry VIII's sixth wife. Father did not like the connotations of Henry VIII and preferred to look elsewhere. These sites were north of London. South of London, we found a beautiful old mansion for sale in Surrey that instantly appealed to Father. The mansion could serve as the home for the temple president and guests, while the lovely wooded site seemed perfect for a temple. Father authorized the mission president to close the deal; and although it was involved in an estate settlement and took over a year to conclude, the final details were at last completed in 1953. Father dedicated this temple in 1958.

Some people have felt that Father had not planned to select temple sites in Europe but felt inspired to do so after he arrived and saw the condition of the Saints. On the contrary, the establishment of temples in Europe was one of his primary motivations in scheduling this tour; and he had told Mildred and me at the time he asked us to accompany him, "We'll pick out the sites for the Swiss and British temples." Thus, I understood that even the countries had already been chosen and authorized by the First Presidency.

The next day saw three full public sessions. Father spoke at all three and "stood in line greeting [afternoon] congregation until after time to start evening meeting," as he wrote in his diary. "Following this closing session stood in line again until 8:50 P.M. . . . Pretty well worn out when we arrived at the Grosvenor Hotel at 10:30 P.M."

Switzerland. Early Tuesday morning, 10 June, we flew to Basel, where President and Sister Samuel E. Bringhurst of the Swiss mission and President and Sister Golden L. Woolfe of the French mission met us.

That evening, Father, Presidents Richards, Bringhurst, Woolf, and I met in "prayer and council regarding the important duty of choosing the city near which a Temple may be built. . . . Bern was decided upon." As I recall the discussion, Switzerland had already been selected as a central location for all of Europe; then we eliminated sites: Zurich might be considered too industrial, Lausanne was too far away from the German sector, and Basel had been too close to the recent war. This left Bern as the most desirable location.

Next morning, Wednesday, 11 June, we all drove the sixty-five miles to Bern to look for sites. Llewelyn and Alice's oldest son, Dick, was a missionary there; and Mother and Father were delighted to spend some time with him. He had a tape recording from home and, during a free evening, we all recorded another message to send back.

Father was serious about finding a temple location that same day, if possible. With Max Zimmer, the architect, we visited several of the sites. Just outside Bern where we had stopped to refuel, Father pointed up to the hills above the little town of Zollikofen and said, "That would be an ideal location for a temple." President Bringhurst agreed, adding, "but it's not available. We can't get it." Another beautiful location was a mansion where Napoleon had stayed during his conquest of Europe; but it was a historic site that could not have accepted a modern building. Another location outside Bern looked ideal, until suddenly a train careened past, and we visualized the unsuitable interruptions this kind of traffic would create.

As we were driving between two or three other potential sites, we came to a location at the junction of a major road between Lausanne and Bern with a third highway from Basel also feeding in. The convenience of this location was obvious, and so was its peaceful setting. Father said, "This is the place, Brother Bringhurst." The property was tied up in a complicated estate settlement, however, and simply didn't seem to be available. Father felt quite clear about his choice, however, and wrote in his diary that they had "chose[n] an excellent site."

The sequel to this story is that settling the estate turned out to be a very complicated process. All of the heirs had to consent to the sale, and one firmly refused because "land in Switzerland is not expandable." After several months, the best choice, the property at Zollikofen, suddenly became available for half the price; and, with the consent of the First Presidency, President Bringhurst promptly closed the deal. Father dedicated the beautiful Swiss Temple in 1955.

When the group returned to the hotel for lunch, Dick arrived, greatly relieved to find us. "I've been looking all over for you," he exclaimed. He had received a telephone call from the mission secretary frantically trying to trace Father for President Donovan H. VanDam in Holland. President VanDam, a former colonel in the army, had said emphatically, "Young man, this is important. You *find* President McKay."

Negotiations had begun before Father left the United States for an audience with Queen Juliana of the Netherlands. Now, word had come that she would receive Father and Mother at 3 P.M. the next day, on the 13th. We huddled over timetables and discovered that there was just time for me to return to Basel, pack our bags, and meet the group at the airport in Zurich.

The Netherlands. The next day found us at Svestdyke, the queen's summer palace. Father made a separate report of this visit, which is not in his journal, but Mother's account is delightfully detailed:

"Two cars went out to the queen's summer palace through rows of very beautiful trees with green trunks. The houses are all mansions in that part of town. Mildred & Lawrence couldn't go in much to my disappointment & to Mildred's. Word was sent that only two were expected by the queen. The guards questioned us closely & after telephoning to the palace found that we were expected. We walked up the stone steps and were met by the queen's private secretary called Baron Von Heeckeren of Venmolecaten. He showed us up a flight of stairs covered by an elegant red carpet into a small reception room and asked us to sit down. In a moment, the queen opened the door. She was dressed in a simple hostess gown—a dainty salmon pink. She asked me to sit down near her and David opposite to her. Before coming in I asked the secretary whether we should curtsy, bow low or what. He said, O no, the queen has done away with the curtsy. She will shake hands with you. And she did.

"She was so gracious, I did not feel the least bit worried but was right at home with her. She offered us cigarettes & when we refused, she and her secretary smoked and puffed very hard filling the room with smoke. She then served tea and cookies and while we were nibbling at the cookies, Dade took the opportunity of explaining the Word of Wisdom. She turned to me and said, 'Do you think tea is a stimulant?' 'Yes,' I said, 'we think we should take nothing into our bodies that is not good for the body.' David also had an opportunity of explaining missionary work. They were amazed. It seemed as though they'd never heard of the Mormons before.

"I said to her, that I wished she had come west to see our mountain scenery when she was in America. 'Oh,' with a flourish, 'I was out there one time and flew over the Great Salt Lake & saw the scenery from the air.' I told her that wasn't the same as seeing it by car etc.

"They were very gracious. He is tall and handsome with features more like an Englishman than a Dutchman. She is better looking than her pictures. As we rose to go, she said, 'O, so soon? Why I have all the afternoon free.' I gave her a card of the Articles of Faith."

At Queen Juliana's summer palace in Svestdyke, Holland, 12 June 1952. With the McKays are Holland mission president Donovan H. VanDam and his wife, Ada

That evening, Father spoke at a banquet at the Palace Hotel at Scheveningen near The Hague on the beach of the North Sea for 140 missionaries and honored guests ("very creditable, dignified occasion," Father noted). Mother recorded that the waiters all stayed in the hall to listen to Father's talk and that the hotel owner made a point of complimenting the behavior of the missionaries.

Father delighted the missionaries with missionary reminiscences, recounting his attempts to sing on street corners with the elders of Glasgow to attract an audience for a street meeting. He demonstrated his repertoire: "Israel, Israel, God Is Calling," "O My Father," and "What Was Witnessed in the Heavens"—all sung to the tune of "Israel, Israel, God Is Calling." The repetition "made no difference," he pointed out, "because we didn't have the same audience at the conclusion that we had at the beginning."

At the meeting for the Rotterdam Saints, 1,027 members and friends crowded into a small hall with "poor ventilation." Before the conference, we visited the site of our former LDS meetinghouse, bombed to rubble "by the Nazis. Beautiful new buildings have arisen and new zoning has prevented our building again on the same spot. Too bad they won't allow it," wrote Mother wistfully.

Denmark. On Saturday, 14 June, we flew to Copenhagen, where President and Sister Edward H. Sorensen and the ubiquitous reporters met us. The airport was flying the United States flag, and a group of about two hundred missionaries and Saints were inside the terminal, singing "Come, Come, Ye Saints" and other songs of welcome. "People around were very curious to know who we are and two women wanted to know whether we were representatives of the United Nations. We informed them," Mother said with mild pride. "It was a great sight to see all of those people singing those songs. We shook hands with many missionaries." A long-time airport employee said it was the first time in his experience that "everything came to a stop for one party."

Sister Sorensen gave us downstairs bedrooms; and at breakfast the next morning, we were astonished to see six or eight missionaries around the table, since we had heard virtually no morning noise. President Sorensen laughed, "Sister Sorensen has had them practicing for days — going upstairs and down in their stocking feet and learning where to place their feet to avoid the squeaks. We didn't want anything to interfere with your night's sleep."

Around conference assignments, we visited Elsinore, the Danish castle in which Shakespeare's *Hamlet* was set. My septuagenarian mother was so excited by the event that she all but sprinted up the stairs to the tower to see where the ghost had walked, and she and Father delightedly recited favorite passages from that play to each other and us.

Norway. In Oslo, we were greeted by President and Sister Sherman Gowans, a youthful couple with young children. Sister Gowans was pregnant, and Mother was pleased that they were almost finished with their missions and would soon be home. They whisked us off to a comfortable hotel for a quiet rest, and then to dinner on a boat restaurant. Mother and Father enjoyed the "beautiful old airs" played on the piano, and Father quite enjoyed astonishing the waiter by assuring him that the whole party indeed wanted milk.

Between conference sessions in which Father again spoke in every meeting and they shook hands with the entire congregation, we visited a ski slope, apparently the first Mother had ever seen, the raft *Kontiki,* in which Thor Heyerdahl had established the possibility of early trans-Pacific travel, and Amundsen's ship, in which he had sailed to Antarctica.

Father also called on the United States ambassador to Norway, Charles U. Bay, accompanied by President Gowans and me, to pay his respects. Later, President Gowans told Mother, "It was just like electricity between those two men." It was an immensely cordial visit. Leon Cowles, son of LeRoy Cowles, president of the University of Utah, was on Bay's staff and had been very instrumental in dispelling some of the prejudice against Latter-day Saints. The ambassador asked Father to send him his photograph, which Father later did, asked if Father would accept his, and expressed personal regrets at the embassy's "failure to arrange an interview with [the] King or Crown Prince. 'If I were king or Crown Prince, I should consider it an honor to have you call on me,'" Bay said.

Sweden. In Stockholm, the missionaries discovered that Father liked yogurt, a good substitute for his beloved clabber. Late at night, they came in and triumphantly announced that they had finally found some yogurt for him. Father was most appreciative.

An energetic missionary, John K. Russell from London, had worked hard on publicity and had scheduled a news conference at which fourteen papers were represented, the most in one group that Father spoke to on the trip. A representative from United Press also phoned to ask "if there were any developments," Mother recorded. "David O. told him that we wanted to build meeting houses and he [the reporter] was surprised when David said the Church would send over 3/4th of the money to build them."

Mother was relieved when a tour of old Stockholm was abbreviated enough to give "my dear husband" a nap before evening meeting. She fretted, "He shouldn't take more than one talk a day. He is too tired taking three." When they walked into the hall, a "wonderful" portrait of Father, painted by Austrian Rudolf Tupsy from photographs, was hanging on the wall. "Since seeing David he wants to put more hair on [the] head and less brown in the eyes," Mother noted. "It is wonderful to do so well never having seen the person he painted."

Father was enchanted by a "beautiful sunset at 9:00 P.M.!" and by the fact that at midnight he "could still see time on watch." (20 June 1952.)

After a full weekend of meetings, Monday was Mother's seventy-fifth birthday, and Father had quietly asked me to arrange for a cake. This was the kind of news that everyone wished to participate in, however; and a group of two hundred, arranged by the indefatigable Elder Russell, sang "Happy Birthday to You" at the airport while Sister Johnson gave Mother a bouquet of red roses. Mother wrote with mixed feelings, "How sweet of them. They came down in four busses. We certainly were the object of all eyes. What an experience!" Father, however, simply beamed. He rejoiced whenever Mother was honored.

Finland. The flight to Finland was extremely bumpy, but an experienced passenger sitting next to Mother noted her initial apprehension and told her to expect roughness when the plane approached a "cone-shaped" cloud. By looking out the window, Mother could thus prepare herself, which greatly contributed to her peace of mind.

President and Sister Henry Matis greeted us and took us to an ultramodern hotel, the Vaakuna, completed just the month before. They were from Chicago, and Brother Matis was a Finn by birth. Sister Matis therefore had had a special interest in participating in a Relief Society project in Chicago to supply clothing and quilts to the Saints in Europe after the war. Then in 1951, Brother Matis had been called to open the Finnish mission with twenty-seven missionaries. Because of conditions, they were advised to take as many of their own household supplies as possible, including all the clothing they might need for the duration of their mission. They had three young children and, due to a mishap en route, arrived in Finland with few belongings and no bedding. The Finnish Saints, hearing their plight, brought them some bedding that had been sent to them from the American Saints. "And there," said Sister Matis, tears gleaming on her cheeks, "were the very quilts I had worked on in Chicago. I never thought I would wrap my own babies in them."

The Matises drove us through "misty weather," as Father called it, to Vahtjarvi Lake where the Church's Boy Scout and Girl Scout units were celebrating Midsummer's Eve with a bonfire. The Scouts were drawn up in impressive formation, around three sides of a square. Songs of welcome, speeches, and the presentation of lilies of the valley followed, "then surprise! They all sang 'Happy Birthday to You' to me," wrote Mother, "and another song that the Finns use for birthdays." The missionaries gave her a bouquet of pink roses, one for each year. The Scouts, who had been working hard all day to make their tents neat and clean, proudly showed the camp to Mother and Father, who praised everything, even though Mother privately wondered "how people could sleep in such a cold, damp place."

Mother was not feeling well, so she stayed in the hotel room while Father conducted the evening meeting, tying his discourse on Christ, the Light of the world with the celebration of St. John's Day on Midsummer Eve. About three hundred fifty members attended the main conference session, and Mother noted approvingly. "Fine showing considering the Gospel has been preached here only 5 years."

On Wednesday, 25 June, Father and President Matis flew to Finland's "Gold Coast," Kuitaranta, to call on the president of Finland, Juho K. Paasikivi, who received them "graciously." After newspaper interviews, and a visit to the United States ambassador, President Matis then took Father and me to the hotel's sauna for a real Finnish experience. Father insisted on going right to the top of the sauna, to experience the hottest temperature. But we were both taken aback when the "scrubber," whose task was to rub us down vigorously with a rough brush, turned out to be a woman. We declined that part of the experience. After we were dressed, the woman was waiting for us. Laughing, she touched Father's white hair and her own gray locks and said in Finnish, "Next time, you'll do this right."

Germany. We left Helsinki for Hamburg on the morning of 26 June. A large group of missionaries and members were on hand to make final presentations of flowers and gifts and to sing, including "God Be with You Till We Meet Again." Touched, Mother wrote: "The air station is round and it was a picture to see them standing in that upper circle. Bless their hearts. How sweet they all are and so happy to have David with them."

President and Sister Edwin Q. Cannon and a party of elders met us in Hamburg and helped us arrange for visas, a time-consuming process. We were quite anxious about being detained, but Father was completely relaxed. For someone who could always be provoked by unpunctuality, he was the least impatient of men. He said, paraphrasing Mark Twain with a twinkle in his eye, "I'm an old man and I've had many worries, but most of them have never happened." He also noted in his diary, "Only time bags have been requested to be opened." (26 June 1952.)

Mother was still not over the slight illness that had afflicted her in

Finland, and wrote, "I was not at all satisfied with the part I took in Hamburg, but I was half sick and it makes a difference." She had started to recite a poem, but some of the words had eluded her and she had to leave it partially finished. The program continued with a song; then before Father spoke, he said, "I'm sure Sister McKay has remembered that poem and will want to give it." Mother gave her poem perfectly, to the satisfaction of all, including herself. She did not mention these details, but instead focused on her sweetheart: "After Dade's talk the people came up in such numbers (there were over 800 there, people standing up all around the sides) that it took two men to hold them back so they wouldn't crush one another. The Germans are so vigorous in everything they do." Father noted, "860 in attendance. . . . Hand shaking until 10:15 P.M. Fatigued after a long strenuous day." (26 June 1952.)

Father always insisted that Mildred and I join the line for hand-shaking along with the mission president and his wife. After we had been shaking hands for some time, Mildred whispered to me, "Have you noticed how many people are left-handed here? It keeps me on my toes to know which hand to put out." I glanced up the line where the Saints were shaking hands with Mother and Father and realized that many of the "left-handers" who came to us were quietly offering their left hands after having shaken right hands with their prophet and president.

In Berlin, Father gave a radio interview, spent an entire morning with two reporters, conducted and spoke at the missionary meeting, dedicated the meetinghouse in Charlottenburg, and then held a full-scale conference in Berlin on Sunday, 29 June. In contrast to the "vigorous" northern crowd in Hamburg, Father noted at the dedicatory service that the audience was "orderly [and] respectful. . . . Arose and remained standing until we left rostrum."

At the Sunday meeting, twenty-six hundred crowded into the hall. The police at first cleared the aisles of all who were standing, but then later allowed them to enter "since the crowd is so orderly," Father noted. The missionaries also explained that Mormons don't smoke so that there would be no danger of fire. Here Father's versatility received an unexpected test. Following a beautiful solo arrangement of "My Peace I Leave with You," I gave a short address on peace. Father leaned over to Mother and said, "He's taken my theme!" So he gave an address on faith.

That evening, he dedicated another church building at Belham and shook hands with the entire congregation except for two men who avoided the line. "Local brethren surmised that they were 'Red' spies, as they shoved past everyone," Father recorded.

Sight-seeing in Berlin was a sobering experience. Mother was heartsick at the devastation of the university, Parliament, and the churches. "So many people here have cause to mourn, and their faces show it," she wrote sorrowfully.

We flew to Hannover on Monday, 30 June. This stop had been added after the call on Queen Juliana had rearranged our schedule for us and turned out to be a direct answer to the fasting and prayers of the Hannover Saints, who had been hoping Father could dedicate their new meetinghouse, rebuilt since the war. The Cannons and the Schreyers had driven earlier and were there to meet us at the airport, to show Father the new meetinghouse, and to delight Mother with a drive around the city's beautiful gardens and lakes. "Daddy enthralled his hearers at night," she wrote, "but it was so hot one woman nearly passed out."

It was a long meeting; and Elder Schreyer, hoping to spare Father and Mother, asked the people to stand and remain in their places until they had left the chapel. As we came through the doors and looked down the garden to the street, Mother and Father looked back. Seeing the expressions on the faces of the people, Mother said, "Dade, we can't do this." Father just beamed. "We surely can't," he said. They returned to the door and shook hands with the entire congregation.

After the meeting, as we neared our hotel, Father saw a soldier in a Scots kilt. It looked like a McKay tartan, and Father insisted on chatting with him. The young man was from Canada and belonged to the Black Watch regiment, which has a similar tartan. This comical conversation ensued:

President Schreyer asked, "Do you know whom you are talking to? This is David O. McKay, president of the Latter-day Saint Church, commonly known as the Mormons. Have you heard of them?"

"Oh yes, I've heard of them," the soldier answered with considerable enthusiasm. "My mother's one of them."

"Well," Father said kindly, "when you write to your mother, tell her you met me."

"Damn right, boy, I will," responded his new friend vigorously.

The next morning, Tuesday, 1 July, we drove to Frankfurt with the Cannons, while President Schreyer and his party followed in another car. Father's agricultural eye appreciatively noted the "luxuriant crops on every hand. Rectangular patches — too small to be called fields — of oats, wheat, rye, beets, potatoes."

Mother was dazzled by the rose gardens which, she felt, made up for coming too late for the tulip season in Holland. Father held two meetings, including one with missionaries and servicemen combined, and gave more newspaper interviews. At the large public meeting in Palm Gardens, it was ferociously hot — the hottest day recorded in the past hundred years. Father's stamina was impressive. We were sitting behind him on the stand and noticed that perspiration had so thoroughly soaked his shirt collar while he was speaking that the black line of his tie was plainly visible.

Switzerland. On 3 July, we drove to Zurich, arriving at midday. Without pausing for more refreshment than a glass of water and some ice cream, Father immediately began visiting proposed temple sites with President Samuel E. Bringhurst.

The next morning, 4 July, Father was awake at 4:30 A.M. and sent a holiday telegram to Thomas E. in Huntsville, transmitting the greetings of all of us, including Richard McKay. Conference sessions were brutally hot ("fans saved our lives," Mother noted), and my parents' unflagging graciousness kept them in line to shake hands with six hundred forty people. At the Sunday School session, Father, as was his custom, spoke to the children, using an illustration that had become a bit of trademark with him. Comparing their lives to a glass of pure water, he would, before their enthralled eyes, carefully release a drop from his fountain pen. As the ink fell into the water and spread throughout the glass, making the water murky, Father would make his point about the importance of purity in personal living. Here we had double translation. A missionary translated Father's English statements into high German, and the Sunday School teachers, each with his or her class clustered about, translated them into low German.

A welcome respite was a two-day expedition into the Swiss Alps, visiting Interlaken, Zurich, the Jungfrau, Grundenwal, the Aletsch Glacier, Chillon Castle, and Lausanne. Father and Mother were both thrilled with the glorious scenery, although Mother loyally noted, "We have magnificent scenery at home, just as beautiful mountains, and more so."

In Lausanne, a high priority was visiting my old friends, the Chappuis family. Sister Chappuis, now widowed, was "delighted to see their missionary once again," Mother wrote. I had made a tape-recorded message from members of the family who had emigrated to America; and when we played it for them, Sister Chappuis "cried, then laughed, clapped her knees and hands. I've never seen anyone more emotionally upset and so happy," wrote Mother.

France. On the afternoon of Thursday, 10 July, we flew to Paris where we met with Brother James Shelby Arrigona, a gracious and knowledgeable guide. President of the Paris branch, he was also chief purchasing officer in France for NATO, supplying all of the European offices. He told us that he had written "Mormon" on page 1 of his application, and the interviewing officer had observed, "I see you're a Mormon. I listen very often to the Mormon Choir. Are you a good Mormon or a jack-Mormon?" When Brother Arrigona answered that he "tried to live up to [the LDS] ideals," he was hired. "It pays to acknowledge that you are a Mormon," he laughed.

Father went through his usual round of interviews, courtesy calls on officials, dictating letters, and correcting sermons. He also admits that while "Ray and others visited the Louvre, I rested for two hours — I am getting more easily fatigued."

It was as well that Father rested, for Sunday, 13 July, was a four-session conference; and again, he and Mother "shook hands with [the] entire audience."

I much enjoyed the opportunity to brush up my French, and I delivered my brief remarks in French and translated for Father. Because Father wanted to use Victor Hugo's *Les Miserables* in his address here, I had spent a frantic day pursuing an English translation until I found the desired object at Brentano's.

The next day, Monday, 14 July, was Bastille Day. Brother Arrigona had arranged for Father to sit in the same reviewing stands as the president of France. Father asked, "Is Sister McKay also invited?" When he learned that there had not been enough space, he quietly asked if the invitation could be declined and joined the rest of the party on the balcony of the Hotel Astoria. I don't think Mother ever knew this story.

Brother Arrigona then conducted us to the Eiffel Tower, and finally hosted us at his home that evening. Mother, who had succumbed to a fit of homesickness the day before and had written that no food anywhere could "compare with our American food," quite forgot herself in raptures over this splendid example of French cuisine: "Boiled eggs were served with a white fish, bread and butter. The eggs and fish were served in a lettuce leaf with a dressing over it. Also potato salad which Mildred thought was especially delicious. Then roast lamb with small baked potatoes, beans, and white beans with a little carrot, and sliced tomatoes. Wild strawberries were served with a whipped sour cream. . . . very delicious!" An evening tour of Versailles was a dazzling finish to the day.

Great Britain. On Tuesday, 15 July, we flew to London, where Father and the two mission presidents, Stayner Richards and newly called A. Hamer Reiser, discussed "church property." Early on Wednesday, 16 July, we all drove to Cardiff, where Father renewed his acquaintance with his cousins, Peggy Powell and Blodwyn Davis. Mrs. Davis kindly took us to the home in Merthyr Tydfil in which Father's mother, Jennette Evans McKay, had been born and found the owner for us, a Miss Morgan. Mother describes this visit:

"We entered the house by an old iron gate and walked a few steps over uneven flagstones into a room about eight by ten. Miss Morgan has a hobby of collecting pitchers and has about twenty of them, all white, a few decorated, and all the same size, hanging on hooks in a beam going along the ceiling. . . . The little bedroom where 'Mama' was born is a little room, 6 by 8, off the large room. The bed, a very old poster, fills up half of the room. Dade was much touched as he walked into that room."

As I recall, he softly said, with tears in his eyes, "I can almost hear that little cry of my mother" when she was born in this room.

In Cardiff that evening, Father presided over two meetings – one for missionaries and one for the public. Stayner Richards spoke on motherhood, "a very sweet stirring talk, bringing in his own and David's mothers. Dade was moved and shook with emotion when I put my hand on his arm," Mother recorded. "When he spoke, he spoke so tenderly of his mother that he had everyone weeping."

My parents received an invitation to the queen's garden party through the good offices of the United States ambassador in London

Birthplace of David O. McKay's mother, Jennette Evans McKay, in Merthyr Tydfil, Wales

and Lieutenant Colonel Jack L. Tueller, who volunteered to give up his own tickets.

Father summarized this royal event crisply:

"Elder Brown drove us to Buckingham Palace where we presented our special invitation and tickets and were soon in the Palace and Grounds with 5,000 other guests. Drenching rain. No formal reception by Her Majesty, although she was on the grounds, b[ut] surrounded by such a dense crowd that it was difficult even to see her. How different from our personal audience with her Majesty Juliana, Queen of the Netherlands!"

This visit ended the official part of the tour. We spent Saturday, 19 July, at Stratford-upon-Avon, where Father's keen eye noticed with disappointment "so many untrimmed hedges and poorly kept farms. Socialism has put a blight upon stable old Britain." On Sunday, 20 July, we went to Glasgow for a last look at Father's old mission field and to Ayr for a visit to "Bobby Burns' " cottage. The caretaker was mightily pleased when Father quoted a Burns poem all the way through.

Leaving for
Queen
Elizabeth's
garden party

We flew back to the United States and separated in New York for different appointments. Mildred and I could fervently echo the little note in Father's diary, "We reluctantly said goodbye to them after constant companionship since June 1st. They have been helpful, congenial, delightful companions!" (24 July 1952.)

Chapter 12

THE
PRESIDENTIAL
YEARS
1953-1970

♦ ♦ ♦ ♦ ♦ ♦ ♦ ♦ ♦ ♦ ♦ ♦ ♦

Although we children were not involved in Father's duties as president of the Church, others told us of incidents that had particularly touched them. Literally hundreds of these reports show Father treating others with the same courtesy, generosity, and sensitivity that we children had always received from him and Mother.

For example, at a dinner party with a group of friends who also knew my parents, the host asked each person to contribute a story about President McKay. Brother Martin Backer of Backer's Bakery said, "Most of you have told stories of how President McKay was with your friends. Let me tell you how he was with tradespeople. We learned to love that man and saw him often, since he would frequently stop in the shop on his way home to pick up something that Sister McKay had ordered. Once she had ordered two dozen dinner rolls, but the girl forgot to write down the order and we sold all our supply. When President McKay called for the rolls, all of us were simply appalled, and the poor girl was crying with embarrassment and distress. President McKay was the calmest person there. Without the slightest expression of annoyance, he said, 'But that's perfectly all right. I'm sure she can use something else. Please just give us what you have.' From my side of the counter, we've seen many so-called ladies and gentlemen who save their good manners for their friends. Not the McKays. They were the same to every individual they met."

One day, a Sunday School teacher in Utah Valley asked Father if

238

McKay family gathering, about 1958

she could take her class to his office to meet him and shake his hand.
He agreed. On the appointed day, however, he was suddenly called to
the hospital to see his brother, Thomas E., who was ailing. Father's
secretary explained his absence; and the children, though disappointed,
understood. Imagine their surprise when he appeared in their Sunday
School class the following Sunday and shook hands with all of them,
explaining that he never liked to break an appointment.

He and Mother were extraordinarily tender grandparents. As the
grandchildren multiplied, overflowing the dining room at our annual
Christmas Eve parties, Mother and Father set up card tables in the hall
and the living room for the grandchildren so that we brothers and sisters
and spouses could enjoy dinner with them. When Teddy Lyn was about
eight, she reproached her grandfather after one of these parties: "What
were you laughing about? We couldn't hear."

He looked at her keenly. "Of course, you couldn't. And Christmas
is for children, isn't it?"

At the next Christmas party, the adults were seated around the
card tables and the children surrounded the dining room table with their
grandparents. (If a child was too young to manage alone at the table,
the mother joined it).

Midene and Teddy Lyn both were tall; and Mildred, who remembered her misery at being the tallest girl in her class at age thirteen,
suffered with them when thoughtless friends joked, "When are you

going to stop growing?" and "How's the weather up there?" We never mentioned this to Father, but he just seemed to know. Teddy Lyn particularly felt self-conscious; but every time Father saw her, he would exclaim, "Oh Teddy, you look more like a princess every day!" In his presence, she never slouched.

Father had never denied us children any request that he could possibly fulfill, and he was the same way with his grandchildren. When our youngest daughter, Joyce, was preparing for her marriage, we felt that it would be helpful for her to have some explanation of the temple ordinances and asked Father if he could spare a half hour to talk with her. He said, "Why, of course. But I can't do it outside of the temple." It happened to be during the month the Salt Lake Temple was closed, so he rearranged his schedule to drive to Logan with us and go through the temple there with Joyce, thrilling her and the others who were in that session with his explanation, given before the ceremony in the chapel.

The 1950s were years of prime activity for Father. For almost a decade, though they were both in their seventies and eighties, their health was good, and Father took full advantage of modern transportation to meet with the Saints, oversee a massive international building project that constructed chapels, schools, and temples, and instill an indelible image of what it meant to be a Latter-day Saint. During his adminstration, the membership of the Church almost trebled, and the number of stakes jumped from 191 to 537. Llewelyn accompanied Father and Mother on another European tour, acting as secretary and translator. Robert joined them on a South American tour, and Edward accompanied them to the dedication of the Swiss Temple.

During the 1950s, Father's pocket diary makes frequent reference to breakfast meetings with Gus Backman, president of Salt Lake City's Chamber of Commerce, and John Fitzpatrick, publisher of the Salt Lake *Tribune*. These three men liked and respected one another, and I think Father's willingness to consult with them on matters of mutual interest involving the community did a great deal toward relaxing old Mormon-gentile enmities.

Father's infrequent diary entries during these years and the journals Mother kept in odd-sized notebooks about her trips with him provide other insights into their characters and relationships. For example, even though we returned from Europe 24 July 1952, by 8 August they were

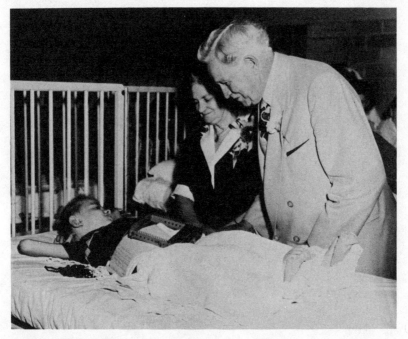

At Primary Children's Hospital, Salt Lake City

in California. Father dedicated a meetinghouse in the San Fernando Valley. Then they went on to the construction site of the Los Angeles Temple, "where Dade met with electricians, builders, architects, etc. to settle matters that have been holding things up for a long time. The men said, 'We have accomplished more this morning in a little while than we have for months.' Dade knows men and knows how to make things go.

"... Drove all the way home Friday.... I think Dade will not do that again. It's too hard on him. I have been asked to talk to Relief Society General Conference in Oct. I dread it. Also in our Sunday School class and at Lizzie's."

From Father's small, red appointment book for 1952 come these notations:

"2 Jan. 1952: 51 yrs ago Ray & I were married. She is 51 times dearer.

"Tuesday, 8 Jan. 1952. Nine important meetings....'.

"Sunday, 2 March 1952. Dedication of Primary Children's Hospital.

"Sunday, 27 April 1952. Dedication Mesa 1st Ward.... Shook hands with over 1,000 people.

"Friday, 16 January 1953. . . . Busy preparing for trip to Washington to attend inauguration of President Dwight D. Eisenhower. . . .

"Tuesday, 10 March 1953. One of the most depressing days that I have experienced for many years. 1. Chinese Mission problems. 2. Decisions in Exp. Committee. 3. Trouble among secretaries. 4. Finally & most depressing, Ray had to go to doctor.

"Saturday, 2 May 1953. Drove to Huntsville, saddled Bess and rode around farm. Much to do. Weather very cold. 6 P.M. Drove Ray around capitol to see cherry trees in bloom. Gorgeous! . . ."

On 30 July 1953, Father and Mother, accompanied by Llewelyn, went to Europe to check progress on the temples, returning 18 August. In Father's conference notebook at the end of the journey he summarized: "Arrived London Monday Aug. 3. 16,600 miles in 21 days, 2 dedicatory services, 6 other meetings (3 in Belfast, 1 in London, 2 in New York)."

Mother kept her usual detailed record, from which these excerpts are taken:

"2 Aug. 1953. . . . President [A. Hamer] Reiser and wife and elders took us with Bro. [Edward O.] Anderson [the temple architect] to the place purchased for a temple to be built. I was amazed to see the beautiful Tudor home and wonderful gardens in the place. I didn't count the numbers of rooms downstairs but on the 2nd floor there were 18 bedrooms. There are 12 bathrooms in the house. Trees of all descriptions from holly to oak trees, tall hedges, lawns, roses, ferns, climbers, everything to make a beautiful old English home. Bro. Anderson and Dade studied it to see just where a temple should be built. . . .

"Aug. 5, 1953. . . . President Bringhurst drove us to the [Swiss] temple site [for the groundbreaking ceremonies]. I've never enjoyed a more beautiful ride. The beautiful hills, crops ready to harvest. Not a leaf or other dirt on the streets. The old castles, the little train, good company, everything delightful. Everything for the program was arranged beautifully. There was a stand for the favored few to sit in the shade but about 300 people had to stand to listen to six people talk and the cook sing. . . . Dade gave the three differences between our church and others and from that led on to the reason for a temple. The people, especially the two outsiders on the stand, were especially interested.

His talk and prayer were wonderful. Everyone felt a marvelous spirit there."

They then returned to England for groundbreaking ceremonies at the Surrey site. Among the speakers were "Llewelyn & my beloved." Everyone "gave good talks, especially David O. McKay," Mother wrote on 11 August 1953. They squeezed in a quick trip to Scotland, driving beyond Thurso to Grandfather's birthplace, where they were disappointed to find that the current owners were "keeping potatoes in the old living room." (13 Aug. 1953.)

They returned to Salt Lake City on 18 August, and Mother wrote: "It's *good* to be home. . . . We had a glorious but strenuous time."

As 1954 began, they were off again, this time on a tour of the missions in South Africa and South America. In many ways, it was a repeat of the European tour, because members had never before seen the president of the Church. At one point in Uruguay Father recorded: "It is not an unusual experience any more for airports practically to be filled with members of the Church — singing either a greeting or a good-bye. Truly, we deeply appreciate the true fellowship, friendship and genuine love manifest by these loyal friends." (31 Jan. 1954.) On another occasion, word had somehow gotten around of which prospective building sites they would be inspecting in Buenos Aires, and at each location the party met "from 25 to 75 or 100 members who, having heard of our intended inspection, had assembled to greet us. In each instance, we took time to shake the hand of everyone, babies included!" (6 Feb. 1954.)

These excerpts from Mother's more detailed journal give a few highlights of their experience:

"Sat., 9th Jan. 1954. . . . Just before we landed [in Johannesburg] an officer came into the plane & said, 'Will President and Mrs. McKay please wait until all the rest of the people are off the plane?' I had a hunch why. When we moved off, several newspaper cameras took our pictures with a little girl who held a large bouquet of flowers for us presented by the Relief Society. It had glads, roses, carnations, and a blue flower. Very lovely. . . . A crowd of about 500 . . . [sang] 'We Thank Thee, O God, for a Prophet.' . . .

"Sunday, 10th Jan. 1954. . . . People were thrilled to meet the President. . . . I had been listening to David and a reporter, one of the Africans, who was very intelligent and asked some very pointed questions about polygamy, the temple, whether the blacks would have the Priesthood, etc. Seemed well satisfied. . . .

"[Thursday], 14 Jan. 1954. . . . Sister Duncan, Bro. Reiser, and Elder Mayo called at the hotel this morning to take us to the Cape of Good Hope. . . . [At the top of] a long cement walk . . . we could see the Cape of Good Hope just a few feet away, the Indian Ocean on one side and the Atlantic on the other side. . . . On the way back we came upon 12 baboons and was Daddy delighted! . . . People are warned to stay in the car and not torment the creatures but Dade insisted on getting out to have his picture taken with the big fellow. I protested and tried to hold him in but couldn't. . . .

"[Friday], 15 Jan. 1954. . . . Went to a concert given by the Saints of Capetown. It was very good. . . . Dade was asked to talk and he gave an excellent one on music. He is always equal to the occasion. We shook hands with people from East London who had driven 600 miles to come to meet the President. . . .

"[Saturday], 16 Jan. 1954. It was testimony day for the missionaries, and they were bearing them from 10 in the morning until 8 o'clock in the evening with an hour at noon for rest. They were fasting all day and so felt pretty hungry by the time eight o'clock came. They still were so interested in the President's testimony that they all reached forward with tears in their eyes. My, but this visit has been wonderful for these people.

"Sunday, 17 Jan. 1954. Sunday session at 10 o'clock. Pres. Barry Mayo, Pres. A. Hamer Reiser, Emma R. McKay, Pres. David O. McKay & President Duncan spoke. Oh, I wish they wouldn't ask me. In bed I can give a pretty good talk but when in pulpit, I'm no good. Such a poor choice of words. . . . David gave the talk of the 'millionaire' with the story of Helen Keller. They just drank it in. He is certainly a wonderful speaker. And at night they were thrilled with him.

"Monday, Jan. 18, 1954. . . . There is a cable that takes you to the top of Table Mountain. You get in a basket and if the wind is blowing you are in great danger. I said I wouldn't go up in it for a hundred dollars [and didn't]. Dade said when he came down that he wouldn't go up [again] for $1,000 which showed to me that he was slightly frightened."

Father commented: "Supposed to be a day of relaxation but proved to be one of the most strenuous of the trip." They signed autographs and shook hands after an evening meeting until 1:30 A.M. Mother's account summarizes: "The President of the Church has done an incalculable amount of good coming down here though it has been hard on him. His back has been bad all the time and last night his legs were both swollen. Phlebitis [has] come back. The English people are known to hide their emotions but they haven't been able to do it here. They shake his hand and rush away crying. Many have said to me, 'You have no.idea what your coming here has done for us.' Over and over they say that.... We feel that we love them very dearly, even though we have been near them only 10 days."

Father and Mother then went on to the second leg of their journey – South America–where my brother Robert joined them at Rio de Janeiro. The heat was very hard on Mother as the tour progressed through the rest of Brazil, Uruguay, Paraguay, Argentina, and Central America. She wrote, apologetically, once, that she was feeling "grouchy" and homesick. They typically arrived one day, did a little sight-seeing, had an entertainment of local talent, and held a missionary meeting. A full day of three or four conference sessions was held on the morrow, and then a second day of official calls, more sightseeing, newspaper interviews, other quasi-official business, and other meetings in the evening. Bob, whose Spanish was as superb as Llewelyn's German, often spoke in sessions with Father.

A highlight at Buenos Aires, where Bob had served his mission, was meeting Juan Peron, chief of state. Mother recorded:

"Wed., 3 Feb. 1954. The meeting with President Peron was most satisfactory.... He said he knew about the Mormons crossing the plains. He admires people who work and fight to get ahead. He said he didn't know what to serve to make them happy. He knew that they didn't drink nor smoke nor drink tea nor coffee. 'What can I do?' Dade replied that to meet him is an honor that to him was all that was necessary and Peron said, 'I am honored.' When the interview was over Peron embraced him and afterwards put his arm about Bob's shoulder and told him he had a fine father, that he is a great man, and slapped his chest and said something about a fine physique. I am sorry I missed that meeting. Pres. Peron wanted to know where the meeting is to be held. He was told of the hall procured and he said, 'No! no! That is too small.' Then he mentioned a theater [Cervantes Theatre] that he said they might have. Pres. Valentine had been to this theatre and they said he couldn't possibly have it because it was being overhauled. All the chairs were out and other repairs would make it impossible. Then Peron sent word that the Mormons were to have the use of that building. They put 60 men at work and it is now ready for Sunday."

Father and Mother also made a point of visiting Santiago, Chile, where the only two members of the Church were Brother and Sister Billie Fotheringham, who combined pioneering for the Church with Brother Fotheringham's work for Kodak. My parents also visited Guatemala and Panama on their way home, making a total of seven Latin American countries in all.

Father and Mother reached Los Angeles on 14 February 1954 and spent two days relaxing at Emerald Bay where Father, after dealing with more reporters and accepting welcome-home telephone calls, wrote thankfully: "Sleeping at intervals all day. It's good to relax and to have no appointments!" (16 Feb. 1954.) Emerald Bay became a beloved refuge during these years. They had already been there for a few days twice in the fall and came back again for a few days before April conference.

That spring, Mother was elected Utah's Mother of the Year. Edward's wife, Lottie, took the nomination procedure in charge, including obtaining letters of endorsement from University of Utah president A. Ray Olpin, apostle Richard L. Evans, and Salt Lake *Tribune* publisher John F. Fitzpatrick. During this time, Mother was traveling with Father in South Africa and South America.

Some of Mother's feelings can be deduced from her speech of acceptance on 11 April 1954, when Governor J. Bracken Lee awarded her the trophy:

"One morning a few days after we returned from that long trip, there was a telephone call. My son was on the telephone. He said, 'Mother, your name is being considered with others for the district honors of Utah Mother of 1954 and your consent is necessary before further action can be taken by the committee.'

" 'Oh no, that cannot possibly be. I will not give my consent because in the first place I do not like publicity, second, I am perfectly content to shine by the reflected light of my husband, and third, I would never receive the honor anyway because I do not deserve it.' Then I went back to bed to nurse a cold, feeling very grouchy.

"That evening, my son Edward and his wife (who is my sponsor) came to my home. . . . She said, 'Mama Ray, I have worked hard on my paper. Will you let me read it to you?' And she read a paper that was so well organized and so beautifully written that I was really delighted. (Of course, she added on quite a bit, I think.) She said with tears in her eyes and voice, 'You will not let me down now, will you, Mama Ray?'

"I said, 'No, indeed I will not. I am very proud of you. I think there is no mother-in-law in the world ever had a greater compliment.' Her being my sponsor means more to me than all the public plaudits I could receive. Lottie lived with us for two years [while Edward was in the navy], and I appreciate very much that she did not name the bad qualifications she found in me then." (This account slightly edited from typescript included in folder, "Information Concerning Emma Ray Riggs McKay.")

In April 1954, Father accompanied her to New York to the national Mother of the Year convention. They stopped in Madison, Wisconsin, to dedicate a chapel. Mother records this loving vignette during the missionary testimony meeting: "We heard every missionary bear his testimony which took six hours. I then bore mine. I told them that I know the President is a prophet, that he is a man of impressions, etc. When I talk of him, Dade weeps and has a hard time to control himself. David talked to the missionaries and they loved it." (23 Apr. 1954.)

In New York, Mother was thrilled to spend some time with Lou Jean while Father attended a conference in Cleveland, and then they checked into the Waldorf Astoria for the convention:

"7 May 1954. . . . I had fun talking our religion with the ladies. I told the lady from Kentucky that she would make a wonderful Mormon & she said, 'That is a compliment.' I was surprised to find how well the Mormons are known in so many places. The Jewess whose husband is studying religions thinks ours is so wonderful with the laity so active in Church work. One mother has Mormons living next to her and she said they are such lovely people. I didn't see one mother smoke."

This honor was one of many that came to Mother during her lifetime of service. Although her chief calling after Father became a member of the First Presidency was to support him in the many demands on his time and to be his companion at the associated public events, she served as a teacher in Relief Society for many years, as president of the Ogden Fourth Ward Relief Society, as first counselor in the Salt Lake Stake Relief Society, and as president of the Relief Societies in Great Britain

The First
Presidency at
the cornerstone
ceremony for
the Relief
Society Building,
30 September
1954. Left to
right: David O.
McKay; Stephen
L Richards, first
counselor; J.
Reuben Clark,
Jr., second
counselor

and Europe from 1922 through 1924. She was president of the Religion Class in Ogden and president of the Seventeenth Ward Primary in Salt Lake City. In 1953, she received an honorary Golden Gleaner Award from the YWMIA "for all she has done to instill Christian principles in the youth." In 1967, Utah State University honored her as "the woman who has most achieved the eternal quest of womanhood." In 1969, five thousand women students from the University of Utah's LDS Students Association sponsored an "Emma Ray Riggs McKay Evening" in the Tabernacle to honor her.

In January 1955, Father and Mother set off again on another major mission tour, this time to the South Pacific. On it, they traveled forty-five thousand miles and visited Tonga, Samoa, Tahiti, New Zealand, and Australia. Father gave seventy-two addresses, including welcoming and farewell talks, instructions to missionaries, and gospel sermons, held

At the
dedication of the
David O. McKay
Building,
Brigham Young
University, 14
December 1954

twenty-six press and radio conferences, and paid courtesy calls on government, tribal, ecclesiastical, and educational leaders.

They stopped in Honolulu between planes long enough for a gathering of friends at the mission home and then flew on to Fiji, where a
hotel steward came to tuck them into their mosquito nets for the night.

At Nukualoafa, Tonga, mission president D'Monte W. Coombs and
his wife met them with "some natives who came 150 miles in a row
boat to meet us." (10 Jan. 1955.) At Liahona College, a Church school,
Father and Mother received a royal welcome, a kava ceremony conducted for them as it would have been for the queen, and they called
on Tongi, the crown prince. They met a man who had been born after
Father, on his first world tour, had blessed a woman past childbearing
age that she would have a baby.

Mother called Pago Pago "the most beautiful harbor I have ever
seen, miles and miles of lovely harbor with hills and rocks in the ocean
crowned with beautiful verdure. As the ship stopped, there was the
church band playing, 'Come, Come Ye Saints.' The Relief Society mem-

bers were all in white and the Primary boys and girls. . . . When all the Saints sat on the floor [of the meeting house] and looked up with their great dark eyes and braided hair, it was a beautiful picture."

The same outpouring of loving welcome, gifts, dances, feasts, and shaking hands occurred over and over again at Samoa, Tonga, and Tahiti ("we were smothered to our ears with these beautiful [leis].") At Apia, Samoa, they inspected a Church school and dedicated a site for a school. They dedicated a new chapel at Sauniatu and visited the David O. McKay Monument, erected in commemoration of Father's and Hugh J. Cannon's 1921 visit. So many of the Saints there wept at parting that Mother "began [to weep] myself, I who seldom cry." (21 Jan. 1955.)

Then the presidential party continued on to Suva, and then Nandi, Fiji, and from there to New Zealand. In Auckland, they visited a new chapel; and in Hamilton, New Zealand, they inspected a Church college under construction. Father selected a temple site in Hamilton, although he did not announce it until 17 February 1955, after he conferred with his counselors. At the meeting in Auckland on 30 January, Mother wrote, "His heart overflowed and we were all weeping willows with him. We shook hands with over 2,000 people and about ten of them, old members from the north of the island, hongied [rubbed noses] with the Pres. and me. . . . People kissed his hand, would look into his face or mine, and burst into tears, and I was weeping with them the whole time. They are so lovable and sincere that you feel you know them in a week. If I were to be with them for two or three years, I should feel as all the other missionaries do that they are the choice people of the world. Their hearts shine through their eyes."

My parents spent a week in eastern Australia, where the Sydney zoo delighted them on the only "free" day they had had during the entire journey, and then they flew back to Honolulu, where they held six days of three or four meetings each, plus receptions, newspaper conferences, and private conferences. Father also broke ground for a new Church college at Laie near the temple, now Brigham Young University–Hawaii.

A note in Mother's hand on a piece of paper slipped in this journal observes: "Times spoken, 82, press and radio interviews, 31, Public leaders (government, generals, chiefs, prime ministers, chief justices, mayors, etc.), 40."

Later that spring, Father had a tumor, fortunately benign, removed

from his left cheek. Then in August 1955, he and Mother, with Edward
and Lottie, accompanied the Tabernacle Choir to Europe to give concerts throughout Great Britain, including singing for the groundbreaking
ceremonies of the temple in Surrey and the dedication of the Swiss
Temple.

Mother's journal records: "Aug. 19, 1955. . . . A few songs were
given by the choir right on the dock. The first was 'Loch Lomond,'
which won the hearts of the people. . . . Then Dade walked over to the
fence behind which stood many nonmembers who had stood from 9 to
11 to hear the choir. They grinned and appreciated the few words he
gave to them. We then went over to the other wire where a crowd of
children had gathered and the President had his picture taken with
them. . . .[The Lord Provost's] secretary rushed out after us and invited
us and Edward and Lottie to come back and sign his book. The Lord
Provost said, "Not on any page with others. I want him on a page by
itself.' . . .

"20 Aug. 1955. . . . When Bro. Reiser drove us to the great Kelvin
Hall, we met in one room to hear the choir, which holds about 3500
people. Every seat was taken and more wanting seats. President Reiser
asked those who had heard the choir before to give up their seats to
those who hadn't. It was heartwarming to see how many arose (husbands and wives of the choir [members]) and gave up their seats to
strangers. . . . The choir was superb! Perfect! . . .

"[London], 22 Aug. 1955. . . . It seemed like getting home to go to
the Grosvenor House where we stayed with Lawrence and Mildred.
Everything reminded us of their charming presence. . . .

"Aug. 24, 1955. We all, except the President, went out to Kew
Gardens. Dade didn't want to go. He just wants to rest. . . .

"Aug. 25, 1955. . . . We met some members of the choir in West-
minster Abbey who said that in Wales the people shouted, whistled,
and stamped in delight and appreciation. As in all other places, they
wanted 'Come, Come Ye Saints' twice and would have liked it even
more. They liked, 'Let the Mountains Shout for Joy.' Jack Thomas told
them he was born in Wales and that pleased them very much. . . .

"Aug. 27, 1955. . . . [At the groundbreaking ceremonies for the
temple] there were seats for us in front and when all was ready the
rain began to come, a very few drops at a time. It was not bad until
nearly through the program, then began to come harder. My umbrella

sheltered Lady Bennett. . . . Bro. [Edward O.] Anderson spoke about
the fine spirit of the Church everywhere, of the beautiful spirit at the
Los Angeles temple & the hopes that he had of having just as fine a
spirit here when the building starts. . . . Dade had autographed people's
books for two hours and was worn out. Went to bed early."

The concert in London, in the Royal Albert Hall, was equally successful.

Robert F. Bennett, who later married our daughter Joyce, was then
president of the Scottish District of the British Mission and recalls some
of the behind-the-scenes tension created by that tour. The Church had
engaged the services of a prestigious public relations firm to handle
publicity and advertising for the concert series, and Bob was appalled
to discover that the young account executive assigned to operations in
Glasgow was both inexperienced and incompetent. As he recalls:

"Tickets just weren't moving. I ended up pulling in all the missionaries from the whole district to put out handbills all over the city.
I also tried to arrange a press conference for President McKay. I went
myself to all of the newspapers in the city and was totally ignored. No
one had heard of President McKay or the choir, and the only feelings
people had about Mormons was a sense of vague distaste left over from
generations of prejudice.

"However, I created enough of a problem that the public relations
company asked a vice president, then vacationing in Scotland, to pull
me in. Well, the account executive and I went to this vice president's
hotel. After I heard what he had to say, he then listened to what I had
to say, and the upshot was that he apologized to me on behalf of the
firm and asked, 'Have you ever run a press conference before?' I said
no. 'Would you be offended if I took personal charge?'

"I, of course, was delighted, because we now had a chance of getting
some coverage. This vice president turned to the much-chastened account executive and started snapping orders, including a list of personal
friends on various newspapers who should be invited, concluding,
' . . . and lay on some refreshments.' When the account executive ea-
gerly suggested tea, the vice president exclaimed, 'My word, man, you
don't serve Scottish reporters tea. Get some scotch.' (When I told this
part of the story to President McKay much later, he roared with laughter.)

"This meeting occurred on a Tuesday. The press conference was scheduled for Friday and the concert was on for Saturday. Representatives from seven or eight of the major Glasgow papers were represented. President McKay's first words were disarming: 'I would like to introduce you to my wife. (pause) My only wife.'

"After that, there simply wasn't a polygamy issue to discuss. The reporters asked their questions, addressing them respectfully to 'Dr. McKay.' (They assumed that he must have a doctor of divinity degree.) At the beginning, they clearly regarded him as an American curiosity. But as the conference continued with President McKay meeting every question, being totally accessible and frank, you could see the reporters recognizing his competence and stature. . . .

"Nearly every paper the next day gave President McKay and the choir front-page coverage, and we filled the hall. This public relations firm, alerted by the vice-president's report, reappraised the arrangements being made at other sites and quickly corrected laxness where it was found. The tour was a great success."

Bob also recalls a special moment with Father walking down the marble staircase from the formal reception area where the Lord Provost of Glasgow, the Scottish equivalent of the Lord Mayor of London, had spoken to the assembled choir and responded to Father's remarks with spontaneous candor and warmth. With his arms around the shoulders of the young missionary who later became his grandson-in-law, Father said, "Brother Bennett, today is the greatest day in the history of the Church in Scotland. Fifty years ago as a missionary, I came into this building and my humble feet were not allowed on these stairs. And today, as representatives of the Church, we have been received formally by the Lord Provost himself."

Then the group moved on to Paris, where Father spent all of Saturday, 3 September 1955, "resting and preparing program for Dedication of Swiss Temple on the 11th." Father's eighty-second birthday on 8 September in Bern was signaled by a flood of cables from "true friends and esteemed associates and some strangers." A cake, flowers, and gifts from many continued to arrive the next day.

Workmen were busy all night before the dedication "with last minute preparations," wrote Father. The service itself "appealed to our spiritual nature so intensely that it seemed that an unseen audience had joined in this most historical and momentous occasion. Indeed, I was deeply impressed that former Presidents of the Church and Father

and Mother were with us, 'listening in.' Many of the audience were
moved to tears."

The rest of 1955 was taken up with October general conference,
the open house of the Los Angeles Temple with its more than 680,000
visitors, the unremitting business of the First Presidency's office, and
the rounds of addresses.

The next diaries in my possession date from 1958, but Father's
Huntsville scrapbook contains the record of a wonderful day's outing
with the Jefferson Hunt Camp of Sons of Utah Pioneers on Saturday,
6 July 1957. Father, then a few months short of his eighty-fourth birthday, rode horseback with them to La Plata, a deserted mining camp
high in the mountain wilderness east of Ogden Valley. In 1891 as a
seventeen-year-old, he had delivered the Ogden *Standard-Examiner*
there, memorizing classics from world literature on the way. He thoroughly enjoyed the program with Boy Scouts that took place on the
site. William Ferrell, president of the Sons of Utah Pioneers camp, later
told me this story:

"We got the other horses into the trailer without difficulty, but
Sonny Boy just stood there. We pulled and pushed, urged him and
slapped him, but he wouldn't budge. He just wouldn't go into that trailer.
We could just see him say, 'Just try and make me.' Then up came a
big black car and your father got out of it. He said, 'I thought you might
be having some trouble with Sonny Boy.' He put his arm around Sonny
Boy's neck, talked to him, turned him around, and walked with him
away from the trailer for several hundred yards. Then President McKay
walked up the plank right into the trailer, and Sonny Boy went in with
him, never tightening the halter rope, and stood calmly. Your father
came out and said, 'He's a one-man horse.' I said, 'You're telling me!' "

Father wrote: "I stood the trip exceptionally well; I was a little
tired, but I was not stiff. I enjoyed every minute of the trip—It was a
delightful experience and will be cherished in memory." (Huntsville
Scrapbook, n.p.)

Father's personal journal resumes in April 1958 when he and
Mother left with a large party for the dedication of the New Zealand
Temple and the Church College of New Zealand at Hamilton, its twenty
academic buildings and twenty residences already in use. The party
traveled first to Hawaii, where Father was buried so deeply in leis,
wrote Mother, that "only David's nose and the top of his head could be

Departing from
Salt Lake City
for Hawaii and
New Zealand,
11 April 1958

seen." (14 Apr. 1958.) Mother found the dedication even more inspiring
than those in Switzerland or Los Angeles and wrote, "All these men
testified that the Pres. is a prophet and did it earnestly and sincerely."
(20–23 Apr. 1958.)

As soon as these dedicatory services were finished, Father and
Mother and their party participated in dedicatory services for the Church
College. Mother was taken on a strenuous tour of the buildings, including a hike up several flights of stairs that ended with the guide's
becoming lost. At the end of the day, she regretfully passed up a sight-
seeing tour to a local cave famous for its glowworms, observing, "I
thought I had walked enough that day. . . . First time I have felt that
old age is upon me." (25 Apr. 1958.)

Father and Mother spent several days at the college as part of the

Lei greeting in Hawaii, April 1958

ceremonies, and Father delighted teachers and students alike by visiting classes without advance notice one afternoon, ending up in a discussion of Robert Louis Stevenson's *Treasure Island*. They left on 1 May for Fiji, enjoying a 136-mile ride through the spectacular mountain scenery of Suva, a marvelous feast, and the ceremonial presentation of a whale's tooth to Father. In Suva, Father also dedicated the first LDS chapel.

In Hawaii, they broke their journey long enough for a tour of the Church College of Hawaii and an address to more than two thousand Saints overflowing the Laie chapel, and then "shook hands for 1 hour 15 min." Father spoke on character: "The greatest thing in the world: a group of young people inspired with an invincible resolution to be true to their faith and spouses." Mother recorded: "People said afterwards it was exactly what was needed, as people always do when Dade talks."

Mother's last entry in her journal reads: "Held 20 meetings in 28 days and Dade talked at every one."

When Father dedicated the London Temple in September 1958, he called Selvoy J. Boyer to be its first president. Later, Brother Boyer told me that during the consultations on temple sealers, Father rapidly ran down the list of fourteen or fifteen names Brother Boyer had given

McKay family reunion, 24 July 1958, Huntsville. Seated: David O. and Emma Ray Riggs McKay; second row, left to right: Edward and Lottie McKay, Frances Ellen McKay (Robert's wife), Emma Rae McKay Ashton, Alice McKay (Llewelyn's wife), Llewelyn McKay; back row, left to right: David Lawrence and Mildred McKay, Robert McKay, Conway Ashton

him, checking the names either yes or no without hesitation. He had never met any of these people. Out of curiosity, President Boyer kept that list for several years. When he examined it again, he found that all of the people who had been checked affirmatively had remained active and faithful members of the Church while those to whom Father had said no had not.

After Father returned from dedicating the London Temple, he had a second cataract operation (recuperation this time was swifter). He also dedicated the Church College of Hawaii at Laie before Christmas 1958.

Father's journals end with brief notations in 1960 about organizing the Manchester Stake, dedicating the Hyde Park Chapel, and organizing the London Stake in 1961, but friends have shared with us vivid memories connected with Father's actions.

When Manchester Stake, the first stake in England, was organized

27 March 1960, Father flew from Africa, where he had been holding conferences, to meet with Elder Harold B. Lee, who had brought with him instructions from the Quorum of the Twelve Apostles suggesting where the boundaries should be drawn to separate the stake from the mission. It was quite a complicated plan, and many factors had been considered in making the proposal.

Father and Elder Lee met in the evening before the first meeting, but Father didn't look at the recommendations. He tapped the folder and said, "I'll want to take this up with somebody else." Elder Lee, who told us this story, said, "I knew whom he meant." So they agreed to meet the next morning.

The next morning, Father showed him a diagram and said, "These boundaries are what I would like to suggest." Elder Lee opened the folder and showed him the recommendations of the Quorum. They were identical.

Another story of Father's influence on Manchester Stake occurred within a few years, related to me only recently by Sister Irene Bates, whose husband was the first English stake president. It was customary for the stake presidents and two bishops, chosen in turn, to be invited to attend general conference, with traveling expenses being paid by the Church. In this particular year, the instructions came to bring all of the bishops and branch presidents.

"Bill was sure this was an error," recalls Sister Bates, and so he waited for the correction to come. It didn't, so he called President N. Eldon Tanner, then president of the European Mission. President Tanner confirmed that the instructions indeed said to invite bishops and branch presidents — 'all of them.' Still Bill hesitated. Finally, President Tanner called him: 'I'm waiting for the names from your stake,' he reminded Bill.

"Bill, still with secret trepidation, obediently issued the invitations. The bishops and branch presidents were delighted with the prospect of coming to Salt Lake City, a once-in-a-lifetime opportunity for most of them. Then, the very next Monday, Bill received word that the first instructions had in fact been in error. He was told to select two bishops and tell the rest that they would not be able to go.

"Bill was heartsick, especially for Brother Vernon, the branch president in the small town of Rawtenstall. The Church was his whole life. He and his wife willingly opened their small home for the branch meetings, and Brother Vernon used to moonlight by digging ditches to earn money for the building fund. People in that tiny branch used to pay tithing and then walk to work so they could make ends meet. Bill knew that the forthcoming trip had been a major celebration, not only in the branch but in the town as well. With great pride, the local paper had featured the forthcoming trip. Brother Vernon's employer had been gracious and eager to give him time off work. Everyone was simply thrilled. It was the innocence of that anticipation that Bill could not bear to think of disappointing.

"Bill lay awake all night, trying to think of a plan. He was willing to give Brother Vernon his own place, but that would have revealed the situation. We would willingly have paid his expenses ourselves; but if he were not officially invited, he wouldn't have a place reserved at the meetings. Finally, in deep distress, he phoned President Marion D. Hanks, president of the British Mission, explained the situation, and said, 'I don't see anything to do but to call President McKay and lay the situation before him.' President Hanks replied warmly, 'I couldn't advise you to do that, President Bates, but here's President McKay's direct number.'

"Bill hung up the phone and looked at the number for a long moment, then said, 'I've got to do it.' He went back in the office while I waited outside. He got straight through to President McKay's secretary, who put him straight through to President McKay. Bill poured out the whole story while President McKay listened without saying a word. At the end, while Bill waited in an agony of suspense, President McKay said, 'I see,' and paused thoughtfully. After the longest ten seconds in Bill's life, President McKay said, 'You're quite right, President Bates. It would be very wrong to do that to that good man. We must have them all come. Please do me a favor and let me call President Tanner.'

"Bill came out of the office with tears streaming down his face. Within a day, he had word from President Tanner that the original instructions were to stand. Brother Vernon and the others went. They had a wonderful experience, particularly Brother Vernon. He came back infused with new life, feeling connected to the Church as he never had before. Proudly the local newspaper reported his experience and views. The whole tiny branch basked in reflected glory. And they never knew.

"No wonder we loved President McKay. He *was* the Church to us in those days. When he came to the London Temple dedication, we went to see him as much as to see our temple dedicated. Afterwards when we were standing in endless lines, waiting to shake his hand, I saw President McKay glance down the line and notice an elderly lady quite far back, bent and tired. He said to the person at the front of the line, 'Please excuse me.' He went to this elderly sister, shook her hand kindly, thanked her for coming, and made sure she could be taken off to rest. How could we help loving such sensitivity and consideration? He made every single one of us feel special when we so easily could have been just one of hundreds.

"Bill all but worshipped him. When he and his counselors came to one general conference, he went to President McKay's office in hopes of seeing him for a few moments. President McKay recognized him and welcomed him warmly. Bill said, 'I know that there are possibilities of buildings, and I just want to share with you some of my feelings about the places some of our people are meeting in and what the situation is in our area.'

"President McKay was delighted. 'Come in, Brother Bates,' he said. 'I'm just looking at plans of chapels.' So they had a long conversation, and Bill was able to describe some of the little rented halls that our Saints were struggling with. President McKay made no promises and didn't remind Bill of any policies, but we ended up with six chapels a-building simultaneously."

In July 1960, when Mother found it difficult to go up and down the stairs in their South Temple home, they rented an apartment in the Hotel Utah. (Until the house sold, Father used to return early each morning to enjoy a bath in its extra-large tub.)

It was my custom to visit them each morning on my way to work. One morning, I was chatting with Father while Mother was snoozing in her chair nearby. Suddenly, she exclaimed, "Lawrence, that's a grammatical error." Father laughed in delight. "Lawrence," he commented, "there's nothing like a grammatical error to wake your mother up."

The decade of the sixties was a time of slowly waning physical health and mobility for both of them, although their loving spirits and their keen intelligences remained unclouded to the end.

Father's sense of humor never left him. On one occasion, he was in the hospital receiving visits from no one but his family. During a visit, I casually mentioned that I had just come from the Genealogical Department of the Church, where executives had suggested that we

The First
Presidency on
President
McKay's
eighty-seventh
birthday, 8
September 1960.
Left to right: J.
Reuben Clark,
Jr., first
counselor; David
O. McKay;
Henry D.
Moyle, second
counselor

do no genealogical work in Scotland for the time being because it was so hard to get genealogy out of Scotland. Father quipped quickly, "It's hard to get anything out of Scotland."

On 10 December 1962 when Father was in his ninetieth year, 462 business and civic leaders of Utah gathered at the Hotel Utah to honor him at a special dinner. Mother was the only woman in attendance. Of the many honors Father received, this banquet had a special place in his heart. No member of the committee that planned the banquet and carried it out was a Latter-day Saint. Rather, they were Protestants, Catholics, and Jews, united in respecting Father's contributions. President John F. Kennedy sent a telegram of congratulations for the event; and the businessmen presented Father with a silver plaque and an organ to be installed in the chapel then being built in Merthyr Tydfil, Wales, the birthplace of his mother.

In August 1963, Father (Mother was ill) went to Merthyr Tydfil to dedicate the chapel for which he had broken ground two years earlier.

The McKay family at the Hotel Utah on Christmas Eve, 1963. Standing behind their parents are, left to right, Robert, Edward, Emma Rae, Lou Jean, David Lawrence, and Llewelyn

Robert Cundick, temporarily serving as organist at the Hyde Park chapel and future chief organist at the Salt Lake Tabernacle, came especially to inaugurate the organ.

This was Father's last long trip. He was over ninety and becoming increasingly frail; however, he was far from retired. At the request of President Lyndon B. Johnson, Father flew to Washington, D.C., in January 1964, only two months after President Johnson took office. Only a few months later on 17 through 21 November came a real high point: the scheduled dedication of the Oakland Temple, in which he had taken a great interest all during the construction. But by then Father's health was a serious concern.

Late that summer Father had suffered a serious stroke that left him weak, barely able to stand. His fluency of speech was gone. When we had dinner with him and Mother in their apartment, the wit and sparkle of his conversation were gone, although his thinking and memory were unaffected. He conducted his First Presidency meetings in his apartment office, and his counselors were among the few who realized the extent of his problem. At October conference, I read his Saturday night priesthood address, and my brother Bob read his opening and closing conference addresses. We began to worry that he might ask one of us to read the dedicatory prayer for the temple dedication, scheduled for 17 November.

"Has he asked you, Bob?" I queried one day in late October.

"No," my brother answered. "Has he asked you?"

"No."

There seemed to be no more to say. President Hugh B. Brown, then Father's first counselor, asked a week or so later, "Lawrence, has your father said anything about who is going to dedicate the Oakland Temple?"

"No," I reported, "he hasn't, President Brown."

November arrived, and still no one was appointed. It became evident that Father was planning to attend the dedication; and the doctors said he would be able to do so if my physician-brother, Edward, went along. Emma Rae accompanied Mother, and Ed, Bob, and I were with Father. Mildred and Lottie also attended. I wrote my daughter Joyce the details of this experience, one of the most inspirational of my life involving Father, on 23 November 1964, a few days after the dedication. The interpolations in brackets include additional details from an address I gave reporting the same incident to the Mormon History Association, 8 May 1982:

"[At] a news conference, it was still hard for [Father] to speak. We realized more than ever the necessity of his getting someone to read his speeches and prayer. Tuesday morning President Brown came in and asked, 'President McKay, have you any instructions for me?' Father said, 'No, President Brown.' It became more and more evident that Father was going to do the whole morning ceremony himself. . . . The President of the Temple and President Joseph Fielding Smith spoke on the history of temples and this one in particular and on their purpose. [Then President Stone electrified us all by announcing, 'We shall all now have the pleasure of hearing from President McKay.' Mildred looked at me and I at her in disbelief. Father was helped over to the rickety temporary pulpit, which he grasped as he stood. Then he began to talk.] . . . He spoke for 30 minutes and then still standing offered the dedicatory prayer for another 30 minutes. His articulation [became] as clear as it was ten years ago. When he finished, his counselors helped him to his seat. Your mother, with tears on her cheeks, turned to me and said, 'Lawrence, we've just seen a miracle.' [I nodded in agreement. Members of the Council of the Twelve were crying.]

"[When the services were over, I asked Dr. J. Louis Schricker, 'Can he do this again this afternoon?' Dr. Schricker answered, 'Lawrence, this is out of our hands. If I hadn't been here to see it, I wouldn't have believed it.']

"It was a miracle, and he repeated it at the second session Tuesday afternoon—except that he seemed stronger and left his notes to ad-lib—and Wednesday morning and afternoon. At the two Thursday sessions he showed fatigue and asked President Brown to read the prayers, but Papa Dade spoke at both sessions. . . .

"All we need is some more temples."

During these final years, Mother was always first in Father's heart, even when the Church came first in his time. Some of our sweetest memories from this time are of their continuing love story. Once, after they were both in wheelchairs, Brother Darcey Wright had wheeled Father out of the apartment door and down the hallway. While they were waiting for the elevator, Father suddenly exclaimed, "We have to go back. I didn't kiss Ray goodbye." Brother Wright dutifully wheeled him back for this loving ritual that had only become more important as the years passed.

Father had an uncanny sense of knowing what was going on with Mother during those closing years. One day, Mildred and I were joining them for dinner. Mother was napping on the couch in the living room, and the cook-housekeeper, Gaby Baruffol, asked Father whether we should start or wait for Mother to wake up. "Oh, she's awake," he said. Gaby went softly into the living room and, sure enough, Mother, who had not made a sound, was sitting up, ready to come to the table.

Even earlier, I recall an incident when Father was in the hospital recuperating from an illness. Mother had been visiting him faithfully each day; but one morning, she woke with a cold and told Lou Jean, "I don't think I'd better go up. It would be too bad to give Father this cold." Mind you, this was earlier than she usually paid her visit; but within a few minutes, the phone rang.

It was Father, who greeted Lou Jean and asked, "What's wrong with your mother?"

Not wishing to worry him, Lou Jean answered, "Oh nothing, she's all right."

Emma Ray
Riggs McKay

"No, she isn't," insisted Father. "What's wrong with her?"

He was much relieved to learn it was just a slight cold.

During one of Mother's illnesses, she was hospitalized at LDS Hospital during an icy spell that made the streets treacherous. We were very concerned because Father got up early in the morning and drove over the glassy streets to spend a few hours with her before his day began, drove up again after his work was over to sit by her bedside, and then drove home over the frozen streets.

We expressed our concern for his safety to Mother's doctors, and they ingeniously solved the problem. They asked Father if he would agree to sleep in a room next to Mother's, explaining, "She rests better if you are near." To Mother they said, "We've asked President McKay to stay nights at the hospital because he'll be under less stress if he can see you oftener." Both of them willingly agreed to a plan that was presented as benefiting the other.

I recall visiting Mother once during this period when Father was there. She was sound asleep, but he sat by her bedside, watching her and holding her hand.

On 18 January 1970, at age ninety-six, he died quietly in his Hotel Utah apartment with Mother and their children present. Mother lingered on, sweet and uncomplaining, for ten months. None of us ever heard her merry peal of laughter again after Father's death, although she always greeted us with her warm smile and loving caresses. When she slipped away on 14 November 1970, despite our heartache, none of us would have delayed that last, permanent reunion with her beloved sweetheart.

HONORS BESTOWED ON DAVID O. McKAY

♦ ♦ ♦ ♦ ♦ ♦ ♦ ♦ ♦ ♦ ♦ ♦ ♦

Honorary Master of Arts degree from Brigham Young University, 2 June 1922

Honorary Doctor of Laws degree from Utah State Agricultural College, June 1950

Honorary Doctor of Humanities degree from Brigham Young University, 4 June 1951

Honorary Doctor of Letters degree from the University of Utah, 9 June 1951

Honorary Doctor of Letters from Temple University, Philadelphia, 14 June 1951

Honorary Master M-Man award, 13 June 1953

Silver Buffalo Award of the Boy Scouts of America, 1953

Honorary membership in the International College of Surgeons at Chicago, 10 September 1954

Cross of the Commander of the Royal Order of the Phoenix bestowed by the acting consul general of Greece representing King Paul of the Hellenes, 29 November 1954

Education building at Brigham Young University named in his honor, 14 December 1954

Honorary life membership from the National Society of the Sons of Utah Pioneers, 12 October 1955

Golden Medal of the Greek Archdiocese of North and South America recognizing "the dignity and glory of unselfish deeds," 20 November 1955. Archbishop Michael, head of the Greek Orthodox Diocese of North and South America, stated that the medal commemorated "the great interest shown and the generous contributions of your church toward both the Greek War Relief drive following World War II and the Ionian Earthquake Drive in 1953." The Church had sent six carloads of clothing and food to Greece. The award was originally presented to Theodore C. (Ted) Jacobsen, president of the Eastern States Mission, representing Father and the membership of the Church on 20 November 1955. When The Fourteenth Biennial Ecclesiastical Congress of the Greek Orthodox Church was held in Salt Lake City on 3 July 1958, His Eminence, the Right Reverend Germonos, Bishop of Nyssa, represented Archbishop Michael in pinning the Golden Medal on Father's coat. In November 1954, King Paul of the Greeks awarded Father the Cross of the Commander of the Order of the Phoenix, acknowledging that the LDS Church had made the greatest single contribution to the earthquake relief fund.

Silver Beaver Award of the Boy Scouts of America, 26 January 1956

Honorary membership in the Blue Key National Honor Fraternity, 5 May 1956

Honorary membership on the Boy Scouts of America National Council, 29 July 1957

All-Church YMMIA Trophy, 12 June 1959

As president of the Church he also served as president of Utah First National Bank, Zion's Savings Bank and Trust Company, Heber J. Grant Company Beneficial Life Insurance Company, Zion's Securities Corporation, Zion's Cooperative Mercantile Institution, Layton Sugar Company, and Utah-Idaho Sugar Company. He was also ex officio president of the board of trustees, Brigham Young University. He had earlier served on the Board of Regents for the University of Utah (1921–22) and as a trustee for Utah State Agricultural College (1940–41).

Member of the Newcomen Society, the Bonneville Knife and Fork Club, and honorary member of Ogden Rotary Club.

A decade after his death, Father was inducted into the Beehive Hall of Fame on 23 October 1981. The tribute to him read: "A tall, stately man with distinguished appearance and flowing white hair in later years, David O. McKay was one of the most universally loved men of his time. Filmmaker Cecil B. DeMille once said of this kind, noble, humble man: 'There are men whose very presence warms the heart. David O. McKay is one of them.' McKay's secular career as a teacher and principal at Weber Academy in Ogden was short-lived. At the age of 33 he was asked to serve as an apostle for The Church of Jesus Christ of Latter-day Saints. He would continue in the service of his church for the rest of his life, the last 19 as its president. Revered by monarchs and masses, David O. McKay received countless tributes, including four Honorary Doctorate degrees and the Silver Buffalo Award in 1953, the highest award given by the Boy Scouts of America for distinguished service. Perhaps the most fitting tribute came from American labor leader Walter Reuther, who said, 'A man like David O. McKay only comes along once a generation.' "

INDEX

◆ ◆ ◆ ◆ ◆ ◆ ◆ ◆ ◆ ◆ ◆ ◆ ◆